P9-AQC-273

Blacksburg

June 1990

Donated by

BUCHANAN LIBRARY
George Mason University

THE

SCIENCE OF RIGHTS.

THE

SCIENCE OF RIGHTS

Grundlage des Naturrechts nach
Principien der Wissenschaftslehre

J. G. FICHTE

TRANSLATED FROM THE GERMAN

BY

A. E. KROEGER

WITH A PREFACE BY

WILLIAM T. HARRIS,

PROFESSOR OF THE SCHOOL OF PHILOSOPHY, CONCORD, MASS.; EDITOR OF THE
"JOURNAL OF SPECULATIVE PHILOSOPHY," ETC.

INTRODUCTION
by Charles Sherover, Hunter College

LONDON
ROUTLEDGE & KEGAN PAUL

First published 1889
by Trübner & Co., London
Reissued 1970
by Routledge & Kegan Paul Ltd
Broadway House, 68–74 Carter Lane
*London, E.C.*4
Reprinted offset in Great Britain by
The Camelot Press Ltd., London and Southampton
No part of this book may be reproduced
in any form without permission from
the publisher, except for the quotation
of brief passages in criticism
SBN 1700 6725 9

PREFACE.

FICHTE's system of philosophy is pre-eminently a philosophy of the free will. Free will is certainly not an object of external perception, but rather of introspection. When we look outwardly, and behold things and events in time and space, we contemplate each thing limited on all sides by other things; each event limited before and after by other events. Such limitation, according to the philosophy of Kant and Fichte, belongs to the category of quality. This category includes affirmation, negation, and limitation: affirmation of the thing or event; negation of it by others which we perceive to exclude it; limitation of the thing or event by others and their limitation by it. This gives reciprocity for the third subcategory of quality. In the "Science of Knowledge" Fichte deduces these three immediate categories of consciousness: the ego, the non-ego, and the mutual limitation of the ego and non-ego. He thus finds the category of quality as the first and most direct form of consciousness. This category of quality considers all manner of objects always under the condition of being limited from outside.

People do most of their conscious thinking in the category of quality, and consequently find all thoughts that do not fit that category "unthinkable." This is the

supreme category with "agnostics." But all people do a
great deal of thinking in the other great category of the
Mind—the category of Freedom, variously called self-
activity and self-determination. While quality or mutual
limitation is the general form of sense-perception and
the understanding, the category of self-activity (called by
Spinoza *causa sui*), or freedom, is the basis of the three
great realms of thought that are accounted supreme in
human life—the realms of rights and morals, of art and
literature, and of the revelation of the divine. The
realm of rights and morals concerns the good, a sub-
category under the idea of self-activity, and itself in-
cluding many subordinate categories, like justice, virtue,
duty, obedience to the authority of institutions, &c.
These categories can have no significance in regard to
inanimate things and none in regard to living beings
which have not developed self-activity to the point of
freedom and responsibility.

The realm of art and literature is governed by the
category of the beautiful, another sub-category of freedom. For the beautiful is the manifestation of free
personality, and the epochs of art take rank in accordance with the adequacy of their manifestation of this
attribute. Homer taught the world how to recognize
freedom under all phases of nature; the essence of the
poetic is trope and personification. It indicates a view
of nature that refuses to see mechanical forces, but
insists that all movement is free and personal. Modern
poetry still imitates Homer, and modern art ornaments
all things by decking them out with shapes that seem
to realize inward purposes. Thus the real intention
(of usefulness for man) is concealed by the appearance
of freedom. The ornamented utensil looks as though

it assumed its form for its own use and not for the sake of usefulness to others.

The realm of religion, finally, implies the same fundamental category of free personality as all in all. For it looks upon all things as creations of an absolute Person who has made all things for the sake of the manifestation of His infinite freedom.

This category of self-activity is the fundamental form of our inward sense—*i.e.*, of introspection—just as quality is the form of our external sense—*i.e.*, sense-perception. Quality is the form of fate, and its insight sees that all things are what they are because the totality of conditions has necessitated them to be so. The category of self-activity is the form of freedom, and its insight sees that the supreme condition of everything is freedom, and that there is no fate except as secondary or derivative from freedom. In other words, the ultimate motive power in all force is will.

Fichte's system of philosophy sets out from the category of quality and proceeds towards the category of freedom, demonstrating at every step that self-activity is the foundation of the qualitative and showing how the qualitative comes to arise from the self-active. Being or existence is not a sort of quiescent substrate underlying all manner of activity, but the very substance of being itself is pure activity. Having shown how the appearance of being and the qualitative arises in the mind through the process of self-activity, Fichte has completed his theory of the intellect and arrived at the beginning of his theory of the will. He calls this the Practical Part of the Science of Knowledge. It is this Practical Part of the Science of Knowledge which furnishes the standpoint of the present work.

The one supreme fact in the universe, from Fichte's point of view, is the free will. To discuss this idea in its relation to civil society and the State, both of which institutions arise from the recognition of freedom as the most sacred object in the secular world, is the object of the book before us—" The Science of Rights," or of jurisprudence.

Mr. Kroeger, the translator, says in regard to it : " The Science of Knowledge having been established as the science of all sciences, Fichte, soon after its discovery and publication, deemed it advisable to illustrate by an example in what manner other sciences take their starting point from it, and apply the form which it prescribes for all sciences. Intensely interested in the political state of affairs in Europe, he naturally hit upon the Science of Rights, or of Law generally, as the science which it would be most congenial for him to treat ; and this preference was strengthened by the reflection that the deduction of the principle of law would involve a circumstantial deduction of the principle of individuality—an extremely difficult and important point in the science of knowledge. . . . . What our law-books and political treatises lack, the *à priori* deduction of our fundamental principle of government and law from the conception of reason as reason (or from the ego), Fichte's Science of Rights supplies."

The present work is a translation of Fichte's first sketch of the Philosophy of Rights which appeared in 1796 under the title : " Grundlage des Naturrechts nach Principien der Wissenschaftslehre von Johann Gottlieb Fichte. Jena and Leipzig."

It seems that Kant published a little later in the same year a work on the Science of Right (Rechtslehre), as the first part of his Metaphysic of Morals. (An English translation of Kant's work, by W. Hastie, B.D., 1887, is published by T. & T. Clark, of Edinburgh).

There is an essential agreement between the two works. Fichte held substantially the Kantian doctrine. The two works deserve the careful study of all who wish to see the profound rational principles that exist in the complex of usages and compromises that have grown into our system of law. Hegel wrote his first sketch of a Philosophy of Rights in 1802–3, and published a more elaborate work in 1821. These three works respectively by the three greatest thinkers in modern times furnish a great storehouse of ideas on the subject of jurisprudence and the constitutional framework of States. As a sample, one may refer to Kant's discussion of the three great fundamental powers into which the government is divided, and especially their co-ordination (see pp. 165–173 of Hastie's translation), as a treatment that cannot fail to be of great interest to Englishmen and to all peoples derivative from England. To the English nation belongs the great honour of having invented local self-government and the complete co-ordination of the three departments of government—the executive, the judiciary, and the legislative. In Great Britain this constitution grew as a natural growth. In English colonies its essential principles are in process of being reformulated with great success.

In the present active state of the public mind on questions of the ownership of property and the socialistic reorganization of society, it is necessary to appeal to reason rather than to tradition, and show the rationale of the institutions that have come down to us from our forefathers. It has become essential to know what this or that right brings with it—what coheres with the ownership of land, what with the use of money, or the right of taxation, or of the ballot. The system is so complex and the interdependences are so subtle that if one link is thrust out there follow entirely unexpected results in apparently disconnected spheres of rights. The reflections of a Kant, a Fichte, or a Hegel will doubtless provoke dissent in the reader's mind. But they will already have served a good purpose when they have been the occasion for so much study as dissent implies. There is one thing that their study will surely produce. This is the conviction that the progress of the world moves from the consolidation of the three powers of government in one person to the co-ordination of those powers in separate departments; from the constitutional forms in which one type prevails (as that of the family prevails in the patriarchal government of China) to the form in which the family, civil society, the State, and the Church are independent and complete in their functions without usurping the functions of one another. This will destroy the illusion of socialism, which wishes the State to absorb civil society, as well as the illusion of the " Nihilist," who wishes civil society to absorb the State.

W. T. HARRIS.

CONCORD, MASSACHUSETTS,
     1888.

ITNRODUCTION TO THE 1970 EDITION

By Charles M. Sherover

In 1796 revolutionary France saw the Directorate complete its first year of rule and appoint Napoleon to command French troops in Italy. The first President of the new American Republic was completing his second term of office. In the Saxon city of Jena, Johann Gottlieb Fichte enjoyed the publication of his third book, a philosophic defense of the nascent principle of free constitutional government.

Published as the *Grundlage des Naturrechts* (*Foundation of Natural Right*)[1] and translated under the title *The Science of Rights*, Fichte's basic work in social theory has been largely ignored and denied the attention which its significance invites. One reason may be that his later political pronouncements were, for the most part, directed to the more dramatic controversies surrounding the struggle to unify the feudal Germanic dukedoms into a modern nation, thus detracting attention from his more fundamental work. Perhaps more

---

[1] The German *Recht* (*s*), as the French *droit*, not only conveys the sense of 'the right' in a political and moral sense; it can also be taken in the sense of lawfulness and of 'justice'.

telling was his insistence on placing it within the context of his own metaphysical system, an early stage in the development of that speculative idealism which Hegel was to preempt and succeed in identifying with his own name.

Born in 1762, Fichte came to public attention in 1792 when his first published work, *Essay Toward a Critique of All Revelation*, which sought to apply principles of Kantian philosophy to religious questions, was at first thought to have been the work of Kant himself. Two years later he was appointed to the chair that Reinhold, an early advocate of Kantian philosophy, had held at the University of Jena; in that same year Fichte completed the first published version of his prime philosophic work, *The Foundation of the Theory of Science*, usually referred to simply as the *Wissenschaftslehre*. Its leading principles were restated in the present work and in the *System of Ethics* published two years later.

In the *Wissenschaftslehre* Fichte's attempt to unify the result of Kant's three Critiques had been guided by the Kantian principle of the irreducibility of selfhood, "the transcendental unity of apperception," and the primacy of the moral self. But morality, as Kant had argued, necessarily presupposes freedom. And Fichte, in an essentially Rousseauean tradition, argues that freedom is essentially social in character, that individual freedom presupposes a free society. As the *Wissenschaftslehre* had, as a prime aim, the vindication of the essential freedom of the moral personality, so Fichte's task in *The Science of Rights* is the determination of the essential principles which provide the necessary conditions for a social order in which individual freedom may be exercised.

His investigation is guided by the essential method of transcendental philosophy, the quest for basic defining possibility, the necessary conditions presupposed by an actual—or desired— state of affairs, the fundamental rational ground of what is taken as real. If one is to look forward to a society of free persons, then the leading question posed is: "How may a community of free beings, as such, be possible?" (p. 126) His point of departure, as well as his method, is essentially Kantian. In the *Critique of Pure Reason*, Kant had defined what Fichte took as the central concern of social theory:

A Constitution allowing *the greatest possible human freedom* in accordance with laws by which *the freedom of each is made to be consistent with that of all others* . . . is at any rate a necessary idea, which must be taken as fundamental not only in first projecting a constitution but in all its laws.[2]

This "necessary idea" of the limitation of the freedom of each so that all may be free is the essential principle of that "constitution . . . [which is] called a *civil community*."[3] Fichte's

---

[2] *Critique of Pure Reason*, trans. Norman Kemp Smith (New York: The Humanities Press, 1950), A316–B373, p. 312.

[3] Immanuel Kant, *Critique of Judgment*, trans. J. C. Meredith (Oxford: Clarendon Press, 1928), II, p. 96.

"fundamental principle" (see pp. 131, 137) is precisely this necessary self-limitation of freedom, and Fichte's awareness of his debt to Kant is quite explicit; Kantian principles define the opening discussion of his book and he confesses to open satisfaction, as a kind of vindication, that what he has had to say comes so close to the cosmopolitan principles which Kant set out in his little essay *Toward Perpetual Peace* published in 1795.

Fichte's book may then be regarded as an attempt to work out the social problematic which Kant had defined. But in doing so, Fichte has suggested an important reversal of priorities. Kant had seen questions of political right to be a consequence of moral freedom; instead of deducing the principles of political right, the principles of what Rousseau had termed a "legitimate" or just society, from the principles of individual morality, Fichte argues their autonomy. He takes the concept, not of morality, but of selfhood as primal and seeks to draw from its essence the criteria defining those basic social regulations or laws which make possible the "relation between rational beings." (p. 81)

The advantage he sees in this procedure is of basic philosophic interest. Morality, in the Kantian tradition, consists in the self-imposition of moral obligations; it commands categorically. A moral commandment does not tell us what we *may* do; it shows us what we morally *must* do. Political laws, in contrast, are concerned with rights which we need not exercise; they open opportunities for action which need not be pursued; in contrast to the moral commandment they are, to use Kant's distinction, of a hypothetical. not a categorical, nature; they tell us what may be permitted if we seek a certain end, but they do not command the end. Moral commandments present obligations; political laws present options. Moral commandments depend upon the "good will," the will to do what is conceived of as morally obligatory; the commands of political laws depend upon the compulsion of the community regarding individual acts, not individual motives. Because of this essential difference, Fichte finds the deduction of political rights from the principles of individual morality to be condemned by the Kantian criterion of self-contradiction. We need not choose to exercise our political rights and, indeed, may conceivably believe on occasion that we have a moral obligation not to. If our rights were merely drawn from our obligations, we would then be in the absurd position of feeling morally obligated not to do what morality commands us to do. Our rights, then, cannot be deduced from the principles of a categorical morality.

Yet they are related. For both political right and morality have a common source in the concept of selfhood; the separate deduction of social freedom has the advantage that it provides the social sanction of individual freedom, the social opportunity to exercise moral freedom in a community of free beings.

In pursuing his investigation, Fichte makes continual use of the Kantian principle of universality to be tested by the possibility of a "law annihilating itself" (see, for example, p. 193); he joins Kant in postulating the necessity of the ultimate goal of a federation of free nations. The structure of the book is patterned after the basic architechtonic structure of the Kantian *Critiques*; the first part, which Kant would have termed "the analytic," establishes the principle of the original rights of man; the second, "the dialectic," looks to their inherent limitation, the ways in which social compulsion is necessary to secure them; both are necessary for the definition of concrete freedom. What results is the thesis that concrete freedom is necessarily finite. Most significantly, in arguing his position, Fichte uses that dialectic method which he developed from sections of Kant's *First Critique* and which Hegel was to make famous—that philosophic method which insists upon the synthesizing power of reason, which sees any conceptual actuality as resulting from the comprehensive unification of thesis and antithesis, of contradictory elements which together constitute a dynamic organic whole.

Hovering in the background, however, is not only Kant, but Rousseau. On the theoretical ground taken from his reading of Kant, Fichte carries forward some essential themes of *Du Contrat Social*. It should be remembered that Rousseau's descriptive subtitle was "Principles of Political Right"; it is Fichte's concern to establish their foundation in human reason. He continues the essential theme that Rousseau had taken from Aristotle: that human rights are essentially social rights; that to speak of right or freedom is to presuppose a community; that man, indeed, "only becomes man ... through intercourse with others" (p. 160); that specific rights are those which the community recognizes as such; and that freedom and responsibility are concomitant. Freedom is not merely freedom of thought or moral determination; meaningful freedom is that of expression, of action in a community of other persons. My freedom presupposes the freedom of others which bounds my own, and the freedom of the community itself to define those specific individual freedoms in terms of its situation at the time. The community is then prior; the political task is the development of a free community in which individual freedoms are maximized, a free community which has found the means of "synthetically uniting the private and the common will" (see p. 206). In such a society the ultimate good of the individual and that of the community at large will be equivalent in a mutuality of freedom and responsibility (see, for example, p. 233).

Fichte's prime amendment to Rousseau is to carry the concept of a free organically unified society beyond the confines of the city-state and town-meeting direct democracy of a council of all citziens. Although he joins Rousseau in refusing to insist on one *form* of government for every society, he concludes that requisite to any free society is the "absolute necessity" of some kind of representative government (see p. 244), operating on the principle of popular sovereignty so that the people may judge the administration of their affairs and, by the curious notion of the Ephorate, be in a position to change government when it is found wanting.

One should be forewarned that Fichte uses the word "democracy" in its traditional Greek sense of direct citizen participation, which he opposes; in its place he suggests "proper democracy" (p. 247), that is, representative government in which some key officials are chosen by the whole people. Whether one prefers a monarchical or presidential system is a matter of local discretion; but, however organized, the basic constitutional law must provide a means for popular judgment of government. Anticipating the development of European parliamentary systems, he rejects the Montesquieuean doctrine of the separation of powers (which had been defended by Kant) and argues that executive, legislative, and judicial powers are really inseparable. Yet he does accept the principle that governmental power must be checked against abuse and suggests an Ephorate, something like a Senate of distinguished elder statesmen, who would have the power of suspending the government when it abuses its constitutional powers. However one may evaluate this notion, or, for that matter, the many specific topics with

which Fichte deals in the closing sections of the
book, it is apparent that he is propounding, not
an omnipotent or total state, but the notion of
the state as the political agency of the community
as such.

If the community is prior to the individuals who
constitute it, if freedom is essentially to be found
in those particular ways in which the community
chooses to honor the free individuality of its
citizens, if freedom and responsibility are mutual
and reciprocal—then the state has an obligation
to its citizens. Its function is the development of
their moral freedom, their maturation as responsible free men. To this end, it must insist on compulsory education of all children; to this end, it
limits the ways in which private property may be
used; each citizen is to be able to live on the fruit
of his labour, and the state is responsible for fore-
stalling dire poverty or suffering from economic
want on the part of those who are unable to work.
Each citizen has a claim on public assistance inso-
far as the state may require him to work if he
is able to do so. Just because each individual
has a responsibility to his community, so the
community has a responsibility to him. Bypassed
here is the Lockean notion of a minimal government
confined to protecting property and putting out
fires. For what Fichte develops out of Rousseau,
by way of Kant, is the concept of the responsible
society—the society which accepts its responsibility
in developing the conditions requisite for individual development; its function, as Thomas

Hill Green was to put it almost a century later, is to "hinder the hindrances" to the development of a free citizenry. The freedom of each community can only be made secure by the freedom of all communities; the necessary goal of any free community must be a world federation of free nations.

In temperament, Fichte was not a detached scholar but a prophet. And, indeed, his work is suggestive of movements of thought which were yet to come. He worked out the dialectic method which, first Hegel and then Marx, were to develop in different ways and claim as their own. In developing Kant's concept of the free causality of the moral self, in the thesis that all reason is ultimately practical, that knowledge is always in the service of action, that one only discovers one's own self in activity, he suggests the development of American pragmatism. In developing the Kantian notion of selfhood into the doctrine of the Pure Ego and then arguing that finite personality is essentially free, that freedom is essentially finite and implies its own limitations as well as the freedom of others, that I find my free moral self only as I recognize myself to be in a community of other selves (as well as passing remarks on the nature of temporal experience), he anticipates much of contemporary existential phenomenology and, in embryo, many of Heidegger's thematic studies.

But *The Science of Rights* is primarily concerned with political thought; its prime significance is for the definition of social problems and suggestions for means of resolving them. As such, its flaws are many: some, such as the discussion of women's rights, may amuse us; some, such as its literary style—although readable—may annoy us. Its attempt, in the concept of the Ephorate, to square the developing notion of European parliamentary government with the need for checks and balances may strike us as curious. In the way it approaches questions involving the dynamics of politics, it is surely naive. But to judge it merely by such criteria is to misjudge it entirely. To judge it on these particulars is to miss the point. For the intent of the book is to develop a statement of principle, and it is the statement of principle which makes it significant.

Fichte was a passionate advocate of the principles of the French Revolution; he wrote while its wounds were still raw. He saw that it was a great historic divide and that the world which was to follow after it would be essentially new. The era of the new nation-state and of democratic ideology was just beginning. With few precedents to guide it, a new examination of the ground of social organization was demanded by the time. He sought to face the prime question posed by these developments of his time: how to reconcile the aspiration for individual freedom, and its responsible exercise, with the social stability that would secure that freedom; how to reconcile the emerging notion of nationhood with the freedom of the citizen. One of the first to see the essential need for a doctrine of constitutionalism, his pioneer work helped to wed it to the notion of patriotism in the synthesis of constitutional democracy or representative government.

His is the first attempt to develop a modern theory of democratic social organization from the new philosophic idealism; his problem, in a sense, was to translate the general principles of Rousseau and Kant into meaningful terms for the new nation-states that were to emerge. He helped to give them an essentially democratic ideology. In pursuing this task, he demonstrated the power of that transcendental idealism he had made his own. Bypassing the laissez-faire anarchy of Adam Smith and the Lockean commonwealth, his principles would have avoided the miseries which attended the industrial revolution. Freedom and responsibility, he insisted, are indivisible and are socially grounded. Anticipating the central social problem of our own time, he suggested that the prime responsibility of a free society is the exercise of its powers of action in order to ensure and enhance the free development of responsible citizens in a world community of free nations. His development of Kant's transcendental idealism was, as Leibniz would have said, "pregnant with the future," the future that is now ours.

INDEX.

———

CONTENTS.

—•••—

INTRODUCTION.

FIRST PART.

BOOK FIRST.

DEDUCTION OF THE CONCEPTION OF RIGHTS.

BOOK SECOND.

DEDUCTION OF THE APPLICABILITY OF THE CONCEPTION OF RIGHTS.

BOOK THIRD.

APPLICATION OF THE CONCEPTION OF RIGHTS.

SECOND PART.

BOOK FIRST.

CONCERNING STATE ORGANIZATION.

BOOK SECOND.

CONCERNING THE STATE CONSTITUTION.

BOOK THIRD.

CONCERNING MUNICIPAL LAW.

FIRST APPENDIX TO THE SCIENCE OF RIGHTS.

CONTENTS.

SECOND APPENDIX TO THE SCIENCE OF RIGHTS.

INTRODUCTION.

————— •◦• —————

I.

HOW A REAL PHILOSOPHICAL SCIENCE IS DISTINGUISHED FROM A MERE FORMULAR PHILOSOPHY.

THE character of Reason consists in this, that the acting and the object of the acting are one and the same ; and this description completely exhausts the sphere of Reason. Use of language has designated this sublime conception for those who are able to think it, that is, for those who are able to abstract from *their own Ego*, by the word *Ego.* Hence, Reason generally has been characterized as *Egohood.* Whatsoever exists *for* a rational being exists *in* it ; but nothing is in it except by virtue of an acting upon itself ; what it contemplates it contemplates in itself, but there is nothing to be contemplated in it but its acting ; and the Ego itself is nothing but an acting upon itself.* To enter into explanations about this matter is not worth

---

* I should not even like to say an *active*, lest I might suggest the conception of a substrate, in which this power of acting would be supposed to be wrapped up. Such a substrate would be again the thing *per se*, only in the present case it would make the Ego itself such a thing *per se.*

while. This insight is the exclusive condition of all philosophizing; and unless a person has attained this insight, he is not yet ripe for philosophy And, indeed, all true philosophers have philosophized from this stand-point; only without being clearly conscious of it.

This inner acting of the rational being occurs either *necessarily* or *through freedom.*

The rational being *is* simply in so far as it *posits* itself *as being;* that is, in so far as it is self-conscious. All *Being*, that of the Ego as well as that of the Non-Ego, is a determined modification of consciousness; and without consciousness there is no Being. Whosoever assumes the latter assumes a substrate of the Ego, which is to be an Ego without being such, and thus contradicts himself. Hence, only those are necessary acts which result from the conception of the rational being, or through which the possibility of self-consciousness is conditioned; but these acts are most certainly all necessary, and result as certainly as there is a rational being. The rational being necessarily posits itself; hence, it necessarily does also all that may belong to this act of positing itself through itself.

The rational being in acting does not become conscious of its acting, since *itself* is *its acting*, and nothing more; but that whereof we are conscious is assumed to be external to consciousness, and hence external to the acting—it is the *object* of the acting. The Ego becomes conscious only of that which *arises* for it *in and through this acting;* and

that which thus arises is the object of consciousness, or the thing. No other sort of thing exists
for a rational being; and since we can speak of a
thing and of being only in their relation to a rational being, no other sort of thing exists at all.
Whosoever speaks of another thing does not know
what he says.

That which arises in a *necessary** acting of the
Ego, but whereof the Ego does not become conscious, from the reason adduced, itself appears as
necessary; that is, in representing it the Ego feels
itself not free. Hence, objects are said to have
Reality. The criterion of all reality is the feeling
of being *forced* to represent something *in the manner* in which it is represented. The ground of this
necessity we have seen; if the rational being is to
be as such, it must act in this necessary manner.
Hence, the expression of our conviction of the
reality of a thing is this: as true as I live, or as
true as I am.

If the object has its ground solely in the acting
of the Ego, and is completely determined through
the Ego alone, it follows that, if there be distinctions amongst the objects, these their distinctions
can arise only through different modes of acting on

---

* When the Science of Knowledge said : Every thing which is
exists through an acting of the Ego, (particularly through the productive power of imagination,) it was interpreted as if the science
had spoken of a *free* acting. Thus it became easy to cry down the
whole system as most visionary. But to say visionary is not to say
nearly enough. To mistake the products of *free* acting for the
products of necessary acting, and *vice versa*, is *insanity*.

B

the part of the Ego. Every object became for the
Ego determined in this particular manner, in which
it is determined, simply because the Ego acted in
the manner in which it did act ; but that the Ego
did so act was necessary, for just such an act was
one of the conditions of self-consciousness. By
reflecting on the object, and distinguishing from it
the mode of acting whereby it arises, this mode of
acting becomes—since the object appears, as we
have shown, as not the product of the *free* Ego—a
mere *comprehending*, a mere taking hold of a given
object. Hence, also, this mode of acting, whenever
it occurs in the (described) abstraction, is called a
comprehension, or a conception.*

Only through a certain determined mode of acting does a certain determined object arise in us ;
but if this acting is necessary, then also this object
surely arises. The conception (or comprehension)
and its object are, therefore, never separated ; nor
can they be separated. The object is not without
the comprehension, for it is through the comprehension ; and the comprehension is not without the
object, for it is that through which the object neces-

---

* A reader—who in his joy at having finally found a well-known
word, should hurry to transfer to it all that he may heretofore have
thought as characterized by this word, conception—would soon be
utterly confused, and unable to understand any thing further ; and
this by his own fault. The word conception is here used to designate neither more nor less than I have described, no matter what
the reader may have heretofore understood it as designating. I do
not appeal to a conception already in him, but wish to develop one
in his mind.

sarily arises. Both are one and the same, viewed from different sides. If you view the act of the Ego as such, that is, in its form, then it is comprehension ; but if you view the content of the act, the *what* is done—abstracting from the *that* is done—then it is an object. When one hears some Kantians speak about *à priori* conceptions, one would believe that they existed in the human mind in advance of all experience, like empty rows of shelves, waiting to have something put on them. What can such people take a conception to be, and what can have induced them to accept KANT's doctrines thus interpreted ?

We have said that, *in advance of that which arises through an acting,* the *acting* itself and the determined mode of acting can not be perceived. Hence, for the common man, and upon the standpoint of common consciousness, there are only objects and no conceptions ; the comprehension vanishes in the object, and becomes one with it. The philosophical genius, that is, the talent to find in and during the acting not only that which arises in it, but also the acting itself, as such, and to unite these utterly opposite directions in one comprehension, thus to catch one's own mind in the act, as it were ; this talent first discovered the conception in the object, and it was thus that a new field was added to the sphere of consciousness.

Those men of philosophical mind made known their discoveries. Nothing is easier than to produce *with freedom,* and under no necessity of think-

ing, every possible determination in our minds, and
to cause our mind arbitrarily to act in every possible manner ; but nothing is more difficult than to
observe that mind as acting in *real*, that is, in
necessary acting. The former mode of proceeding
gives us conceptions without objects, or an empty
thinking ; and only in the second manner does the
philosopher become the observer of an actual thinking of his mind.* The former is an arbitrary re-
petition of the original modes of Reason's acting,
after the necessity, which gave them significance
and reality, has passed away; the latter alone is
the true observation of reason in its modes of proceeding. From the former arises an *empty, formular-philosophy*, which considers itself as having

* The formular-philosopher thinks this or that, observes himself
in this thinking, and then places the whole series of thoughts,
which occurred to him, before the public as truth, and this simply
because he could think them. The *object* of his observation is himself, in his *free* productions, which he either undertakes without any
clear direction, as chance may determine, or with a direction given
him externally. But the true philosopher has to observe Reason in
its *original* and *necessary* procedure, by which his Ego, with every
thing which exists for it, has first derived Being. But since he can
no longer find this originally acting Ego in empirical consciousness,
he, by the only act of arbitrariness which is permitted to him,
namely, by the free resolve to philosophize, places that Ego back
at its first starting-point, and then causes it to describe all its acting from that point after its own laws, which to the philosopher
are well-known. Hence, the object of his observation is general
Reason itself, following its own laws of development, and having
no external object in view. The former observes an individual,
(his own,) lawless thinking ; the other, Reason itself, in its necessary acting.

done enough when it has proved that one may think any thing without being anxious concerning the object, that is, concerning the conditions of the necessity of this thinking. A real philosophy posits conception and object together, and never treats one without the other. To introduce such a real philosophy, and to abolish all merely formal philosophy, was the object of KANT's writings. I can not say whether this his object has as yet been observed by but one philosophical author. But I can say this, that the misunderstanding of that system has shown itself in a two-fold manner: firstly, through the so-called Kantians in this, that they also conceived KANT's system to be such an empty formular-philosophy, and held the difference to be only that it was the former one reversed ; and hence they continued to philosophize in the same empty manner, as had always been done before— only from an opposite side ; and secondly, through some sharp-sighted skeptics, who saw clearly enough where philosophy was at fault, but who did not see that KANT had remedied this fault. Mere formal thinking has been indescribably injurious in philosophy, in mathematics,* in the natural Sciences, and indeed in all pure Sciences.

* In mathematics this is shown, particularly in the abuse of algebra by mere formal minds. Thus, to cite an example, it has not yet been rightly comprehended that it is impossible to square a circle, and that this is contradictory to the conception of a circle. A critic has asked me, " Whether the squaring of the circle is impossible because *straightness* and *crookedness* have nothing in common ?" He thinks he has been very smart in having asked this

II.

WHAT THE PROBLEM OF THE SCIENCE OF RIGHTS,
AS A REAL PHILOSOPHICAL SCIENCE, WILL BE.

To say, therefore, a certain determined conception is originally contained through and in Reason,

question, looks around, laughs, and leaves me to sink under my
disgrace. But I look at him and laugh at his question. "Most
truly, such is my serious opinion, dear sir !" "*Ansam philosophiæ
non habes !*" says he pityingly ; and I reply, "Your great wisdom
has run away with your common sense. Knowledge on this point,
my dear sir, I do not lack exactly ; but understanding of it—most
sorely. When I was still at college, I heard often enough that the
circumference is equal to a polygon of an infinite number of sides,
and that we can square the circle when we get the content of that
content. But I never could understand it. And I hope to God
that I shall never understand how it is possible to measure that
content. For what is the conception of an Infinite ? I suppose
that of a *problem*, to divide infinitely the side of the polygon ; and
hence the problem of an *infinite determining?* But what, then, is a
measure, for which you want to use the infinitely-sided polygon?
I suppose a *determined something.* Now, if you keep on dividing
ad infinitum, as the problem requires you, you will never get to
measuring it. But if you proceed to measure it, you must first
stop dividing, and then your polygon is finite, and not, as you have
posited it, infinite.—But because you can take hold of your manner
of acting in describing an Infinite, that is, because you can seize
the empty comprehension of the Infinite, and designate it, for instance, as A, you now pay no further attention, to whether you have
really accomplished the act—no, not even to whether you can accomplish it ; you take your A calmly and proceed to business.
Common sense looks at your doings admiringly, and cheerfully confesses it its own fault that it does not understand you ; but when
some one who is not *so* modest takes it upon himself merely to
utter his opinion on the subject, you can not explain his inability to
understand a matter which to you seems so very clear, except on
the presumption that the poor man has not gone through the rudi-
ments of the Sciences."

can only signify : a rational being, as sure as it is such, acts in a determined manner. The philosopher has to show of this determined act, first, *that it is a condition of self-consciousness,* and this furnishes the deduction thereof ; but he has also to describe this determined act as well in regard, secondly, to its form, to *the manner of acting in it,* as, thirdly, in regard to its content, to that *which arises in this act for the reflection.* He thus furnishes at the same time the proof of the necessity of this conception, determines it, and shows its application. None of these parts can be separated from the others, without wrongly treating even these separates, and without falling into formal philosophy. The conception of Rights is assumed to be an original conception of Reason ; it must, therefore, be treated in the above manner.

1. Now, in regard to this conception of Rights, it results—as we shall hereafter show in its deduction—that this conception becomes a necessary condition of self-consciousness, because a rational being can not self-consciously posit itself as such, without positing itself as an *individual,* or as one of many rational beings, which many it assumes outside of it by assuming itself.

2. What the manner of acting in the positing of the conception of Rights is, can be even sensuously represented. I posit myself as rational, that is, as free. In doing so I have the representation of freedom. In the same undivided act I posit other free beings. Hence, I describe through my power

of imagination a sphere of freedom, which these many separate beings divide amongst themselves. I do not ascribe to myself all the freedom which I have posited, because I must also posit other free beings, and must ascribe part of it to them. Thus, in appropriating freedom to myself, I at the same time restrict myself, by leaving freedom to others. The conception of Rights is, therefore, the conception of the necessary relation of free beings to each other.

3. Finally, as regards the *content* of the conception of Rights. The conception of freedom involves originally only the power, through absolute spontaneity, to form conceptions of our possible causality ; and it is only this power which rational beings necessarily ascribe to each other. But that a rational individual, or a person, *should find himself to be free* requires something more, namely, that a result in the external world should follow the thinking of his activity, or that he should perceive the effect of his free causality.

Now, if the causalities of rational beings should work upon the same world, and should thus be able to influence, check, and oppose each other, as is indeed the case, then freedom—in the latter signification of the word—would be possible for persons who stand under this reciprocal influence, only on condition that all of them restrict their causality within certain limits, and divide the world, as it were, amongst them. But since they are posited as free, such a limit to their freedom could not lie beyond freedom—since then the limit would *cancel,* but not restrict it *as* freedom ; but must rather be *freely* posited by all ; in other words, all must have made it their rule, not to disturb the freedom of those with whom they are placed under reciprocal influence.

And thus we have the *whole object* of the conception of Rights, namely, *a community between free Beings as such.* It is necessary that every free being should assume other free beings as existing ; but it is not necessary that all these free beings, *as free beings*, should coexist together ; the thought of such a community and its realization are, therefore, altogether arbitrary. But *when* it is thought, through what conception or determined mode of acting is it thought ? It appears that it is possible in thought to have every member of this community so restrict his own external freedom through inner freedom as to make it possible that all other members shall also be free. Now, this is the conception of Rights.—If this conception is thought as a practical conception—because the thought as well as the realization of such a community is arbitrary—then it is purely of a technical-practical character ; that is to say, the conception of Rights does not demand *that* such a community be erected, but merely demands that, if it be erected, it shall be established on the basis of the conception of Rights.

In all this our representation of the conception of Rights we have refrained from expressly refut-

ing those who attempt to deduce the conception of
Rights from the Moral Law, because, as soon as the
true deduction of that conception has been established, every impartial mind will accept it as the
true one without demanding that the incorrectness
of other deductions be shown up. But for parti-
sans and narrow-minded disputants, it would be
lost time to write. The rule of law, Restrict your
freedom through the conception of the freedom of
all other persons with whom you come in contact !
receives, it is true, a new sanction for conscience
through the Moral Law ; but the deduction of this
sanction forms a part of the Science of Morality,
and does not belong to the Science of Rights. It
might be said that many learned men, who have
written systems of natural law, have treated in
them without knowing it that very part of the
Science of Morality, had they not forgotten to state
why obedience to the Moral Law always conditions
absolute inner harmony of the rational Being. Indeed, most teachers of morality seem not to have
considered that the Moral Law is purely formal,
and hence empty ; and that a content for it must
not be surreptitiously obtained elsewhere, but must
be thoroughly deduced. We can state at once how
the matter stands in our case. I must necessarily
think myself in contact with the men nature has
placed me amongst, but this I can not do without
thinking my freedom as restricted by their freedom,
and hence I must act in accordance with this neces-

sary thinking, or my thinking and my acting* are in contradiction, and I am not in that absolute harmony with myself which constitutes morality. I am, therefore, bound in conscience, through my knowledge of what *shall* be, to restrict my freedom; or, in other words, morally bound to respect the conception of Rights. Now, it is this moral aspect of the question which belongs to the Science of Morality, and not to the Science of Rights; in the latter science men are bound only by their arbitrary resolution to live in community with others; and if any one is not willing to restrict his arbitrariness at all, the Science of Rights has nothing to say to him other than this: that he must, in that case, remove from all human society.

In the present work the conception of Rights, as the condition of self-consciousness, is deduced at the same time with its object; it is derived, determined, and secured in its application, as should be done by a real science. This has been done in the first, second, and third books of our science. It is then further determined in the second part, and the manner stated, in which it must be realized in the sensuous world.

* I have read somewhere that the fundamental principle of the Science of Morality is, that "The manifold acts of the free will should be in harmony." This is a very unfortunate application of my statement of the absolute self-harmony of rational beings in my *Lectures on the Vocation of the Scholar.* For if it were correct, a man might merely resolve to be a very thorough and consequent rascal —in which case all the acts of his free will would perfectly agree, being, all of them, opposed to the condition of what *shall* be; and he would have done enough to satisfy such a morality.

III.

CONCERNING THE RELATION OF THE PRESENT THE-
ORY OF RIGHTS TO KANT'S SCIENCE.

With the exception of some excellent suggestions in recent writings by Mr. EHRHARDT and Mr.
MAIMON, the writer of this had discovered no trace
of a distrust in the manner in which the Science of
Rights had been heretofore treated, until—after
the completion of the present work—he was most
agreeably surprised by KANT's important work, *A
Perennial Peace.*

A comparison of KANT's doctrines of Rights, as
they appear from that work, and the principles of
the present science may not be disagreeable to
many readers.

It can not be clearly seen from KANT's work,
whether he deduces the conception of Rights, according to the usual method, from Morality, or whether he assumes another deduction. But some remarks (page 15) concerning the conception of a
Law of Permission make it very probable that his
deduction agrees with our own.

A Right is evidently something which one may
use or not use, and is, therefore, the result of a
pure Law of Permission ; of a law which simply
allows you rights, leaving you at liberty to use them
or not as you please—a law, moreover, which, being
restricted to a certain sphere, permits the conclusion, that beyond that sphere each one is left to his
own free will. This permission does not lie ex-

pressly in the law, but is merely argued from the limitedness of the law. The limitedness of a law shows itself in this, that it is a conditioned law. Now, it is absolutely not comprehensible how from the unconditionally commanding and thus universal Law of Morality it were possible to derive a Law of Permission.

KANT'S assertions that the state of peace or of law amongst men is not a condition of nature, but of art ; and that we have the right to compel persons, though they have not attacked us, to submit to the supremacy of government as the only security against future possible attacks from them ; agree wholly with our science, and are deduced in our science in the same manner as in KANT'S work.

Our science also agrees with KANT'S work in its deduction of the principle, that a state government can be erected only on the basis of an original but necessary compact ; and, furthermore, of the principle, that the people must not themselves exercise the executive power, but confer it, and that hence a Democracy, in the pure significance of the word, is an utterly unlawful form of government.

But I differ with KANT in his statement, that the division of legislative and executive power is sufficient to secure the maintenance of rights in a state. The chief points which I hold on this subject, and which are developed at length in the present work, I shall here state as concisely as possible.

The conception of Rights involves that when

men are to live in a community, each must so restrict his freedom as to permit the coexistence of
the freedom of all others. But it does not involve
that this particular person, A, is to restrict his freedom by the freedom of those particular persons,
B, C, and D. That it has happened so that I, A,
must conform myself particularly to the freedom of
these, B, C, and D, of all other men, is purely the
result of my living together with them ; and I so
live with them, simply by my free-will, not because
there is an obligation for me to do so. Thus it
is originally within the free-will of every citizen,
whether he chooses to live in this particular state
or not—though he *must* live in some state, if he
wants to live at all with other men. Now, as soon
as he expresses the resolve to enter a particular
state, and is accepted as a member of it, then he is,
by this simple, natural declaration, subjected to all
the restrictions which law prescribes for that state.
By his mere statement, I will live in this state, he
has adopted all its laws. The laws of the state
become *formally* his laws by his resolve to live in
the state ; but, *materially*, they have been determined without his consent by the conception of
Rights and the position of the state. Again, the
law, Restrict your freedom by the freedom of all
others, is a purely formal law, and as such not capable of application. For how far is the sphere to
extend, within which no one may hurt him, but beyond which he may also not go, without being regarded as a disturber of the freedom of others ?

This the parties must arrange amongst themselves.
Applying this to the state : each one, on entering
the state, must arrange with the state what is to be
his particular sphere of free activity, (his property
and his civil rights.) When he has so arranged, by
what has his sphere been determined ?   Evidently,
by his own free resolve ; for without it he would
have had as much right to what the others possess
as they have themselves. But how is it determined,
how much can be allowed to each individual ?
Clearly, by the common will in accordance with the
rule : This number of men are to be free in this
particular sphere of general freedom, hence, each
one has as his share so much.

Now, within these self-imposed restrictions, the
citizens must be kept by force, and a certain threat
of punishment, should they transgress them, must
keep them from such transgressions. It is also
clear that this punishment must be known to them
if it is to affect their wills ; that they must have
consented to receive such punishment for a transgression of their sphere of freedom upon entering
the state. (In other words, no *ex post facto* laws are
admitted.)

But who is to *proclaim* the common will, thus determined in all respects, regarding the rights of the
individual citizen as well as regarding the punishment to be inflicted upon their transgression ? Who
is to *interpret* this necessary arrangement and
agreement ? The masses themselves would be the
most improper body for it, and by counting together

the expressed wills of the individuals, the true common will could scarcely be obtained in its purity.

This business can only belong to him who continually overlooks the whole community and its requirements, and who is responsible for the continuous supreme rule of the law : to the administrator of the executive power. He proclaims the *matter* of the law, as given in the conception of Rights and in the geographical position of the state ; which matter receives its *form*, that is, its binding power over each individual, only by that individual's consent, that is, his consent to remain in the state, but not expressly his consent to any particular law.

From these reasons we, in our theory, have asserted, that in civil law the legislative and the executive powers are inseparable, and not to be divided. Indeed, civil legislation is itself a branch of the executive, if the law is really to be executed. The administrator of the executive power is the natural interpreter of the common will, announcing the relations of the individuals to each other in the state ; not exactly of the will which they actually nave, but of the will which they must have, to make heir coëxistence in a community possible.

Of quite a different nature is the law concerning the manner in which the laws are to be executed, or the *constitution*. The constitution must be adopted by the vote of every citizen, and can be adopted only by unanimity ; since it is the guarantee which each one has given him by all others for the security of all his rights in the community. The essential component of every constitution is the *ephorate*, explained in our work. Whether this is sufficient to secure the rights of all—without the separation of the legislative and executive powers, which to me seems inadmissible, I must leave to the judgment of more competent men.

First Part of the Science of Rights.

Part First.

DEDUCTION

OF THE

CONCEPTION OF RIGHTS.

A FINITE, RATIONAL BEING CAN NOT POSIT ITSELF WITHOUT ASCRIBING TO ITSELF A FREE CAUSALITY.

PROOF.

A. *If a rational being is to posit itself as such, it must ascribe to itself an activity which shall have its last ground in itself.*

An in itself returning activity (Egohood, subjectivity) is character of the rational being. The positing of itself (reflecting about itself) is an act of this activity. Let this reflection be called A. The rational being posits itself through the act of such an activity. All reflection reflects something as its object ; let this object be called B. Now, what sort of a something must this object be as object of the reflection A ? In A the rational being is to posit itself, is to be its own object ; but its character is in itself returning activity. The last highest object (B) of its reflection must therefore also be *in itself returning,* or *itself determining activity,* since otherwise it would not posit itself as a rational being, and hence would not posit itself at all.

This assumed rational being is a *finite* being ; but

a finite rational being is one *which can reflect only upon a Limited.* Hence, the in itself returning activity B, must be a limited activity, that is, beyond this activity B there must be, and must be posited by the reflecting, a C, which is not this in itself returning activity, but rather its opposite.

B. *Its activity in contemplating the world can not be posited by the rational being as such an activity, which has its last ground in itself:*

For this contemplating activity is posited by its very conception as an activity which does not return into the Contemplating, but rather has an externality, an opposite of the Contemplating, a World for its object.

(After the contemplation, the *activity* in this contemplating may certainly also be ascribed by the rational being to itself, or raised into its consciousness; that is, the rational being may posit itself as the Contemplating. Nay, from the stand-point of transcendental philosophy, it appears quite clearly that even this Contemplating is nothing but an in itself returning Ego, and that the World is nothing but the Ego contemplated in its original limits. But if the Ego is to ascribe that activity in the contemplation of the world to itself, it must already have existence; and, at present, the question is only, how the Ego can originally be for itself, and this we can not explain from the world-contemplation, since, on the contrary, the latter becomes possible only through the former, which we are in search of.)

C. *But the rational being can opposit such an ac-*

tivity as we are in search of, to the world, as that which limits this activity, and in order to opposit it can generate it. Moreover, if such an activity is the sole condition of the possibility of self-consciousness, and if self-consciousness must be ascribed to a rational being, as indeed that which constitutes it a rational being, then it must opposit and generate such an activity.

The activity of the rational being, in contemplating the world, which must be known to the philosopher, when his speculation has advanced to the Science of Rights, but which may not yet be known to the rational being, about which he philosophizes, is *necessitated* and *bound*, if not in regard to its form, that is, that it occurs at all, at least in regard to its content; that is, that, if it occurs, it must occur in such or such a manner. We must represent objects as they are—in our belief—without our coöperation; our representation must be determined by their being. An activity opposed to this activity would therefore, in order to be its opposite, have to be free in regard to its content; or, there must be in it a possibility of acting thus *or otherwise.*

Again, this free activity is to be limited by the activity in contemplating the world; that is, the activity in the world-contemplation is itself that free activity, but in, a state of limitedness; and *vice versa,* the free activity is the activity in the world-contemplation, whenever that limitedness falls away. In other words, objects are objects merely in so

far as and through this, that they do *not* exist
through free activity ; and this free activity must
be checked and limited, if objects are to be. For
free activity tends to cancel these objects, in so
far as they bind it. Hence, free activity is *causality*
upon the objects, and contemplation is cancelled
causality, causality voluntarily renounced by the
rational being itself.

We have now described what the activity B is
in its relation to the world-contemplation, and to
the world itself. But it is also to be a return of the
rational being into itself, and in so far as it is directed upon objects, it is not this. Hence, when
related to the rational being itself, it must be a free
determining of itself to have causality. Only in so
far as this activity is directed upon objects, is it determined in its content. But originally, and in its
essence, it must not be so determined. Hence, it
must be determined through itself—must be determined and determining at the same time, and is,
therefore, most truly, an in itself returning activity.

What we have just said may be systematically
expressed thus : The activity B, which we were in
search of, must be *posited as an opposite* to the contemplation, and is, in so far, absolutely free, precisely because that contemplating activity is not
free ; this activity B, moreover, is directed upon
the rational being, or, which means the *same*, returns
into itself, precisely because the contemplating activity is directed upon something external to the
rational being ; and in so far this activity B is the

creating of the conception of an intentional causality outside of us, or of the conception of an end, (object.) At the same time, this activity B must be *related* to the contemplation, that is, *posited as equal to it;* and in this relation it is a causality directed upon objects. But it is to be carefully remembered that this causality upon objects follows immediately from that conception of an end, and is the very same, only viewed from another point of view.

By means of such an activity B the required self-consciousness becomes possible. B is something which has its last ground in the rational being itself, and can, as such, be posited only by means of the possible opposition of a something which has not its ground in the rational being. The Ego (the rational being itself as such) is thus now limited and determined, and hence, can be taken hold of by reflection ; that is to say, the practical Ego is the Ego for the reflection ; the reflection takes hold of this practical Ego, which is posited through itself, and which, in the reflection, must be posited as through itself ; and of this Ego, as logical subject, a possible predicate may assert something, as, for instance, in our case—the contemplation of the world.

It is only by means of such an activity that self-consciousness becomes possible ; for our result involves only the characteristics, which, at the commencement, we showed to be the conditions of self-consciousness ; namely, first, the existence of such an in itself returning activity, or of an activity which should have its last ground in the rational being itself ; secondly, the *finity* and limitedness of this activity ; and thirdly, the being *posited* of this activity in opposition and relation to the limiting ; as which it is posited indeed by merely being *reflected* about.

Hence, such an activity, and the positing thereof, is necessarily assumed when self-consciousness is assumed ; and both conceptions are identical.

COROLLARIA.

1. It is here maintained, that the practical Ego is the Ego of original self-consciousness ; that a rational being perceives itself immediately only in Willing, and that it would not perceive itself, and hence would also not perceive the world, and that it would therefore not be Intelligence, if it were not a practical being. Willing is the real essential character of reason ; and representation—although in the insight of the philosopher it stands in reciprocal causality with willing—is posited as the accidental. The practical faculty is the inmost root of the Ego ; to it every thing else is attached, and with it connected.

All other attempts to deduce the Ego in self-consciousness have failed, because they must always presuppose what they wish to deduce ; and we here see why they must fail. How was it indeed possible to assume, that the Ego arises through the connection of many representations, in none of which the Ego is contained? that an Ego is produced by the mere connection? On the contrary, only after the Ego is, can any thing be connected in it. The Ego must, therefore, exist *—of course *for the Ego* —in advance of all connection.

2. Willing and Representing are, therefore, in continual and necessary reciprocal causality, and neither is possible unless the other is at the same time. The first assertion, that willing is not possible without representing, will be admitted without much trouble : I must represent what I will. The other, that every representing is conditioned by a willing, may, however, meet difficulties. But a representation can not be without a Representing subject, and can not be posited in consciousness unless this representing subject is posited. This repre-

---

* The Ego, *which* is to reflect, or which is to determine itself to have causality, or *which* is to contemplate the world, is the prior— of course, for the philosophizing Ego, which, however, let us hope, is also an Ego, and follows the laws of its being—*by virtue of those very laws ;* and it is this prior Ego, of which the first fundamental principle of the Science of Knowledge speaks.

Now *another* Ego is to be object *for* this reflecting Ego ; that is, this Ego is to be object for itself. How is this possible? Such is the question we are here answering.

Attentive readers must pardon this note. It is not for them, but for the careless and superficial readers, who need such a reminder ; and these are requested to recall it to mind whenever they need it hereafter.

senting subject is—not *accidentaliter*, in so far as it now represents, but *substantialiter*, in so far as it is at all, and as it is a somewhat—either a really Willing, or, at least, a something, which is posited and characterized through its ability to will. Not Intelligence alone constitutes a rational being, for it alone is not possible ; nor does the practical activity alone constitute a rational being, for it also is not possible alone ; it is only both united which complete it and make it a Whole.

3. It is through this reciprocal causality between the Contemplation and Willing of the Ego, that the Ego and every thing which is for the Ego, that is, every thing which is at all, first becomes possible.

First of all, the Ego itself. It might be said, that a reciprocal causality between the Contemplation and the Willing of the Ego must precede the possibility of the Ego itself ; that there must be something in the Ego, which stands in reciprocal causality, before the Ego is itself ; and that this is a contradiction. But here lies the very deception which we wish to remove. Contemplation and Willing neither precede nor follow the Ego, but are the Ego ; occur only in so far as the Ego posits itself ; occur only in this positing and through this positing of its occurrence ; and it is nonsense to think of any occurrence outside of and independent of this positing. *Vice versa*, the Ego posits itself in so far as both occur and in so far as it posits the occurrence of both ; and it is equally nonsense to think of any other positing of the Ego. It is, at any rate, very unphilosophical to believe, that the Ego is something else than both *its deed and product* at once. Usually, however, as soon as we hear the Ego spoken of as an active, we hasten to picture a substrate, of which we proclaim this activity to be mere power or faculty. This substrate, however, is not the Ego, but is a product of our own imagination, which we sketch in consequence of the demand made upon us to think the Ego. The Ego is not something, *which has* powers ; it is no power at all ; but it is simply *Acting ;* it is what it acts, and when it does not act, it is not at all.

It has been asked : How does the Representing subject arrive at the conviction that there exists an object of its representation outside of it, and that this object is determined precisely as it represents it ? If those who asked this question had but considered what it really meant, they would themselves have arrived at the correct conception.

The Ego itself, through its acting, makes the object ; the form of its acting is itself the object, and no other object is to be thought of. That, the manner of acting whereof necessarily becomes an object, is an Ego ; and the Ego is nothing but that, the mere manner of acting whereof becomes an object. If it acts with its whole power—I must use this expression if but to express myself—then it is object to itself; but if it acts only with part of its power, then it acts upon something which is external, or upon an object.

To grasp itself in this identity of acting and being acted upon—not in the acting, nor in the being acted upon, but in the *identity* of both ; and to surprise itself as it were in this act of grasping itself, is to comprehend the pure Ego and to get possession of the stand-point of all transcendental philosophy. This talent seems to be altogether deficient in some men. He who can only view each apart and separate, and who, though he takes the greatest pains, always grasps either the active or the object of the activity, obtains through both in their separation utterly distinct results, which can only be seemingly united, because they have not been so united from the beginning.

§ 2.

THROUGH THIS POSITING OF ITS POWER TO HAVE FREE CAUSALITY, THE RATIONAL BEING POSITS AND DETERMINES A SENSUOUS WORLD OUTSIDE OF ITSELF.

A. It *posits* this external sensuous world. Only the absolutely self-active, or practical, is posited as subjective, as belonging to the Ego, and by its limitation the Ego is limited. Whatsoever lies beyond this sphere of the absolutely self-active, is posited, for the very reason that it lies beyond it, as not produced nor producible through the activity of the Ego ; hence, it is excluded from the sphere of the Ego, and the Ego is excluded from its sphere ; and thus there arises a system of objects, that is, a

world, which *exists independently of the Ego,* that is
to say, of the practical Ego, which here stands for
the Ego generally, and independently of which
world *the Ego* (also, of course, the practical Ego,
which determines its ends) *exists likewise;* both of
which, therefore, exist independently and externally
of each other, and have both their separate ex-
istences.

COROLLARIA.

1. The transcendental philosopher must assume
that every thing which is, is only *for* an Ego ; and
whatsoever is for an Ego, can only be *through* the
Ego. But common sense, on the contrary, claims
an independent existence for both ; and maintains
that the world would be, though it (common sense)
were not. The latter has no need to take cognizance of the assertion of the philosopher, and can
not do so, for it stands on a lower stand-point ; but
the former must certainly take cognizance of common sense ; and his assertions are indefinite, and
hence, in part, incorrect, until he has shown *how,
from these very assertions, the precise results of common sense follow, and how they can indeed only be
explained by those assertions.* Philosophy must deduce our conviction of the existence of a world.

Now, this has been done here from the possibility
of self-consciousness ; and that conviction has been
shown up as a condition of this self-consciousness.
The Ego must posit an external world, because it

can posit itself in self-consciousness only as practical activity ; and because, since it can not posit any thing but a limited, it must posit a limit to this, its practical activity. This is the original procedure of every rational being, and is, doubtless, also the procedure of the philosopher.

Now, although the philosopher immediately afterward sees that the rational being must first posit its suppressed practical activity before it can posit and determine the object, and that thus the object itself is not immediately given, but is originally produced only by virtue of another—this need not disturb common sense ; for it can not become conscious of the just now postulated process, since that process conditions the possibility of all consciousness, and is therefore beyond its sphere ; it even does not disturb the philosopher as soon as he gets to the sphere of common sense.

It might be asked, What reality shall be ascribed to those acts which lie beyond the sphere of consciousness, and are not posited in consciousness, if reality is properly ascribed only to that which is necessarily posited by the Ego ? Of course, no reality, except in so far as it is thus necessarily posited. Those acts beyond common consciousness have reality, therefore, only for the philosopher who posits them. *If* the activities of the human mind are to be systematically united in an ultimate ground, *then* this and that must be assumed as necessary acts ; such, and nothing more, is what the philosopher asserts. Those original deed-acts have the same reality which the causality of things upon each other in the sensuous world, and their universal recipro-cal relation, claim to have. For those primitive peoples, of which we still have memorials, who little united their experiences, but rather allowed their observations to lie scattered and separate in their consciousness, no such causality or universal rela-tion of things had existence. They gave sepa-rate life to almost every object of the sensuous world, and thus made those objects first free causes, as they were themselves. The universal connection we speak of, had not only *no reality* for them, it even *did not exist* for them. But the man who connects his experiences into unity—and this problem lies in the way of the synthetically progressive human reason, and had to be taken up sooner or later—must necessarily connect in such a determined manner ; and for him the whole connection thus obtained has reality. Moreover, as soon as this problem had been taken up and solved, and as hu-man reason had once again returned into itself—as it did for the first time with clear consciousness, and completely, in one of its sublimest representatives, KANT—and had thus discovered, that all its seem-ing external perceptions were, after all, produced by itself ; the following additional problem proposed itself to the still synthetically progressive reason : namely, to unite all these, its modes of acting, also in an ultimate ground ; and this proceeding had reality from the same ground which gave reality to the category of causality, of a universal connection of

D

objects, etc. etc. This final problem for the synthetical faculty, moreover, after the solution of which
mankind returns forever again to analysis, which
analysis has thus, however, received quite a different
significance—had also to be solved sooner or later ;
and all we might wish is this, that those persons
who are not called by their talents to take part in
this branch of science, would also take no notice of
it, would leave, as has been heretofore customary,
philosophy to the philosophers, and would not be
so foolish in their anxiety for the reality of the results of that science, as to demand that we ought to
give to those results the same kind of reality which
alone is known to them.   To say, " A pure Ego and
its acts have no reality prior to consciousness," is as
foolish as if a savage were to say, " Your causality
and your reciprocal connection have no reality, because I can not eat them."

2. From the deduction of our conviction of the
existence of a sensuous world, it results at the same
time, how far this conviction extends, and in what
condition of mind it occurs : for no grounded goes
further than the ground, and as soon as we know
the ground of a certain mode of thinking we also
know its extent.   It extends so far as our practical
faculty is distinguished from and opposed to the
theoretical faculty ; so far as our representation of
the influence of things upon us and of our reaction
upon them extends, since only by this representation is our practical faculty posited as limited.   This

is the reason why philosophers have always proved
the reality of an external world by its influence upon
us ; a proof which certainly presupposes what it
would prove, but which pleases common sense, because it is the same proof common sense makes use
of for itself.

But how does the speculative philosopher proceed in order to remove this conviction for some
time, so that he may investigate beyond its range ?
Evidently by not drawing the distinction which conditions this conviction. As soon as we look merely
at the activity in the representation and seek only
to explain it, a necessary doubt regarding the existence of external things will arise. The transcendental idealist comprehends the practical and theoretical
activity at the same time as activity generally ; and
hence—there being now no passivity in the Ego, as,
indeed, there can not be—he arrives at the result,
that the whole system of objects must be produced
for the Ego by the Ego itself. But for the very
reason that he has thus comprehended both activities, he can also, at the proper time, distinguish
both, and show up the stand-point which common
sense must necessarily occupy. The dogmatic
idealist excludes the practical activity wholly from
his investigations, looks only at the theoretical activity, which he desires to ground through itself;
and hence he naturally makes the theoretical activity unconditioned.

But these speculations are possible for both sorts
of philosophers only so long as they remain in the

solitude of thinking ; as soon as their practical activity is excited, both immediately forget their speculative convictions and return to the ordinary human view of things, simply because they must. There never has been an idealist who extended his doubts or his certitude to his actions, and there never will be one ; for if he did, he could not act at all, and hence could not live at all.

B. The rational being also *determines* the sensuous world by that positing of its free activity ; that is, in positing that sensuous world it at the same time invests it with certain general and unchangeable characteristics.

Firstly. The conception of the causality of the rational being is produced through absolute freedom ; and hence the object of this causality in the sensuous world, being its opposite, must be fixed and unalterably determined. The Ego is infinitely determinable ; the object, because it is an object, is once and for ever determined. The Ego is what it is in *Acting ;* the object is what it is in *Being.* The Ego is incessantly becoming, and there is nothing permanent in it ; the object is, as it is, forever ; is what it is and is what it will be. In the Ego lies the ultimate ground of its acting ; in the object lies the ultimate ground of its being ; for it has nothing but being.

Secondly. The conception of causality, produced through absolute freedom, and which, under this same circumstance, might be infinitely different, tends upon a causality in the object. Hence the object must be infinitely changeable through an infinitely changeable conception ; that is to say, it must be possible to make out of the object whatever one may possibly will to make out of it. The object is fixed, is permanently determined, as we said at first, and may, therefore, by virtue of this its permanency, *resist* the causality of a rational being ; but it can not change itself through itself, (it can not *commence* any effort ;) and hence it can not *act* contrary or in opposition to this causality of a rational being.

Finally, the rational being can not posit itself as having causality, without positing itself, at the same time, as representing ; it can not posit itself as acting upon a determined object, without constantly representing this determined object ; it can not posit a determined causality as completed, without positing the object upon which it was directed. For, since the object is posited as annihilating the causality, although the causality must remain together with the object, there arises here an opposition, which can only be mediated by a floating of the imagination between object and causality, through which floating there arises a *Time.* Hence, the causality, in its working upon the object, occurs successively in Time. Now, if the causality is directed upon one and the same object, and if thus the causality is regarded in every present moment as conditioned by the previous moment, then the condition of the object is also regarded in each moment as conditioned by its condition in all previous moments, beginning at the first cognition of the object; and thus the object remains the same, although it is incessantly changed; that is to say, the substrate produced by imagination, in order to connect in it the manyfold of the qualties, or in other words, the basis of the incessantly each other excluding accidences, which is called their substance, always remains the same. This is the reason why we can posit ourselves only as changing the form of the things, and not their substance, and why we are well conscious of the power to infinitely alter the shapes of things, but also of our inability to produce or annihilate them, and, likewise, why matter can be neither increased nor diminished for us. On this stand-point of common consciousness —but by no means on the stand-point of transcendental philosophy—it is true that matter is originally given to us.

§ 3.

THE FINITE RATIONAL BEING CAN NOT ASCRIBE TO ITSELF A FREE CAUSALITY IN THE SENSUOUS WORLD, WITHOUT ASCRIBING THE SAME TO OTHERS, AND, HENCE, WITHOUT LIKEWISE ASSUMING OTHER FINITE RATIONAL BEINGS OUTSIDE OF ITSELF.

PROOF.

A. We have shown in § 1 that a rational being can not posit (perceive and comprehend) an object, without, in the same undivided synthesis, ascribing to itself a causality.

But it can not ascribe to itself a causality without having posited an object, upon which that causality is directed. The positing of the object, as a something determined through itself, and in so far checking the free activity of the rational being, must be posited in a previous time-moment, and it is only through this positing of a previous time-moment, that the time-moment, in which we comprehend the conception of causality, becomes the present. All comprehending is conditioned by the positing of a causality of the rational being, and all causality is conditioned by a previous comprehending of the same. Hence, every possible moment of consciousness is conditioned by a previous moment of the same ; and thus, in the explanation of the possibility of consciousness, consciousness is already presupposed. Consciousness can only be explained through a circle ; hence it can not be explained at all, and appears impossible.

The problem was to show : how self-consciousness can be possible. Our reply was : self-consciousness is possible, when the rational being can ascribe to itself a causality in one and the same undivided moment wherein it opposes something to this causality. Let us suppose this to occur in the time-moment Z. You ask now, under what condition this occurrence is possible? and it appears at once that the causality, which the rational being is to ascribe to itself, can be posited only in relation to a determined object, A, upon which it is directed. For no one must say that a *general* causality, a merely *possible* causality might be posited, since such would be an indefinite thinking; and Philosophy has already received injury enough from this sort of arguments. Such a merely possible causality, or causality in general, is posited only through abstraction from a certain or from all *actual* causality; but you can not abstract from any thing, unless it has been previously posited; and hence here, as ever, the indefinite conception of the *general* is preceded by a definite conception of a definite *actual*, and the former is conditioned through the latter. Nor must any one say that the causality might be posited as directed upon the object B, which is posited in the same moment, Z, for B is posited *as object* solely in so far as no causality is directed upon it.

Hence, the moment Z must be explained from another moment, in which the object A must have been posited and comprehended; but A also can be comprehended only under the same conditions under which alone B could be comprehended; that is to say, the moment in which A is comprehended, is also possible only on condition of a previous moment, and so on, *ad infinitum*. We find no possible point wherein we might connect the thread of self-consciousness, through which all consciousness first becomes possible, and hence our problem is not solved.

It is important for the whole science which is

here to be established, that the reader should obtain a clear insight into this argument.

B. The ground of the impossibility of explaining self-consciousness, without constantly presupposing it as already existing, lay in this : that in order to be able to posit its causality, the subject of self-consciousness must previously have posited an object, merely as such ; and that thus, whenever we wanted to connect the thread of self-consciousness to a time-moment, we were always forced to go to a previous moment, wherein the connections must have been already made. This ground must be removed ; but it can be removed only by assuming that the *causality of the subject* is synthetically united with the object in one and the same time-moment ; that the causality of the subject is itself the perceived and comprehended object, and this object that causality of the subject, and that thus both are the same. Only from such a synthesis can we not be driven to a previous one ; only it contains all the conditions of self-consciousness, and gives us the point in which we can connect the thread thereof. Only on this condition is self-consciousness possible. As sure, therefore, as self-consciousness occurs, must we make this assumption. The strict synthetical proof is, therefore, completed ; for what we have stated has shown itself to be the absolute condition of self-consciousness.

The only question is yet, what our synthesis may signify, or what it may involve, and how its requirements may be possible. Our business now is therefore to analyze what has been proven.

C. It seems as if the synthesis we have undertaken, in place of dispelling the mere incomprehensibility which it undertook to clear up, proposes to us a complete contradiction. That which the synthesis has established, must be an object; but it is the characteristic of the object, that the free activity of the subject in taking hold of it be posited as checked. Now, the object in the present case is to be a causality of the subject; but it is the character of such a causality that the activity of the subject be absolutely free, and determine itself. The activity of the subject is therefore by this synthesis required to be both checked and absolutely free. How is this contradiction possible? It is possible, and both activities are united, when we think *the subject as being determined to determine* itself; or when we think a requirement addressed to the subject to resolve on manifesting its causality.

In so far as that which the synthesis establishes is an object, it must be given in sensation, and in *external*, not in internal sensation; for all internal sensation arises solely through reproduction of an external sensation, and hence presupposes the latter; and thus, we should again by the assumption of such sensation, presuppose that self-consciousness, the possibility whereof is to be explained. But that object is comprehended, and can be comprehended only as a requirement addressed to the Ego to act. As sure, therefore, as the subject comprehends it, it has the conception of its own freedom and self-activity, and of this freedom and self-activity as given to it externally. It obtains the ¯conception of its free causality, not as something which in the present moment *is*, for this were a real contradiction ; but as something which in the future moment *shall be*.

The question was, How can the subject find itself as object? To find *itself*, it could find itself only self-active ; for else it would not find *itself ;* and since it does not find at all unless it is, and is not unless it finds itself, it would not find at all. Again, in order to find itself as *object*, (of its reflection,) it could not find itself as *determining itself* to be self-active,* but as determined to self-activity through an external requirement, which requirement must leave it, however, in possession of its full freedom of self-determination ; for otherwise, the subject would not find itself as Ego.

To make the latter point clearer, I shall here pre-state some future results. The subject can not find itself compelled to act ; for then it would not be free, would not be Ego ; nor, when it resolves to act, can it find itself necessitated to act in this or that determined manner ; for then, again, it would not be free, would not be Ego. How, then, must

* The question here is not how the matter may be when viewed from the transcendental stand-point, but simply, how it must appear to the subject under investigation.

we think it as determined to be active, in order to find itself as object ? Only in so far, that the subject finds itself as something which may be active or not, to which a requirement is addressed to be active or not, but which may *also* not follow that requirement.

The rational being shall realize its free activity ; this requirement addressed to it lies in its very conception, and as sure as it comprehends that conception it realizes that free activity. This it only can realize either through *actual acting*. All that is required is activity in general, but the conception expressly involves that the subject must choose in the sphere of possible acts one act through its free self-determination. It can act only in *one* way ; can *determine* its power of sensation, which is here the power of sensuous causality, only in *one* manner. As sure as it acts, it chooses through absolute self-determination this one way, and is in so far absolutely free and a rational being ; and posits itself as such.

Or it can realize that free activity through *not acting*. In this case it is also free, for according to our presupposition, it has comprehended the conception of its causality as something required of it. Now, in resisting this requirement and *not* acting, it chooses freely between acting and not acting.

The conception here established is that of a *free reciprocal causality,* in its greatest precision, and is, therefore, nothing but this. I could add, for instance, to any free causality a free opposing causality as *accidental ;* but that would not be the precise conception here required. In our conception *Causality* and a *Counter Causality* can not be thought apart at all. Both are the integral parts of a whole event ; and such an event is now postulated as the necessary condition of the self-consciousness of a rational being. It must occur, as we have shown.

Only to such an event is it possible to attach the thread of consciousness, which can then, we apprehend, pass through all other objects without difficulty.

This thread has been attached by our present representation. Under this condition the subject can and must posit itself as a free acting being : such was our proof. If it does posit itself as such, then it can and must posit a sensuous world and must opposit itself to the sensuous world. And now, after the chief problem has been solved, all the workings of the human mind proceed according to the laws thereof without further difficulty.

D. Hitherto our analysis of the established synthesis has been simply *explanatory :* all we had to do was to make clear to ourselves what the mere conception of that synthesis involved. This analysis still continues, but it now begins to *draw conclusions;* that is to say, perhaps the subject must posit many other things in consequence of the posited influence upon it ; if so, how does it posit this other, or what does it posit, by virtue of the laws of its being, in consequence of its first positing ?

The described influence was necessary condition of all self-consciousness ; it occurs as sure as self-consciousness occurs, and is, therefore, a necessary fact. If, by virtue of the necessary laws of rational beings, something else must be posited at the same time with this influence, then the positing of this other is a necessary fact like the former.

In so far as the described influence enters sensation, (is felt,) it is a limitation of the Ego ; and the subject must have posited it as such ; but there is no limitation without a limiting. Hence the subject, in positing that influence, must have posited at the same time something *outside of itself* as the determining ground of that influence. This is evident at a glance.

But again : This influence is *determined*, and through the positing of it as determined there is posited, not merely a general ground, but a *determined* ground of it. What sort of ground must this be, or what must be its characteristic as ground of this determined influence ? This is a question we shall have to dwell upon more at length. The influence was comprehended as a requirement addressed to the subject to manifest free causality ; and (which is of all-important significance) it could not be at all comprehended otherwise, and could not have been comprehended, had it not been comprehended in this manner.

This requirement to act, is the content of the influence, and its ultimate end is a free causality of the rational being, to which that requirement is addressed. The rational being is not determined or necessitated to act by this requirement—as in the conception of causality the effect is necessitated by the cause—but merely seizes this requirement as occasion to determine itself to act. To do this, however, it must first have understood and comprehended the requirement, and this previous cognition of it is taken into calculation. Hence the posited ground of the influence, or of the requirement addressed to the subject, must, at least, presuppose the possibility, that the subject can understand and comprehend it, for otherwise its requirement would have no End in view at all. Its having such End is conditioned by the understanding and freedom of the rational being, to whom it is addressed. This ground must, therefore, necessarily have the conception of reason and freedom, and must, therefore, be itself a being, capable of comprehending, that is, an intelligence, and since this is also not possible without freedom, it must be a free and hence a rational being, and must be posited as such.

In regard to the manner of drawing a conclusion, which has here been established, as a necessary manner, which is originally grounded in the nature of reason, and which most assuredly follows without our conscious coöperation, we add a few words of explanation.

The question has justly been asked : What effects can be explained only as the effects of a rational cause ? The answer : Those effects, which must be necessarily preceded by a conception thereof ; is true, but not sufficient, for the higher and more difficult question remains : What, then, are effects, of which it must be said, that they were possible only after a previous conception thereof ? Every effect can be taken up in conception, after it once exists, and the manyfold of the effect arranges itself under the unity of the conception more easily and happily only as the observer himself has more sense and understanding. Now, this is a unity, which the observer himself has transferred into the manyfold through what KANT calls his reflective power of judgment, and which he must so transfer, if only *one* effect is to exist for him. But who guarantees him that, just as he now arranges the actual many-fold under the unity of his conception, so, previously to the effect, the *conceptions* of the manyfold, which he perceives, were subordinated by an understand-ing to the conception of that unity, which he now thinks ; and what may justify him in arriving at such a result ? There must be a higher ground of justification, or the conclusion, that the effect is that of a rational cause, is false throughout.

There is no doubt : a rational being, as sure as it is this, sketches out for itself the conception of the product, which is to be realized through its activity ; and by the conception thus traced out, it guides its activity, always looking at it in acting, as it were. This conception is called the conception of an end.

Now, a rational being cannot at all obtain a con-ception of its causality, *unless it has a cognition of the object of this causality.* For it cannot determine itself to act—of course, with a consciousness of this self-determination, for only thereby does it become a free activity—unless it has posited this its activity as checked ; and when it posits a determined activity as checked, it posits an external object as the checking. This is the reason, by the by, why nature, even if we should claim for her intelligence and freedom, cannot have the power to form the conception of an end, (and for that very reason, no one should claim for her intelligence and freedom.) For there is nothing external to nature, upon which she could direct her causality. Every thing upon which causality can be directed, is itself nature.

A sure criterion of the effect of a rational being would, therefore, be this : that the effect could only be thought possible on condition of a cognition of its object. Now, there is nothing which can not be thought possible through mere force of nature, and which must be thought as possible only through cognition, except cognition itself. Hence, when the object—and here also the end of an effect—can only be, to produce a cognition, then it is necessary to assume a rational cause of the effect.

But the assumption, that a cognition was intended, must be necessary ; that is, it must be impossible to think any other end of the act, and the act itself it must be possible to comprehend only when it is comprehended as intending to produce a cognition.

(To illustrate by the contrary: Nature, we say, teaches us this or that by an event ; but in so saying, we do not mean to assert that nature had not

E

quite another end in view in producing the event
than to teach us ; we only wish to say that, if any
one chooses to regard the event from such a point
of view, it may be instructive for him to do so.)

The above case arises here.   The cause of the influence upon us has no end at all, unless it has,
above all, the end in view, that we should recognize it as such cause.   Hence we must assume a
rational being as this cause.

We have now proved what was to be proved.
The rational being can not posit itself as such, unless a requirement to act free is addressed to it.
When such a requirement to free self-determination
is addressed to it, it must necessarily posit a rational
being outside of itself, as the cause thereof; and
hence it must posit a rational being outside of itself
generally.

COROLLARIA.

I. Man becomes man only amongst men ; and
since he can only be man, and would not be at
all unless he were man, it follows, that *if man is
to be at all, there must be men.*   This is not an
arbitrary assumption, not an opinion based on past
experience or on other probability-reasons ; but it
is a truth to be strictly deduced from the conception of man.   As soon as you proceed to determine
this conception fully, you are driven from the thinking of a single man to the assumption of another
one, by means of which to explain the first.   Hence,

the conception of man is not at all the conception of a single one, for such a one is unthinkable, but of a race.

The requirement addressed to the rational being to manifest its free self-activity, is what is called education. All individuals must be educated to be men ; otherwise, they would not be men. The question here forces itself upon every one : If it should be necessary to assume an origin of the whole human race, and hence a first pair of human beings—and from a certain standpoint of reflection this assumption is assuredly necessary—who educated that first pair ? They must have been educated, for our proof is universal, and a man could not educate them, since they are assumed as the first men ; hence it is necessary to assume that another rational being, not of the race of men, educated them ; of course, only so far, until they could educate each other. A spirit took them in his charge, precisely as it is represented in an old and venerable chronicle, which, indeed, contains throughout the profoundest, sublimest wisdom, and establishes results, to which all philosophy must, after all, return.

II. Only free, reciprocal causality upon each other through conceptions and after conceptions, only this giving and receiving of knowledge, is the distinguishing characteristic of mankind, through which alone every person shows himself to be man.

If man is, then there must also be necessarily a world, and precisely a world like our own, which contains irrational objects and rational beings. This is not the place to proceed further, and to show up the necessity of all determined objects in nature, and their necessary classification, which, however, can be demonstrated quite as strictly as the necessity of a world generally.*

The question concerning the ground of the reality of objects is now answered. The reality of the world—of course for us, that is, for all finite reason—is a condition of self-consciousness ; for we can not posit ourselves without positing something outside of us, to which we must ascribe the same reality which we ascribe to ourselves. To ask for a reality which shall remain after having abstracted from all reason, is contradictory ; for he who asks that question, has also, in all probability, reason, and is impelled by reason to ask his question, and desires a rational answer ; hence he has not abstracted from reason. We can not go out of the sphere of our reason ; this has been well taken care of ; and philosophy desires only that we shall become aware thereof, and shall not believe that we have gone beyond it, when we are always, as a matter of course, within it.

§ 4.

The finite rational being can not assume other finite rational beings outside of itself, without positing it-

---

* Readers who can not see this, should have patience, and should draw no other conclusions from their not seeing, than the only legitimate one, that they do not see it.

*self as occupying a determined relation toward them,
which is called the Legal Relation.*

A. *The subject must distinguish itself through opposition from the rational being, which it has assumed outside of itself.* The subject has posited itself as one, which contains in itself the last ground
of something that is *in it*, (for this is the condition of Egohood, or of Rationality generally ;) but
it has also posited a being outside of itself, as the
last ground of this something in it.

It is to have the power of distinguishing itself
from this other being ; and this is, under our presupposition, possible only, if the subject can distinguish in that given something how far the ground
of this something lies *in itself* and how far it lies
outside of itself.

The ground of the acting of the subject lies both
in the being *outside of it*, and in itself ; that is, the
ground of the form of that acting, or that the subject did act. For if the outside being had not influenced the subject and thus called upon it to act,
the subject would not have acted. Its acting, as
such, is conditioned by the acting of the outside
being.

But moreover, its acting is also conditioned *materialiter ;* for to the subject is assigned its general
sphere of action.

Within this sphere, however, the subject has
chosen with freedom, has absolutely given to itself

the further determination of its acting ; and of this further determination of its activity, the ground lies solely *in the* subject itself. In so far alone, therefore, can it posit itself as an absolutely free being, and as the sole ground of something ; in so far alone can it separate itself utterly from the free being outside of itself, and ascribe its causality to itself only.

Within that sphere, that is, from the end point of the product of the outside being, X, to the end point of its own product, Y, it has chosen amongst the possibilities, which that sphere contains ; and from these possibilities and from this comprehension of them, as possibilities which it might have chosen, the subject constitutes for itself its freedom and self-determination.

Within that sphere the subject had to choose, if the product, Y, was to become possible as a separate one of the effects given through that sphere. Again :

Within this sphere *only* the subject could choose, and *not the other being ;* for the other being had left that sphere undetermined, according to our presupposition.

That, which chose exclusively within this sphere, is *its* Ego, is the individual, is the rational being determined as such through opposition to another rational being ; and this individual is characterized through a determined utterance of freedom, pertaining exclusively to it.

B. *In this distinction through opposition the conception of the subject as a free being, and the conception of the outside rational being, as also a free being, are mutually determined and conditioned through the subject.*

Opposition is not possible unless in the same undivided moment of reflection the opposites are also posited as equals, related to each other, and compared with each other : this is a formal theoretical proposition, which has been proved in its place in the Science of Knowledge, but which we trust will be accepted here as self-evident by common sense, even without that proof. We shall now apply this proposition.

The subject determines itself as an individual and as a free individual through the sphere wherein it has chosen one of the possible acts given in that sphere ; and the subject also posits another individual outside of itself, as its opposite, and as determined through another sphere, wherein this other individual has chosen. Hence the subject posits both spheres at the same time, and only thus is the required opposition possible.

The being outside of the subject is posited as free, hence as a being, which *might* also have overstepped the sphere by which it is now determined, and might have overstepped it in such a manner as not to leave to the first subject the possibility of a free acting. It has voluntarily *not* overstepped that sphere, and has, therefore, itself restricted its own freedom, *materialiter*, that is to say, the sphere of the acts, which its formal freedom could have realized ; and all this the subject also posits necessarily in that stipulated oppositing, (as indeed it posits every thing that follows, which the reader will please bear constantly in mind.)

Again : This outside being has addressed a requirement to the subject to manifest free activity ; hence it has restricted its freedom by a conception of an end entertained by the subject, wherein the freedom of the subject, be it only problematically, was presupposed ; it has therefore restricted its freedom through the conception of the (formal) freedom of the subject.

Now, through this self-restriction of the other being its cognition by the subject as a rational and free being is conditioned. For the subject has posited a free being outside of itself only by virtue of a requirement addressed to itself to manifest free activity, hence only by virtue of that self-restriction of the outside being. But again : This self-restriction was conditioned also by the cognition on the part of the outside being of the subject as a possibly free being. Hence the conception, which the subject has of the outside being, as a free being, is conditioned by the same conception on the part of the outside being of the subject, and by an acting, determined through this conception.

On the other hand, the completion of the cognition on the part of the outside being of the subject, as a free being, is conditioned by the same cognition and a correspondent acting on the part of the

subject. If the subject had not cognized a free being outside of itself, then something would not
have resulted, which, according to the laws of reason, ought to have resulted, and the subject would
not be rational. Or, if this cognition did result in
the subject, but was not followed by a correspondent restriction of its freedom, in order to leave to
that other outside being also the possibility to act
free ; then the other outside being could not have
concluded the subject to be a rational being, since
that conclusion became necessary only by the subject's self-restriction of freedom.

Hence the relation of free beings to each other is
necessarily determined in the following manner and
is posited as thus determined : The mutual cognition of individuals is conditioned by this, that each
treat the other as free, (or, restrict his freedom
through the conception of the freedom of the other.) But this manner of treatment is conditioned
by the manner of acting of each toward the other ;
and this by the manner of acting and by the cognition of the other, and so on *ad infinitum*. The relation of free beings toward each other is therefore
the relation of a reciprocal causality upon each
other through intelligence and freedom. No free
being can recognize the other as such, unless both
mutually thus recognize each other ; and no one can
treat the other as a free being, unless both mutually
thus treat each other.

The conception, here established, is very important for our purpose ; for it is the basis of our whole

theory of Rights.   We shall try, therefore, to make
it clearer bv the following syllogism :

———

I.

*I can suppose that a certain rational being will re-
cognize me as a rational being only in so far as I
treat it myself as such.*

The *Conditioned* of this proposition is, *not* that
that being in itself, and apart from me and from
my consciousness, as, for instance, in its own conscience, (which falls within the sphere of Morality,)
or before others, (which is a matter for the State,)
should recognize me as such a rational being ; but
that it should recognize me as such according to
its own consciousness *and mine* synthetically united in one, that is, according to a consciousness
common to us both ; and in such a manner, that
I should be enabled to compel it to acknowledge,
as sure as itself wishes to pass for a rational being,
that it knows me to be one also.

The *Conditioned* of this proposition moreover is,
not that I can prove generally that I have been recognized by rational beings as their *equals*, but that
this particular individual, C, has recognized me as
such.

The *Condition* of this proposition is, *not* that I
merely entertain the conception of C as a rational
being, *but* that I actually *act* in the sensuous world.
For the conception remains in my most inner consciousness, only *mine*, not accessible to the outside

individual. It is only through experience that the individual, C, obtains something ; and this experience I can excite only through acting. What I *think*, the other one can not know.

The *Condition* is, moreover, *not* that I shall only not act in opposition to that conception, *but* that I shall really act in conformity to it, or shall really enter into mutual causality with C. For otherwise we should remain separate, and should not exist the one for the other.

The ground of the connection is :

Unless I exercise causality upon him, I can not know, or can not prove to him, that he has even a representation of myself or of my existence. Even assuming that I appear as object in the sensuous world and that I am within the sphere of his possible experience, the question still remains, whether he has ever reflected upon me ; and this question he can answer only himself.

Again : Unless I act upon him according to the conception of a rational being, I can not prove to him that he must necessarily have taken me for a rational being. For every manifestation of power can be the result of a power of nature working by mechanical laws ; and only the moderation of power through conception is the sure and exclusive criterion of reason and of freedom.

II.

But I must assume that all rational beings out-side of me will in all possible cases recognize me as a rational being.

The necessity of this universal requirement must be shown up as condition of the possibility of self-consciousness. But self-consciousness is not with-out consciousness of individuality, as has been shown. All that needs, therefore, to be proved now is, that no consciousness of individuality is possible without this recognition, or that the latter necessarily results from the former. We proceed to establish this proof.

A. I posit myself in opposition to C as individual only by ascribing exclusively to myself a sphere for my free activity, which sphere I deny to him.

I posit myself in opposition to C as a rational and free being only by ascribing also to him freedom and reason, hence only by assuming that he has also chosen a sphere of his free activity different from mine.

But I assume all this only on the presupposition that he, in choosing *his* sphere, has taken my free choice into consideration, and has voluntarily and with fixed purpose left my sphere open to me. (Only by positing him as treating me like a rational being do I posit him at all as a rational being. My whole judgment proceeds from me and his treatment of me, as could not well be otherwise in a system which has the Ego for its basis. It is only from this *determined* manifestation of his reason that I draw a conclusion as to his rationality generally.)

But the individual, C, can not act upon me in the described manner without first, at least problematically, recognizing me as such rational being ; and I can not posit him as thus acting upon me unless I posit him also as recognizing me (at least problematically) in that manner.

Every thing problematic becomes categorical when the condition is added. The condition was, that I should recognize the individual, C, as a rational being in a manner valid for *him and me ;* that is, that I should *treat* him as such, *for only acting is such a universally valid recognition.* Now, *I must* necessarily treat him thus, as sure as *I* posit *myself* in opposition to him as rational being—of course in as far as I proceed at all rationally or logically in my cognitions.

As certain, therefore, as I now recognize, that is, treat him as a rational being, he is *bound* or *obliged* by his first problematical recognition to recognize me *categorically*, and to recognize me thus in a universally valid manner, that is, to treat me as a rational being.

There occurs in this instance a uniting of opposites into one. Under the present presupposition, the point of union lies in *me*, in *my consciousness ;* and the uniting is conditioned by this, that I am capable of consciousness.

He fulfills the condition under which I am to recognize him, and prescribes now on his part the condition to me. I, on my part, add the condition by actually recognizing him ; and thus I compel him, in virtue of the condition established by himself, to recognize me categorically, whilst I also oblige *myself*, by thus recognizing him, to treat him as such.

COROLLARIUM.

The conception of individuality is, as we have shown, a *Reciprocal Conception*, that is, a conception which can be thought only in relation to another thinking, and which in its *form* is conditioned by this other thinking, and moreover by the *same* thinking of it. This conception is possible in every rational being only in so far as it is posited as *completed* through another individual. Hence the conception of individuality is never *mine;* but by my own confession and the confession of the other individual, it is both *mine and his;* and *his and mine;* a common conception, wherein two consciousnesses are united into one.

Each one of my conceptions determines its next succeeding one in my consciousness. Through the given conception of individuality a *community* is determined, and the further results thereof depend not only upon me, but also upon the individual, who, by its means, has entered into community with me. And since the conception is necessary, this necessity COMPELS US BOTH TO AGREE TO AND ABIDE BY ITS RESULTS : we are both now *bound* to each other and *obliged* to each other through our very existence. There must be a law common to us both, and which we both must recognize in common as necessary, which determines us both in common to abide by the results of that conception ; and this law must lie in the same character, which led us to enter that community, namely, the character of *Rationality*. This law, which compels us to agree to the same results of a conception, is called *Consequence*, and is scientifically established in common *Logic*.

The whole described union of conceptions was possible only in and through acts. Hence, the continued consequence also is such only in acts ; and can be required and is required only for acts. The acts stand here for conceptions ; and of conceptions in themselves, without acts, we do not speak, because we can not speak of them as such.

———

B. I must appeal to that recognition in every relation which I may occupy to the individual, C, and must always judge him by that recognition.

It is presupposed that I am placed in many relations, connections, and mutual communications with that one and the same individual, C. Hence, I must be able to relate given effects to *him*, that is, to connect them with other effects, which I have already accepted as *his*.

But when he is posited, he is posited both as a determined, sensuous being, and as a rational being ;

both characteristics are synthetically united in him. The former, by virtue of the sensuous predicates of his causality upon me ; the latter, solely by virtue of my having recognized him as such. Only in the union of both predicates is he posited at all through me, and has he become an object of cognition for *me.* Hence, I can relate an act to *him* only in so far as it is partly connected with the sensuous predicates of his previous acts, and partly connected with his recognition through me ; and in so far as it is *determined* through both.

Assuming him to act in such a manner as to make his act determined through the sensuous predicates of his previous acts, (which, indeed, the mechanism of nature itself has provided for,) but not determined through the recognition of him by me as a rational being ; that is to say, assuming him to treat me as an object, and thus to deprive me by his act of the sphere of freedom belonging to me : in that case I am nevertheless still forced to ascribe the act to *him*, to that same sensuous being, C. Now the conception of this sensuous being, C, has heretofore, through the common recognition—and perhaps also through a series of previous acts, which were determined by that recognition—been united in my consciousness with the conception of rationality, (he has been accepted by me as not only a sensuous but also a rational being,) and what I have once united I can not separate again. Those conceptions were posited in my consciousness as necessarily and essentially united ; I had posited sensuousness and rationality in union as the essence of C. But in this new act, X, I am called upon, necessarily, to separate these conceptions ; and hence I can now ascribe rationality to him only *accidentally*. My own treatment of him, as a rational being, becomes now *accidental* and conditioned, and holds good only if he should treat me as one. Hence, I can *in this case* treat him in strict logic, which is here my only law, as a mere sensuous being, until *sensuousness and rationality* shall again be united in the conception of his act.

My assertion in such a case would be : Your act, X, contradicts your confessed recognition, that I am a rational being ; you have acted inconsequently. I, however, acted logically previous to your act, X ; and act now logically in treating you as a mere sensuous being, because by your act, X, you have confessed yourself such.

By making such an assertion I place myself on a higher stand-point over us both, go beyond my individuality, appeal to a *law* which is valid for us both, and apply it to the present case. Hence, I posit myself as *judge*, that is, as his superior. This is the source of the superiority which every one claims, who believes to be in the right over his opponent. But, by appealing to this common law, I invite him to judge with me, and demand that in the present case he shall himself acknowledge my conduct toward him to be logical, and shall, forced by the laws cf thinking, approve my conduct. The community of consciousness continues always. For I judge

F

him by a conception, which I hold that he must have himself.

This is the source of the *Positiveness* which lies in the conception of Rights, and whereby we believe we *oblige* our opponent not to resist our treatment, but even to approve it. This obligatoriness arises by no means from the Moral Law, but from the law of thinking ; and hence there enters here a practical validity of the syllogism.

C. Whatsoever is valid between me and C, is valid between me and every individual with whom I am placed in mutual causality.

Every other rational being can be given to me only in the same manner and under the same conditions as C was given ; for only thus is the positing of a rational being outside of me possible.

The new individual, D, is another one than C, in so far as its free act, *in its sensuous predicates*, is not relatable to the sensuous predicates of the acts of other individuals posited by me.

The condition of the cognition of the identity of the acting individual was the possibility of connecting the characteristic signs of his present act with his previous acts. Where this possibility does not exist, I can not refer the act to any of the rational beings known to me ; and since I must relate it to a rational being, I posit a new one.

Perhaps it may be well to gather the point of the proof here undertaken—which has been somewhat diffused by its numbers of links—into a single view. What we had to prove was this : As sure as I posit myself as an individual, I require all rational beings known to me to recognize me in all cases of reciprocal causality as a rational being. A certain positing of myself is therefore assumed to involve a postulate for other individuals, a postulate extending to *all* possible cases of its application ; and this postulate, if involved in it, we must be able to discover in it by a mere analysis of that certain act of self-positing.

I posit myself as individual, in opposition to another individual, by ascribing to *myself* a sphere for my freedom, from which I exclude the other, and by ascribing to *him* a sphere, from which I exclude myself—of course, only in the thinking of a fact and by virtue of this fact. Hence, I have posited myself as *free* a side of him without danger to the possibility of his freedom. Through this positing of my freedom I have *determined* myself; to be free constitutes my essential character. But what does *to be free* mean? Evidently to be able to carry out the conceptions of acts I may entertain. But the carrying out always *follows* the conception, and the perception of the desired product of my causality is always—in relation to its first conception—a matter of the *future*. Freedom is therefore always posited in the future ; and if it is to constitute the character of a being, it is posited for *all* the future of the individual; is posited in the future as far as the *individual himself* is posited in the future.

Now, my freedom is possible only if the other

individual remains within his sphere; hence, as I demand my freedom for all the future, I also demand his restriction to his sphere, and since he is to be free, his restriction through himself for all the future; and all this I demand immediately in positing myself as an individual.

But he can restrict himself only in consequence of a conception of me as a rational being. Nevertheless, I demand this his self-restriction absolutely; hence I demand of him *Consequence,* (logical consistency,) that is, that all his future conceptions shall be determined by one certain previous conception, namely, his cognition of me as a rational being.

And since he can recognize me as such only if I myself treat him as such, by virtue of such a conception of him, I require of myself the same *Consequence,* and thus his acting is conditioned through mine.

III.

The conclusion has been discovered already. It is this: *I must recognize the free being as such in all cases, that is, must restrict my freedom through the conception of the possibility of his freedom.*

The deduced relation between rational beings —namely, that each individual must restrict his freedom through the conception of the possibility of the freedom of the other—is called the *Relation of Legality,* Legal Relation; and the formula given to it is called the *Fundamental Principle of the Science of Rights.*

This relation has been deduced from the conception of the individual. We have therefore proven what was to be proven. Again: the conception of the individual has been proven to be the condition of self-consciousness; hence, the conception of Law (of Rights) is itself condition of self-consciousness; and hence, this conception has been properly deduced *a priori,* that is, from the pure form of Reason, from the Ego.

COROLLARIA.

I. Our deduction, therefore, asserts that the conception of Law lies in the conception of Reason, and that no finite rational being is possible wherein it does not occur. It does not occur in consequence of having been taught, nor through experience, nor in virtue of arbitrary arrangements among men, etc., but in consequence of man being a rational being. It is a matter of course that the *manifestation* of this conception in empirical consciousness is conditioned through a given case of application; and that this conception does not lie originally—like some empty form—in our soul, waiting for experience to put something into it, as certain philosphers seem to hold in regard to *a priori* conceptions. But that the case of application *must* occur, because man can not be man isolated, has also been proven.

Likewise have we shown that a certain conception, that is, a certain modification of thinking, a certain manner of judging things, must be necessarily pertaining to the rational being as such. Let us call this conception for the present X, if the reader so chooses. This X must operate wherever men live together, and must manifest itself among them and have a designation in their language ; and will do this of itself, without the laborious deduction of the philosopher. Whether this X is precisely what the use of language has named *Law,* is a question which common sense—that is to say, common sense when left to itself, and not when confused and led astray by the arbitrary explanations and interpretations of philosophers—has to decide. For the present we declare, as we have a perfect right to do, that the deduced conception, X, the reality whereof has been proven in our deduction, is to be called in this our investigation the conception of *Law* or *Rights,* holding ourselves responsible to prove by it whatever questions common sense may raise concerning Law.

II. The deduced conception has nothing to do with morality ; nay, has been deduced without it, and since only *one* deduction of a conception is possible, this fact is already in itself sufficient to prove that the conception of Law is not to be deduced from the conception of Morality. Indeed, all attempts to so deduce it have failed utterly. The conception of *Duty,* which is involved in Morality, is in most of its characteristics utterly opposed to

the conception of Law. Morality commands cate
gorically ; Law merely permits, and does not command you to make use of your rights. Nay, Morality often prohibits you to exercise what is your
Right, and what, in the admission of all the world
will, nevertheless, remain your Right. You have a
Right to it, undoubtedly, the world will say, but
you ought not to have used your Right. Now, if
the conception of Law were derived from Morality,
Morality would be in contradiction to itself, since in
such a case it would first grant a Right and then
prohibit its exercise.

Whether, however, Morality may not give a new
sanction to the conception of Law is another question ; but this question belongs to the Science of
Morality. On the field of Natural Law a good will
is counted for nothing. It must be possible to carry out the conception of Law though not one individual had a good will ; and it is the very business
and object of the Science of Rights to establish
such a condition.

And thus we need no artificial measures to separate Natural Law and Morality ; for both Sciences
are originally, and without any coöperation of ours,
separated and completely opposed to each other
through and in Reason.

III. The conception of Law is the conception of
a relation between rational beings. Hence it results only when such beings are thought as in relation to each other. It is nonsense to speak of
rights between man and nature, or between man

and the ground, soil, or animals, etc., as such ; nonsense to speak of such rights as existing direct between Man and Nature. Reason has only *power* over Nature, not a *right* in relation to Nature ; for the conception of Rights does not arise at all in such a relation. It is quite a different thing, when the question is asked, Whether we may not have conscientious scruples as to enjoying this or that portion of Nature? For this is not a question which we ask because we feel that we may have invaded the rights of the things of Nature, but we ask it because we are afraid we might hurt ourselves by indulging in such enjoyments of things ; it is a moral, not a legal question.

It is only when two persons are related to one and the same thing that a question arises as to the *Right to the thing*, or, more properly expressed, as to the *Right which the one person has against the other*, to exclude him from the use of such thing.

IV. It is only through acts, through manifestations of their freedom in the sensuous world, that rational beings are placed in mutual causality with each other ; hence the conception of Rights relates only to what manifests itself in the sensuous world ; and that which has no causality in the sensuous world, but remains in the interior of the Soul, is not subordinated to the conception of Right, but to Morality. It is, therefore, nonsense to speak of a *right* to freedom of thinking, freedom of conscience, etc. You have a *power* to do these internal acts, and you may have duties concerning them, but you can not speak of rights in reference to them.

V. Only in so far as rational beings are really placed in relation to each other and can really act in such a manner that the acting of the one can have results for the other, is a question of rights possible between them. Between persons who do not know each other, or whose spheres of action are utterly separated, a legal relation is not possible. It involves an utter misapprehension of the conception of rights, when people speak of the rights of the Dead upon the Living. We may have moral duties, to remember them, etc., but in no way legal obligations toward them.

Book Second.

——•——

DEDUCTION

OF THE

APPLICABILITY

OF THE

CONCEPTION OF RIGHTS.

§ 5.

THE RATIONAL BEING CAN NOT POSIT ITSELF AS
AN INDIVIDUAL, HAVING CAUSALITY, UNLESS IT
ASCRIBES TO ITSELF A MATERIAL BODY AND
THEREBY DETERMINES THAT BODY.

PROOF.

ACCORDING to our previous result, the rational
being posits itself as a rational individual, or, as we
shall say hereafter, as a *person*, only by *ascribing
exclusively to itself a sphere for its freedom*. It says :
I am the person which has exclusive freedom within
this sphere, and I am no other possible person ; and
no other person is *myself*, that is, no other person
has freedom within this sphere ascribed to me.
This constitutes its individual character ; through
this determination the person is this or that person,
bearing this or that name, and is no other one.

All we have to do is to analyze this act; to see
what takes place when it does take place.

A. The Subject ascribes this sphere to itself ; determines itself through this sphere. Hence it oppos-
its the sphere to itself. Itself is the logical subject,
(in any possible proposition,) and the sphere is the

predicate; but subject and predicate are always opposed to each other.

The first question is: Which is the true subject? Evidently that which is active purely in and upon itself; that which determines itself to think an object or to will an end; the Spiritual, the pure Egohood. To this is *opposed* a limited, but exclusively its own sphere of its possible free acts. By ascribing this sphere to itself, it limits itself, and changes from the absolute formal to a determined material *Ego* or to a person; and I hope that these two distinct conceptions will not be mixed up with each other by the reader.

The sphere is opposed to the subject signifies: it is excluded from the subject, posited outside of it, separated from it. Thinking this still more definitely, it signifies: the sphere is posited as *not existing* through the in itself returning activity; and the latter is posited as *not existing* through the sphere; both are mutually independent of and accidental for each other. But that, which is thus related to the Ego, as independent of it, belongs—according to our previous deductions—to the *World*.

This sphere is therefore posited as *a part of the World*.

B. This sphere is posited through an original and necessary activity of the Ego, that is, it is *contemplated*, and thus becomes a Real or an actual somewhat.

As certain results of the Science of Knowledge

can not be supposed to be known to all readers of this work, I here append such as relate to this paragraph : Those persons have not the least conception of the Science of Knowledge and of KANT's system who believe that in contemplating, there is, besides the contemplating subject and the contemplation, moreover, a thing, a somewhat, upon which the contemplation is directed, as common sense generally holds in regard to bodily seeing. On the contrary, through the contemplating and only through it does the contemplated arise. The Ego returns into itself, and this act furnishes contemplation and contemplated object together. In contemplation, reason (or the Ego) is by no means passive, but absolutely active. In contemplation, reason is the *productive power of imagination.* Through the seeing, or contemplating, something is thrown out from the Ego, as it were, somewhat in the manner that the painter throws out from his eye the completed forms upon the canvas, (*looks them,* so to speak, upon the canvas,) before the slower hand can draw their outlines. In the same manner the sphere is here posited, or contemplated.

Again : The Ego in contemplating itself as activity contemplates its own activity as a *line-drawing.* This is the original scheme of activity in general, as every one will discover who wishes to excite in himself that highest contemplation. This original line is the *pure extension,* the common characteristic of Time and Space, out of which Time and Space arise only by distinction and further determination. This line does not presuppose space, but space presupposes it; and the lines in space, that is, the limits of the extended things in space, are something utterly different.

In the same manner the sphere is here produced in the form of lines, and thus becomes an *Extended Somewhat.*

C. This sphere is *determined;* hence the producing has its limits, and the product is taken hold of in the understanding as a completed whole, and thus first becomes truly posited, that is, fixed.

This product determines the person; the person is the same person only in so far as the product is the same, and ceases to be the same when the product ceases to be the same. But, according to our previous results, the person must posit himself continuing, as sure as he posits himself free. Hence he also posits that product as continuing the same; as permanent, fixed, and unchangeable; as a whole, completed at once. But a fixed and forever determined extension is *extension in space.* Hence that sphere is necessarily *posited*, as a limited body extended in space and filling up its space; and it is necessarily *found* as such body in the analysis, the consciousness whereof alone is possible to us; since the synthesis, now described, or the production of that sphere is presupposed only for the possibility of the analysis, and thus for the possibility of consciousness.

D. The deduced material body is posited as *the sphere of all possible free acts of the person*, and as nothing else. Therein alone does its essence consist.

That a person is free, signifies, according to our former results : through his generating a conception of an End he at once becomes the cause of an object exactly corresponding to that conception ; or in other words, only and merely through his will does a person become a cause ; for, to trace out a conception of an end is, to will. Now, the described body is to contain the free acts of such a person ; hence it is in that body that the person is cause in the manner stated. Immediately through his will, and without any other means, the will is realized in the body ; as the person wills, so is the will accomplished in the body.

Again : Since the described body is nothing but the sphere of free acts, the conception of the body must exhaust the conception of that free sphere, and *vice versa*. The person can not be absolutely free cause, that is, can not have a causality resulting immediately from the will—outside of his body.* If a determined will is given, a corresponding determined change in the body is the necessary result. On the other hand, no change can occur in the body except through the will of the person ; and hence you can with equal certainty conclude

---

* How this result is apparently contradicted by the phenomena of Mesmerism, and yet only apparently, this is not the place to explain.—TRANSLATOR.

G

from a given change in the body, as to a determined conception of the person, corresponding to the change. This last result will attain its proper determinateness and full significance only in the future.

E. But how and in what manner can the changes in a material body be made to express a conception ? Matter, in its essence, is imperishable ; it can not be annihilated, nor can new matter be produced. The conception of a change in the body can not apply to matter in this sense. Again : The posited body is to continue uninterruptedly ; hence the same parts of the matter are to remain together and to continue to constitute the body. It seems, therefore, as if the conception of a change could also not be applied to the body in this sense.

The body is matter. Matter is infinitely divisible. Now, the material parts of the body would remain, and yet would also undergo change, if they changed their relation to each other. The relation of the manyfold to each other is called *the form.* Hence the parts, *in so far as they constitute the form,* are to remain ; but the form itself is to be changed. (I say in so far as they constitute the form ; and hence these parts may constantly separate themselves from the body—provided they are replaced in the same undivided moment by other parts—without thereby destroying the required permanency and sameness of the body.) Our result is, therefore, that the change produced in the body through the conception is in the form of *motion of the parts of the body*, and is, therefore, a change of the form.

F. In the described body the conceptions of the person are expressed through a change in the relation of the *parts* to each other. These conceptions, or the will of the person, may be infinitely different; and the body, which is to contain the sphere of freedom of such person, must be able to express this infinite difference. Hence, each part must be able to change its position in relation to the other parts, that is, must be able to move while all the others are at rest; to each infinite part of the body must be assigned a mobility of *its own*. The body must be so constituted, that it will always be a matter of freedom to think a part larger or smaller, more complicated or more simple; and likewise to think each multiplicity of parts as a whole, and then again as a part in relation to the more extended whole, etc. It is altogether for thinking to determine every time what is to constitute a part. Again: When thinking thus determines what is to be a part for the time, a peculiar motion of such part must be the immediate result.

Something, which is thought as a part in such a relation to a whole, is called a *member*. Each member of the body contains, therefore, members within itself; and these again contain members; and so on *ad infinitum*. Whatsoever is to be regarded for the moment as a member depends altogether

upon the causality-conception. The *member* moves
when it is regarded as such ; and that, which is
the whole in relation to it, is then at rest ; and
again, that which is a part in relation to this member, rests also ; that is, it has no motion of its own,
only the motion in common with the member. This
is called *Articulation.* The deduced body is necessarily articulated, and must be posited as such.

Such a body, to the continuance and identity
whereof we attach the continuance and identity of
our personality, and which we posit as a complete
articulated whole, and in which we posit ourselves
as having causality immediately through our will,
is what we call *our body.* We have thus proved
what was to be proved.

§ 6.

THE PERSON CAN ASCRIBE TO ITSELF NO BODY,
WITHOUT POSITING SUCH BODY AS UNDER THE
INFLUENCE OF ANOTHER OUTSIDE PERSON, AND
WITHOUT, THEREFORE, FURTHER DETERMINING
SUCH BODY.

PROOF.

A. We have shown that the person can not posit
himself at all with consciousness, unless he posits
an influence as having occurred upon him. The
positing of such an influence was the exclusive condition of all consciousness, and was the first point
to which the whole consciousness was attached.
This influence is posited as having occurred upon

the *determined person, the individual, as such;* for
we have shown that the rational being can not posit
itself as a rational being generally, but can posit
itself only as an individual ; hence an influence
posited by the person upon himself is necessarily
an influence upon himself as such individual, because he is nothing for himself and can be nothing
else for himself than an individual.

We have also shown, that the proposition : an influence occurs upon a rational being, signifies the
same as : its free activity has been canceled in part
and in a certain respect.   Only through this canceling of its activity does an object become *for* the
Intelligence, and does the Intelligence conclude
that there is something which exists not through it.

An influence has been directed upon the rational
being, as individual, signifies, therefore : an activity,
which belongs to it, as an individual, has been canceled.   Now the whole sphere of *his* activity, as
an individual, is his body.   Hence the causality of
the individual in this body, or his power to be cause
in it, through his mere will, must be canceled ; in
other words, the influence must have been directed
upon the body of the person.

If we, therefore, assume that one of the acts
which lie within the sphere of the possible acts of
a person has been canceled, or rendered impossible
for the moment, we have explained the required influence.

But the person is to refer this influence *to himself,* that is to say, the person is to posit that mo-
mentarily canceled activity as one of his possible

activities, as contained in the sphere of the utterances of his freedom. Hence, the person must
posit that canceled activity in order to be able to
posit it as canceled; or, that activity must really
exist, and must not be canceled. The same determined activity of the person must, therefore, in the
same undivided moment, *be canceled*, and also *be
not canceled*, if a consciousness is to be possible.
Let us examine how this can be.

B. All activity of the person is a certain determination of the articulated body; that an activity
of the person is checked, signifies, therefore, that a
certain determination of the articulated body is impossible.

Now the person can not posit at all that his activity is checked, or that in his articulated body a
certain determination is impossible, without positing at the same time such a determination as possible; for only on the condition that a determination in the body through mere will is possible,
does he posit something as his body. Hence, the
person must posit the very determination, which is
to be impossible, as possible; and since the person
can posit nothing, unless it *is*, (for the person,) it follows that the person must actually produce this determination. And yet this activity, although it is
thus actually produced, must always remain checked and canceled; for the person only produces it in
order to be able to posit it as canceled. It thus appears that the same determination of the articulation is both actually produced through the causality

of the will and canceled through an external influence. Again: The person is to find himself in this moment as free in his sphere, is to ascribe the whole of his body to himself. It is, therefore, necessary that even in the sense in which he posits a certain determination of his articulation as canceled, the person should retain the power through his mere will to remove that canceling influence ; for else the person would not ascribe the body at all to himself, in this sense, and would thus not posit an external influence as having occurred upon it. In short, the fact that the canceling remains, must depend upon the free-will of the person ; and the person must posit it as possible to remove that canceling.

How can he posit this possibility ? Clearly not in consequence of a previous experience, for we have here the beginning of all experience. Hence, in positing, that the production of that determination, in the manner in which it actually is produced, would certainly remove the canceling, did not the person restrain his will to thus remove it.

In positing this, there is evidently discovered and posited a double manner of determining the articulation, which may be also called a double articulation, or a double *organ ;* and the relation of this duplicity is this : The first mode of determining the articulation—wherein the person *produces* the canceled movement, and which we shall call the *higher organ*—may be modified through the will without the other—which we shall call the *lower organ*—being thereby modified. Higher and lower organs are in so far distinguished. But again : If the modification of the higher organ is not at the same time to modify the lower one, then the person must restrain the will to have the lower organ thus modified. Hence, higher and lower organ are also unitable through the will, and are in so far one and the same organ.

The perception of the required influence upon the person requires, therefore, the following : The person must give himself up to the influence, must not cancel the modification produced thereby in his organ. He has the power of thus canceling that influence through his mere will, and must restrict the freedom of his will if he does not want that influence canceled. But furthermore : The person must internally reproduce that modification of his organ, caused by the external influence upon it.

We have said a possible manifestation of the freedom of the person is canceled by that influence. This does not mean that the activity of the person has been made impossible in a certain direction and for a certain purpose, but merely that something has been produced in the person which the person might himself have produced, but which has been produced in the person in such a manner that the person must ascribe it, not to his own, but to the causality of a being outside of himself. Indeed, nothing occurs within the perception of a rational being, which it does not believe itself capable of producing itself, or the production whereof it may not

ascribe to iteslf; for any thing else the rational being has no *sense*. What has thus been produced
within its organ, the rational being reproduces with
freedom through its higher organ, but in such a
manner that the reproduction does not influence
the lower organ ; for if it did—although it would result in precisely the same determination of the articulated body—it would now no longer be a perceived determination, but a determination produced
by the person himself. It would no longer be the
product of a foreign and external object, but of the
own causality of the subject. You can not *see*, for
instance, unless you first give yourself up to an influence, and then internally reproduce the form of
the object and actively trace out within you its outlines. You can not hear, unless you internally imitate the tones through the same organ through
which, in speaking, the same tones were produced.
If, however, this internal causality should extend to
the external organ, you would no longer hear, but
speak.

In so far as the relation is as we have described
it, the articulated body of man is *Sense*. But it is
sense only, as every one must see, in relation to an
influence upon it on the part of a causality, which
might be its own, but which, in such a case, is not
its own, but is the causality of an external cause.

The person under this sort of an influence remains perfectly and completely free. That which
the external cause has produced in the person may
be immediately removed by the person ; and the

person posits expressly this power of removing it, and hence posits, that the existence of the influence depends upon himself. Again, if such an influence is to occur, the person must with freedom imitate it, and *must thus expressly realize his freedom in order to be but able to perceive.* (We have here, by the by, described and extensively determined the *absolute freedom of reflection.*)

And thus the articulated body of the person has indeed been further determined. For it has also been posited as Sense; and to enable it to be posited as such, higher and lower organs have been ascribed to the body; of which the lower organ, (sense) through which it is related to external objects and to rational beings, can be placed under a foreign influence, but the higher organ (reflection) never.

C. The described influence upon the subject is to be such that only a *rational* being outside of the subject can be posited as its cause; namely, under the assumption that the purpose of that outside rational being was thus to influence the subject. But it has been shown that no influence can occur upon the subject, unless that subject through its own freedom causes the impression made upon it to halt, and does then reproduce it internally. The subject itself must act with a fixed end in view; that is to say, it must limit the sum of its freedom, which might cancel that impression, to the attainment of the proposed end of the cognition, which self-limitation is indeed the exclusive criterion of Reason. Hence, the subject must complete through itself the attainment of the end of the other outside being ; and thus the outside rational being must have calculated upon this completion of its purpose through the subject, if it really had an end in view. It must, therefore, be considered as a rational being, in so far as it has *limited* its own freedom to the manner of the given impression, through this presupposition of the freedom of the subject.

But it always remains possible that the manner of acting on the part of that outside being was the result of chance or of necessity. There is, as yet, no ground to assume self-limitation on the part of that outside being, unless it can be shown that it *might* have acted differently ; that the fullness of its power, if exercised, would have resulted in quite a different mode of acting ; and that that fullness of power must, therefore, have been restricted, to have resulted in the manner it did.

It must, therefore, be possible for that outside being to influence or treat the subject also in an opposite manner.

What is this opposite manner ? The character of the first kind of causality was such that it depended altogether upon the freedom of my will, whether an influence should be exerted upon me or not ; for that influence could not occur unless I passively submitted to it and then reproduced it as having occurred. The character of an opposite causality would, therefore, be that it no longer depended upon my freedom, whether I chose to observe the influence or not ; its character implying that I *must* observe it. How is such an influence possible ?

The first kind of influence was dependent upon my freedom, because through that mere freedom of will I could destroy the produced form of my articulated body if I chose ; under the second kind of influence this must, therefore, be impossible. The produced form of my body must be firm, indestructible—at least, not destructible through the higher organ—my body must be tied to this form, and be utterly checked in its movements. From such a complete check the reflection upon this check would also result necessarily ; not in its form, as the result of the check, but in its content, as following and directing itself upon the check. For a free being finds itself only as free. As sure, therefore, as it reflects, it imitates, internally, an influence produced upon it, under the presupposition that it has the power to break off this influence at any moment. It restricts its own freedom. But if that influence can no longer be broken off by the mere causality of the will, then such a self-limitation is also unnecessary. Something is wanting which belongs in the reflection of a free being, as such, and thus the compulsion is felt. Reflection is always accompanied by the feeling of compulsion ; for in the articulated body every thing is connected, and each part influences all others, in virtue of the conception of articulation.

This checking of the free movement in my body I must necessarily posit as possible ; and thus my body is further determined. As its condition I must posit outside of me a tough, compact matter, capable of resisting the free movement of my body ; and thus through the further determination of my body, the sensuous world has also been further determined.*

That tough, compact matter can check only a part of my free movements, but not all ; for in the latter case the freedom of person would be utterly annihilated. Hence, I must be able, through the free movement of the other part of my body, to remove the check from the limited part, and hence to exercise a causality upon the tough matter. The body must have physical power to resist the impression of that matter, if not immediately, through the will, at least mediately, through Art, that is, through application of the will by means of the free parts of the body. But in that case the organ of this causality itself must be composed of such a

* A deduction of such an empirical determination signifies as follows : The philosopher shows *a priori*, that, if one person is to influence the other, and each one to know and treat the other as rational being, then such persons must have a common sphere of action, a sort of independent body, and outside of this body must be, amongst other powers, one power to check its free movement. He then looks around in the sensuous world, points to tough matter, and says, Here we have found what reason required. It was sure to be found, but I could not tell *a priori what* it was ; could merely say it must be somewhere and of some character ; and now *a posteriori* I can tell you, it is tough matter.—TRANSLATOR'S REMARK.

tough substance ; and the superiority of a rational being over matter arises only from the freedom to work out conceptions. Matter works only by mechanical laws, and has thus only one mode of working, whereas the free being has many modes.

If my body consists of tough, hard matter, and has the power to modify all matter of the sensuous world, and to form it after my conception, then the body of the person outside of me consists of the same matter and has the same power. Now, my body itself being matter, it is, as such, an object of the physical influence of the other person ; a possible object, whose free movements he can check altogether. If he had considered and treated me as such mere matter, in the presupposed case, he would have treated me thus. But he has not done so ; hence he has not conceived me to be mere matter, but to be a rational being, by the conception whereof he has restricted his own freedom ; and from this his treatment I am now authorized to draw the conclusion, that the influence exercised upon me was the influence of a rational being.

We have thus established the criterion of the reciprocal influence of rational beings upon each other. That influence always presupposes, *that the object of the influence has sensuousness*, and is not, like mere matter, to be modified by physical power.

D. In the described influence, the organ of the Subject has been actually modified through an external person. This has been done neither through

the immediate bodily touch of that other person nor
through some firm matter ; for the latter would not
involve the conception of the influence of a person.
How then ?

The organ is, at all events, something material,
the whole body being material ; and the organ must
therefore have been modified, brought into and retained in a certain form, and likewise through some
external matter. The mere will of the subject would
cancel this form ; and he must restrain his will, not
to destroy it. The matter through which this form
has been produced is, therefore, no tough, firm matter, the parts whereof could be separated by the mere
will, but a finer, more subtle matter. Such a subtle matter must be necessarily posited as condition
of the required influence upon the sensuous world.

The modification of the organ for the influence
through freedom is not to affect at all the organ for
the influence through compulsion, but is to leave it
utterly free. Hence, the finer matter must influence only the former and not in any way the latter
organ ; it must be a matter, the component parts
whereof have no connection perceptible to the lower organ, that is, to the organ under compulsion.

In the described condition I assume the power to
react upon this subtle matter through the mere will,
by means of an affection of the higher through the
lower organ ; for it has been expressly stated, that
I must hold back such a movement of the lower organ, in order not to destroy the determination produced in the higher organ ; hence, I must also hold

back the power, to give another determination to that more subtle matter. *The subtle matter is therefore for me modifiable through the mere will.*

To meet in advance any possible misapprehension, I add a few words. A double organ has been posited ; a higher and a lower organ. The higher organ is that which is modified through the subtle matter ; the lower organ is that which can be checked by the tough and hard matter.

Two cases are possible :

Either the person is influenced as a free being. In that case the higher organ is modified through a certain form of the more subtle matter ; and if the person is to perceive this influence, he must restrain the movement of the lower organ in so far as it is related to that part of the higher organ, but must at the same time—only internally, however— imitate the particular movement which he would have to make, in order to produce himself that particular given modification of the higher organ. For instance, if you perceive an object in Space through Sight, you internally—but with the quickness of lightning, and hence imperceptibly—imitate the feeling of the object, that is, imitate the pressure which would be needed to produce that object through plastic ; and the impression in the eye is retained, as the scheme of this imitation. This explains why uneducated people, people who have not yet attained facility in executing the functions of mankind, when they wish to look carefully at an elevated body, or even at a painting, engraving, book, etc., always want to touch what they see. Again : A person, who hears, can not possibly at the same time speak ; for he must, in hearing, imitate the tones which he hears, through his organ of speech, by reproducing them. This explains why some people often ask you to repeat what you have said. They heard it well enough, but did not become conscious of it, because they did not reproduce your words internally. Frequently such people must repeat your words loudly to themselves before they can understand them. In this case, therefore, the body serves as organ, as sense, and as *higher* sense.

Or, the second case, a modification is produced in the higher organ through the mere will of the person, accompanied by the will that the lower organ shall be correspondingly moved by this will. In that case, if the lower organ is not checked, the intended movement results, and through that movement the intended modification of the subtle or tough matter also results. Thus, for instance, you form in the eye, as an active organ, the figures you intend to sketch or the words you intend to write, and throw them outside of you, long before the hand, which obeys your eye, can draw or write them. In this case the body serves as tool.

If the intended movement of the lower organ does not result—the movement of the higher organ always results so long as the person is alive—then

H

the lower organ is checked ; and in that case, the body serves as sense, but as lower sense.

When one rational being affects another rational being as mere matter, then the lower sense of that being is also affected, it is true, and is so affected necessarily and altogether independently of the freedom of that being, (as the lower sense is indeed always affected ;) but it is not to be assumed that this affection was in the intention of the person who produced it. His intention was merely to attain his purpose, to express his conception in matter, and he never took into consideration whether that matter would feel it or not. Hence, the reciprocal influence of rational beings upon each other, *as such*, always occurs by means of the higher sense ; for only the higher sense is one which can not be affected without having been presupposed. Our criterion of this reciprocal influence remains, therefore, correct.

E. As condition of self-consciousness an external influence has been posited, and by virtue thereof a certain nature of the body has been posited, and as a result of this nature of the body a certain condition of the sensuous world has been posited. Our argument was : If consciousness is to be possible, then the sensuous world must be constituted in that manner and must have that relation to our body which has been specified.

We have also shown up, as condition of self-consciousness, a community of free individuals, and from this necessary condition we have deduced the further determination of the body, and, by its means, of the sensuous world. The argument here was: Because there is to be in the sensuous world a community of free beings, therefore the world must be thus or thus constituted. But such a community of free beings *is* only in so far as it is posited through these beings—on no account with *freedom* on their part, but with absolute necessity; and whatsoever is thus posited has reality for us.

F. I ascribe to myself a higher and lower organ, related to each other as stated above; and in consequence thereof assume in the sensuous world outside of me a coarser and a finer matter, related to my organs as stated above. Such a positing is, as we have shown, a necessary condition of self-consciousness, and hence is involved in the conception of a person. If I posit, therefore, a person outside of me, I must necessarily assume that that person posits the same, or, in other words, I must ascribe to that person also, as I did to myself, the possession and use of two such distinct organs, and must assume *for that person also*, as I assumed for myself, the real existence of such a determined sensuous world.

This transferring my necessary thinking to another person, is also involved in the conception of a person. Hence, I must also assume of the other person, that in the same manner he assumes of me what I assume of him, and that he also assumes that I assume the same of him. In other words, the conceptions of the determined articulation of rational beings and of the sensuous world outside of them, are necessarily exchangeable conceptions ; conceptions concerning which all rational beings agree beforehand, without any previous understanding, and thus agree necessarily, *because the personality of each involves the same manner of contemplating.* Each one can justly assume of the other and claim that that other must have the same conceptions on these matters, as sure as the other pretends to be a rational being.

G. But a new objection arises, which must be answered before the body of a rational being can be completely determined. It has been asserted that I can not attain self-consciousness except through the influence of a rational being outside of me. Now, although it depends solely upon my freedom whether I choose to surrender myself to that influence or not, and although the manner of my reacting upon that influence is altogether within my free will, still, the possibility of my thus giving utterance to my freedom is conditioned by the occurrence of the influence from without—no such external influence, no possibility for me to manifest my freedom. Hence, so far as actuality is concerned, I am *made* a rational being. True, so far as the *power* of freedom is concerned, I am free before ; but in actuality I can not become a free or rational being unless that external influence is directed upon me. Hence, my rationality depends upon the arbitrariness or the good-will of another—upon chance; and all rationality depends upon chance.

But this can not be ; for if it were, I could not be independent as a person ; I could only be the accidence of another person, who again would be the accidence of a third, and so on *ad infinitum.*

This contradiction can not be solved otherwise than by the presupposition that the other has already been *compelled,* in that original influence upon me, to treat me as a rational being, (*compelled,* of course, as a rational being, that is to say, he has felt himself consistently bound,) and that he has been compelled to treat me thus by *me ;* that, therefore, in that first original influence upon me, which made me dependent upon him, he was also, at the same time, dependent upon me ; that, therefore, that very first and *original* relation between us was already a relation of reciprocal causality.

But this seems impossible. For previous to that influence *I am not at all I ;* have not posited myself ; since the positing of myself is possible only on condition of that external influence upon me. How then can I have causality upon the other person before I have posited myself ? I am to have causality without having it ; to influence the other person without being active. How is this thinkable ?

1. *To influence without influencing* signifies to

have a mere power to influence. This mere power is to influence, is to have causality. But a power is only an ideal conception, and it would be an empty thought to ascribe to such a power the exclusive predicate of reality, namely, causality, without assuming that power as realized.

Now, the whole power of the person is assuredly realized in the sensuous world, in the conception of his body, which body is as sure as the person is, and continues as long as the person continues, and which body, moreover, is a completed Whole of material parts, and has, therefore, a determined original form.

It is, therefore, required that my body should have causality, should be active, and yet that *I* should not be active in that activity.

2. But my body is *my* body only in so far as it is placed in motion by my will, and otherwise it is only a mass of matter ; my body is active as my body only in so far as *I* am active through it. Now, in the present case I am not to be active, am not even to be I. Hence, my body can not be active.

It must, therefore, be thus : Through its mere existence in space, and through its form, my body must exercise an influence of such a nature that every rational being will be bound to consider me as a being gifted with reason, and hence to treat me as such.

3. The first and most difficult question is, now,

How can any thing exercise an influence through its mere existence in space, without any motion ?

The influence is to be exercised upon a rational being, *as such;* hence, it must occur, not through an immediate touching and checking of its lower organ, but must be brought to bear upon its higher organ, hence by means of the more subtle matter. Now, it is true that, in our above description, we have assumed this subtle matter to be a means whereby rational beings influence each other, in modifying it through their higher organ. This is not, however, to be the case here. In our case, the human body is to produce an influence in its state of repose, without any activity ; and accordingly the more subtle matter must be posited in our case as modifiable by the mere form of the body in its state of repose, and as modifying the higher organ of another rational being through this its modification. In so far, moreover, as the human body is here regarded merely as form, the same must be the case in respect to every other form.

(It has not been proved, that the here deduced more subtle matter, by means of which the mere reposing form in space is to exercise an influence, is specifically different from the previously deduced more subtle matter, but simply that the more subtle matter must have these two predicates. For if we had wished to prove the former, we should have had to show that the subtle matter, whereby the repos ing form is to exercise an influence, could not be possibly placed in motion by the movement of the higher organ, and hence must be specifically distinct. Now, although this proof is not exactly necessary here, I will append it, as follows :

The form of the person outside of me must continue to be the same, as we have shown. Now, if we reciprocally influence each other only by means of a subtle matter, which can be placed in motion, (*Air,*)—that is to say, only by speaking with each other—then that matter, A, would continually change, and if *it* received the impression of our forms, would continually change those forms, and hence those persons. But as those persons must remain the same, it is requisite that the matter in which our forms are impressed must remain immovable amidst all the motion of the other matter. A must, therefore, be not modifiable through our organ, and in so far distinct from A. Let us call it B, or *Light.* (The appearances in light can, therefore, be modified by us only indirectly, namely, in so far as we can modify that appearance itself, or the form of our body.)

4. My body must be visible to the person outside of me, must appear and have appeared to that person through the medium of the light, *as sure as that other person exercises an influence upon me.* Thus our first question is answered.

But now comes the second question. For, according to our necessary presupposition, this appearance is to be of such a nature that it absolutely can not be understood and comprehended except by assuming it to be the appearance (form) of a rational being. My form must be of such a character that I can say to each other person: As soon as you see this (my) form, you are necessitated te consider it as the representative of a rational being in the sensuous world, if you are yourself a rational being. How is this possible?

First of all, what does this signify, to understand or comprehend? It signifies to fix, to determine, to limit. I have comprehended an appearance, when I have received through it a perfect whole of a knowledge, which, in all its parts, is grounded in itself; whereof each part is explained and grounded through all others, and *vice versa.* (So long as I am still explaining, still floating and undetermined in my belief, still driven from one part of my knowledge to other parts, I have not yet comprehended. I have not comprehended A as an accidental until I have ascertained its cause; and as A is a determined accidental, its determined cause.)

To say, therefore, I can not understand an appearance except in a certain manner, signifies: each separate part of the appearance impels me onward to a certain point, and only when I have arrived at this point can I place the several parts in order and gather them all into a whole of knowledge.

To say, therefore, I can not comprehend the appearance of a human body except by assuming it to be the body of a rational being, signifies: in gathering together its several parts, I can not stop until I have arrived at the point which forces me to consider it the body of a thinking being.

I shall proceed to the strict genetical proof of this result ; sketching, however, only its chief features ; for, as a whole in its completeness, it forms a science of its own, the science of *Anthropology.*

I. It must be necessary to think the human body as a Whole, and impossible to think its parts separately as we can think coarse matter, sand earth, etc.   What must thus be thought as a Whole, in order to be thought at all, is called *an organized product of nature.*   The human body must, therefore, be firstly such an *organized* product of nature. The distinction of such an organized product of nature from a *product of art*, which also can only be thought as a Whole, lies in this : In both products each part exists only for the sake of the others, and hence for the sake of the whole ; and our judgment in considering either product is forced to proceed from one part to the other, till all have been gathered together.   But in the product of nature the Whole also exists for the sake of the parts, and has, as a Whole, no other purpose than to produce these determined parts ; whereas, in the product of art, the Whole does not thus refer back to the parts, but refers to an external purpose.   The product of nature exists for its own sake ; the product of art for the sake of a purpose, or as a tool. Again : In the product of nature each single part produces itself by its inner power ; but in the product of art, before even it can become such, this inner power of self-development is killed off, and in the composition of its parts this inner power is not at all taken into calculation. It is composed simply according to mechanical laws ; and hence it refers to an external originator, whereas the product of nature produces and maintains itself.

II. An appearance has been completely comprehended by the presupposition that it is a product of nature, if all that occurs in it refers back to organization and can be completely explained by the end and aim of this determined organization. For instance, the highest and last manifestation of the organizing power in plants is the seed. Now, this seed is completely explainable from the organization as its end, that is, as the means of propagating the plant ; and through this seed the power of organization returns into itself and recommences its career. The act of organization thus never closes, but always rushes along in an endless circle.

But that an appearance has not been completely comprehended by that presupposition, signifies, that the highest and final product of the power of organization can not be referred back as means to that power, but rather points to quite another purpose. True, you continue the explanation according to the laws of organization for some time, (whereas, in the product of art you can not apply this law at all,) but after a while you discover that you can no longer use it to explain ; that is, its final product

can not be again related to it.   Hence, the circle is
not closed, and the comprehension not completed ;
that is to say, nothing has been *comprehended*, the
appearance has not been understood.   (It is true,
man also completes the circle of organization by
the propagation of his species.   He is a perfect
plant, but he is also something more.)

Now, such a final product of the power of organization, which can not be referred back again to it,
is *Articulation*.   Articulation is both visible and a
product of organization ; but articulation does not
again produce organization, and rather refers to
another end ; that is to say, it can only be gathered together completely in another conception.
This other conception can be the conception of
free movement, and in so far man is an *animal*.

III. But this presupposition of free movement
also must be insufficient for the comprehension of
the human body.   Its articulation, therefore, must
be incomprehensible in any *determined* conception.
It must not refer to a definite, *determined sphere* of
arbitrary motion, as in the case of the animal, but
to all infinitely thinkable motions.   There must be,
not a determinedness of articulation, but an infinite determinability of articulation ; not development, but developability.   In short, all animals are
perfect and complete ; man, however, is merely suggested.   A rational observer of the human body
can unite its parts in no conception, except in the
conception of a rational being like himself, or in

the conception of freedom as given to him in his self-consciousness. He must subsume the conception of his own Ego to his contemplation of that other human body, because that body expresses no conception of its own, and can only be explained by that conception of his own Ego. Every animal *is* what it is ; man alone is originally nothing at all. What man is to be, he must become ; and as he is to be a being for himself, must become through himself. Nature completed all her works ; only from man did she withdraw her hands, and precisely thereby gave him over to himself. Cultivability, as such, is the character of mankind. The impossibility of subsuming to the human form any other conception than that of his own Ego, is it, which forces every man inwardly to consider every other man as his equal.

COROLLARIA.

I. It is a vexatious question, which, so far as I know, Philosophy has never yet solved : How do we come to transfer to some object of the sensuous world the conception of rationality and not to others ; or what is the characteristic distinction of both classes ?

KANT says : " Act so that the principle of thy will can be the principle of a universal legislation." But who shall belong to the empire which is governed by this legislation, and who shall enjoy its protection ? I am required to treat certain beings in such a manner that I can desire them to treat me according to the same principle. But I act every day upon animals and lifeless objects without ever seriously entertaining that rule. I am told : Of course, the rule applies only to beings who are capable of being conscious of laws, hence of rational beings. But who is to tell me what specific objects in nature are rational beings ; whether, perhaps, only the white European or also the black negro, whether only the full-grown man or also the child, can claim the protection of that legislation ; or whether, perhaps, the faithful house-dog may not likewise claim it ? Until this question has been answered, KANT's rule has neither applicability nor reality, however excellent it may be.

Nature has decided this question long ago. There is probably no man who, at the first glimpse of another man, will take to flight, as at the view of a wild animal, or prepare to kill and eat him like a piece of game ; or who would not, on the contrary, endeavor to enter into mutual communication with him. This is so, not through habit and education, but through nature and reason, and we have just shown up the law by virtue of which it is so.

Let no one believe, however, that man must first go through that long and tiresome process of reasoning, which we have just gone through, in order to arrive at the comprehension that a certain external body is his equal. That recognition either does not take place at all, or it occurs at once without consciousness of the ground thereof. It is only the philosopher's business to discover these grounds.

II. Every animal, a few hours after its birth moves to seek nourishment at the breasts of its mother, guided by the *animal instinct*, or the law of certain free motions, which is likewise the ground of the so-called art-instinct of animals. Man also has instinct, but not animal instinct in the above significance ; he has only plant-instinct. He needs the free help of men, and without it would die a few hours after his birth. As soon as he leaves the womb of his mother, nature withdraws her hands from him and casts him aside, as it were. PLINIUS and others have been very bitter against man's creator on that account. This may be rhetorical, but it is not philosophical. For the very abandonment of man proves that he is not, and is not to be, the pupil of nature. If man is an animal, then he is a very imperfect animal ; and for that very reason is he no animal. It has often been considered, as if the free spirit existed in man to take care of the animal. Such is not the case. On the contrary, the animal exists to bear the free spirit into the sensuous world, and to connect him with it.

This utter helplessness throws mankind back upon itself, maintains and unites the species. As the tree keeps up its species by casting off its fruits, so man, by taking care of and educating the helpless new-born child, maintains himself as species. Thus reason produces itself, and only thus is the progress of reason toward perfection possible. In this manner are the links connected with each other, and each future one contains the spiritual results of all previous links.

III. Man is born naked ; the animals are born covered. In creating animals, nature has completed her work and impressed upon it the seal of completion, by protecting the finer organization, through a coarser covering, against the influence of the coarser matter. But in man, the very first and most important organ, that of touch, which is spread over his whole skin, has been left utterly exposed to the influence of the coarser matter, not through any neglect on the part of nature, but because of her respect for us. That organ was destined by nature to touch matter immediately, in order to make it most proper to our purpose ; but nature left us perfectly free to determine in what particular part of our body to locate that power of moulding matter, and what part of our body we might choose to consider as mere matter. We have located that power in the tips of our fingers, from a reason which will soon appear. It is there because we so willed it. We might have given to each part of our body the same delicate touch, if we had so willed it. This is proven by those men who write and sew with their toes, who speak with their bellies, etc.

IV. Each animal has, as we remarked before, inborn powers of motion ; for example, the beaver, the bee, etc. But man has nothing of the kind, and even the new-born child's position on the back is given to it in order to prepare it for the future walk. The question has been asked : Was man intended walk upright or on four feet ? I believe he was not intended to do either. It was left to man as species, to choose its mode of motion. A human body can run on four feet ; and men grown up amongst animals have so run with incredible swiftness. I hold that the species has, by its own choice, freely lifted itself up from the earth, and thus acquired for itself the power of looking around in every direction and of surveying one half of the universe in the skies, whilst the animal is, by its position, chained to the soil which brings forth its nourishment. By thus lifting himself up from the ground, man has won from nature two tools of freedom ; the two arms, which, no longer required to do animal functions, now hang down, awaiting merely the command of the will, and cultivated solely with a view to carry out those commands. Through his daring gait, which is an everlasting expression of his boldness and expertness, man continually keeps his free-will and reason in practice, always remains a *becoming*, and expresses this, his character. This gait of his lifts up his life into the region of light ; by its means he touches the earth with the least possible part of his body. Animals use the earth as their bed and table ; man lifts his bed and table above the earth.

V. What characterizes the cultivated man above

I

all is the spiritual eye and the mouth, which betrays the most secret feelings of the heart in its movements. I mention the eye, not because it is moved about by the muscles wherein it is fixed, and can cast its glances hither and thither; a mobility, which the erect walk of man serves to heighten, it is true, but which, in itself, is mechanical. I speak of it, because the eye is to the man not merely a dead, passive mirror, like the plane of a sheet of water, or like an artificially prepared looking-glass, or like the eye of an animal, but rather a mighty organ, which self-actively sketches and reproduces the forms in space; which self-actively creates, looks out of itself, the figures, which are to be hewn out of the marble or painted upon the canvas before chisel or brush has been touched; which self-actively creates a picture for the arbitrarily sketched spiritual conception. Through this infinite living and moving of the parts amongst each other, that what they have of earthly substance in them is, as it were, stripped off, and the eye, clearing itself into light, *becomes a visible soul.* Hence, the more spiritual self-activity there is in a man, the more spiritual does his eye become; and the less spiritual activity, the more does the eye remain a dark, fog-covered mirror.

The mouth, which nature formed for the lowest and most selfish occupation, nourishment, becomes, through self-culture, the expression of all social sentiments, as it is also the organ of communication. As the individual or the race is more animal and selfish, does the mouth protrude more ; as the race grows nobler, the mouth recedes behind the arch of the thinking forehead.

All this, the whole expressive face, is nothing, as we come out of the hands of nature ; is merely a soft, impressible substance, wherein you can, at the utmost, discover what is to become of it by transferring the picture of your own culture upon it ; and this very lack of completion makes man capable of culture.

All this—and not in the separate parts, wherein the philosopher represents it, but seized in its surprising connection as a whole, as which it appears to the senses—is it, which forces every one, who bears a human face, to respect and recognize every one who bears a human face, whether it be merely suggested in dim outlines or already elevated to a certain degree of completion. The human form is necessarily sacred to man.

§ 7.

PROOF THAT, THROUGH THE FOREGOING SIX PROPOSITIONS, THE APPLICABILITY OF THE CONCEPTION OF RIGHTS HAS BECOME POSSIBLE.

A Persons, as such, are to be absolutely free, and dependent only upon their will. Again : as sure as they are persons they are to be reciprocally influenced by each other, and hence not to be dependent solely upon their will. How both these requirements may be possible, it is the task of the

Science of Rights to determine ; and its problem is, therefore, *How may a community of free beings, as such, be possible ?*

We have shown the *external* conditions of this possibility. We have explained how, under this presupposition, persons, who mutually influence each other, and how the sphere of this their reciprocal influence, the sensuous world, must be constituted. The proof of our results rests altogether on the presupposition of such a community, and that presupposition is again based on the possibility of self-consciousness. Hence, all our previous results have been deduced by mediated conclusions from the postulate, I am I, and are, therefore, as certain as that postulate is. Our systematic procedure leads us now to develop the *internal* conditions of such a reciprocal influence.

The last point which we reached, and from which we now proceed further, was this : All arbitrary reciprocal causality of free beings has for its basis or ground an original and necessary reciprocal causality of those beings, which is, that each free being, by its mere presence in the sensuous world, compels all other free beings to recognize it as a person. It furnishes the fixed appearance ; the other free being furnishes the fixed conception. Both are necessarily united, and there is not the smallest play-room for freedom. Through this there arises a common recognition, but nothing further. Both internally recognize each other, but they remain isolated as before.

Each has this conception of the other: that the other is a free being, and must not be treated as a mere thing. Now, if this conception did in both determine all their other conceptions, and, since their will belongs to their conceptions, did determine also their will, and through it all their actions; in other words, if they could not think and will otherwise than under this conception, then it would be impossible for them even to will to influence each other arbitrarily, or as things; they could not *ascribe* to themselves the power of influencing each other as things, and hence could neither *have* that power.

This evidently is not the case. For each has also posited the body of the other as matter, as modifiable matter, and each has ascribed to himself the power to modify matter. Each can, therefore, clearly subsume the body of the other, in so far as that body is matter, to that general conception of modifiable matter; can think himself modifying the body of the other through physical power; and hence—since his will can be limited only through his thinking—can also *will* thus to modify the other's body.

But for that very same reason, that is, because he is free, can every one restrict the exercise of his power, can he give a law to that exercise, and hence can he give to it the law, never to treat the other's body as a mere thing. The validity of that law depends, therefore, upon the fact whether a man is consistent or not. But consistency in this case depends upon the freedom of the will ; and there is no more reason why a man should be consistent, unless he is compelled to be so, than there is why he should *not* be consistent. The law must, therefore, be applied to this freedom ; and thus we have here the boundary-line between necessity and freedom for the Science of Rights.

B. We have said that no absolute ground can be shown why the rational being should be consistent, and hence why it should adopt that law for its freedom. Perhaps, however, an hypothetical ground might be discovered.

It certainly can be shown that, *if* an absolute community is to be established between persons, as such, each member thereof must assume the above law ; for only by constantly treating each other as free beings can they remain free beings or persons. Moreover, since it is possible for each member to treat the other as not a free being, but as a mere thing, it is also conceivable that each member may form the resolve, never to treat the others as mere things, but always as free beings ; and since for such a resolve no other ground is discoverable than that such a community of free beings *ought to* exist, it is also conceivable that each member should have formed that resolve from this ground and upon this presupposition.

If it could, therefore, be moreover shown that each rational being must necessarily desire such a community, then the necessity of the postulated consequence would also appear, namely, that each individual must form that resolve, and must be consistent. But that desire can not be proved from our previous premises. True, it has been shown that, if a rational being is to attain self-consciousness, and is, therefore, to become a rational being, another rational being must necessarily have affected it as a rational being. In fact, these are exchangeable, identical conceptions ; no such affection or influence, no rational being.

But it does not follow that, after self-consciousness has been posited, rational beings must always rationally influence each other ; nor can this be deduced from the former without using the result, which is to be proved, as proof.

The postulate, that a community of free beings is to remain permanent, appears, therefore, to be an arbitrary postulate ; or a postulate which each person may adopt for himself, if he so wills. If he adopts it, he is, of course, also bound to submit himself to the above law, that is, always to treat all other persons as free beings.

We are here, therefore, as before remarked, on the boundary-line between necessity and freedom, the line which separates the Science of Morality from the Science of Rights. The proposition which forms the line is : The rational being is not absolutely bound by its character of rationality, to desire the freedom of all other rational beings.

The Science of Morality shows that every rational being is absolutely bound to desire the free-

dom of all other rational beings. The Science of
Rights does not show this, but says : Each rational
being has the freedom to desire it or not to desire
it ; and then shows the result of either act.

C. Let us suppose that I have resolved with full
freedom to enter into a community with free beings,
say with the free being C. What is the result of
this resolve ? Let us *analyze* it.

I intend to enter into a *community* of mutual
rational treatment with C. But a community involves *many*. Hence I add, in thinking, the person C to my resolve, and assume, in my conception
of C, that he has the same resolve ; and since I
framed that resolve with freedom, I also assume C
to have framed his voluntarily. I therefore posit
necessarily our community as dependent equally
upon the free resolve of C ; hence as accidental, as
the result of a *mutual willing*.

I desire nothing further than to be in this community of rational intercourse with C ; we both to
treat each other alike ; he me, I him. Hence, in
case *he* should not treat me thus, I have posited
nothing. For I have posited in that resolve only
that we are mutually to treat each other as free beings ; but have posited nothing for the case, that
he may treat me otherwise. I have neither posited
that I shall treat him as a rational being, if he does
not treat me as such, nor that in such case I shall
treat him not as a rational being. In short, I have
posited nothing for such a case. As soon as *his*

treatment no longer corresponds to my conception of him as a rational being, that conception falls to the ground, and the law, which I formed in consequence of that conception, also falls to the ground. I am no longer bound by that law, and again am dependent solely upon my free-will.

D. Our present result is, therefore, as follows : It is impossible to show an absolute ground why any one should make the fundamental principle of the Science of Rights, "Limit thy freedom in such a manner that others can also be free," the law of his will and of his actions. It can be shown, however, that a community of free beings, as such, can not exist, unless every member is subjected to this law ; and that, therefore, each person who desires such a community must also desire this law. That law has, therefore, only hypothetical validity ; namely, if a community of free beings is to be possible, then the principle of Rights must be valid.

But even the condition, the community of free beings, is again conditioned by a common desire. No one can, by his own mere will, realize such a community with another unless the other has the same will, and by virtue thereof subjects himself to the principle of law conditioned thereby. If the other one has not this will, as is most clearly proved when he treats the other person contrary to that principle of law, then the first person is absolved by the law itself from the law. For the law had validity only under condition of the lawful behavior of the other ; and this condition not being given, the law, by its own conception, is not applicable to the case, and the first person—unless there is another law ; but this the Science of Rights does not presuppose—is now no longer bound by the law ; he can act toward the other as he chooses ; he has a right against the other.

The difficulty, which previous treatments of the Science of Rights generally have left unsolved, is this : How can a law command by not commanding, or how can law have causality by utterly ceasing to exist ; or, how can it comprise a sphere by not ·comprising it ? The answer is, it must result thus necessarily as soon as the law prescribes to itself a definite sphere and carries with it the quantity of its validity. As soon as it utters the sphere whereof it speaks, it determines thereby also the sphere whereof it does not speak, and confesses expressly that it does not prescribe for that other sphere.

For instance, the law commands that the other person shall treat me as a rational being. He does not do so ; and the law now absolves me from all obligation to treat him as a rational being. But by that very absolving it makes itself valid. For the law, in saying that it depends now altogether upon my free-will how I desire to treat the other, or that I have a compulsory right against him, says, virtually, that the other person can not prevent my compulsion ; that is, can not prevent it through the mere *principle of law*, though he may prevent it through physical strength, or through an appeal to morality, (may induce me to forego my compelling him, or prevent me from compelling him by superior strength.)

CONCLUDING REMARKS.

The applicability of the Conception of Rights is now completely secured, and its limits have been definitely fixed.

A sure criterion has been established, to which of the sensuous beings the Conception of Rights applies, and to which it does not apply. Each being, which has human form, is internally compelled to recognize every other being which has the same form as a rational being, and thus as a possible subject for the Conception of Rights. But whatsoever has not that form is to be excluded from the sphere of rights, and can not be said to have rights.

The possibility of a reciprocal causality of free and rational beings, which causality the Conception of Rights must determine, has also been proved. It has been shown that such beings *can* have causality upon each other and still remain free.

The fundamental principle of law, as law generally, has been determined. It has been shown to be, not a mechanical law of nature, but a law for freedom ; the ground being this, that it is quite as possible for rational beings to treat each other without mutual respect for each other's freedom, and

simply as things of nature, as it is for them to re
strict their freedom by the conception of Rights.
It has also been shown that, if this fundamental
principle of law is to be valid and realized, this can
only be done if every free being constantly and freely makes it the law (or rule) of all its actions.

The quantity of the applicability of this law has
also been definitely ascertained. It is valid only on
condition and in case that a community of reciprocal intercourse between free beings, as such, is
to be established. But since the purpose of this
community is itself conditioned by the behavior of
those with whom some one intends to enter into a
community, its validity for each such some one is
again conditioned by the fact, whether the others
subject themselves to that law or not ; and if they
do not thus subject themselves, then the law obtains validity through its very invalidity, since it
authorizes that some one to treat these others, who
have not subjected themselves to the Conception of
Rights, as he may choose to treat them.

Book Third.

APPLICATION

OF THE

CONCEPTION OF RIGHTS.

§ 1.

SYSTEMATIC DIVISION OF THE SCIENCE OF NATU-
RAL RIGHTS.

A.

IF reason is to be realized in the sensuous world, it must be possible for many rational beings to live together as such ; and this is *permanently* possible only if *each free being makes it its law to limit its own freedom by the conception of the freedom of all others.* For each free being having the physical power to check or destroy the freedom of other free beings, and being dependent in its free actions only upon its will ; it is only when all free beings have voluntarily made it their law (rule of action) never so to check the freedom of all others that a community of free beings becomes possible, wherein such a check never occurs.

What we have here stated is nothing but the judgment of the reflecting philosopher concerning the possibility of a community of free beings, and is to signify nothing more. If free beings, as such, are to exist together, then it can be thought possible only in the above manner ; but *whether* they are so to exist together, and whether the condition of their living together, namely, the *Law*, has really been acknowledged by each—this we do not take into account.

At present we can, at the utmost, say : it is nature that desires free beings to live together in the sensuous world, and hence produces a number of bodies capable of reason, culture, and freedom. It is not to be understood as if we thus asserted nature to possess understanding and will, ordesire ; we merely say : if nature is assumed to have a will, then her end and purpose in the production of many such bodies can have been only that they should live together in the indicated manner. Under that assumption, it is nature who wills that the freedom of each free being shall be restricted by the freedom of the others. But since in that case she likewise must will each rational being to be free generally, she must will that they restrict their freedom *voluntarily*, and that this law of restriction shall not be one of her own mechanical laws, but a law of freedom. What other arrangements nature may have made to realize her end in spite of that freedom, we shall see hereafter.

The above law is to be a *law ;* that is, it is to be impossible that an exception should occur to it ; the law must command universally and categorically after it has once been assumed.

In consequence of this law, each one is to limit

his freedom; that is, the sphere of his voluntarily resolved acts and utterances in the sensuous world. The conception of freedom here is, therefore, *quantitative and material.*

He is to limit his freedom thus by the possibility of the *freedom* of all others.

Here the same word has another meaning, and its significance is altogether *qualitative and formal.* Each of these others is to have the privilege of freedom, of being a person; but *how far* the sphere of their possible free acts is to extend, the law does not determine. In other words, no one has the right to do an act which would make impossible the freedom and personality of another; but all other free acts each has a right to commit.

The first question would, therefore, be : What constitutes a free person, or what is requisite to make a person free? And, since the whole of this requisite is here considered only as condition of the possibility of a living together of free beings, it is in so far termed a *Right.* For the same reason we shall here demonstrate the conditions of freedom and personality only in so far as a violation thereof is possible through physical power.

Now this right, or these rights, are involved in the mere conception of the person, as such, and in so far are called *Original* (or inalienable) *Rights.* The Science of these Rights arises through the mere analysis of the conception of personality, in so far as that which this conception involves *can* be violated by the free acts of others, but *must*

K

not be so violated in virtue of the conception of Rights.

The first division of our Science of Rights will, therefore, treat of the *Original Rights of Men.*

B.

Our established result is *hypothetical.* If free beings, as such, are to exist together, then each one must subject himself to the described law. The latter part of the sentence is, therefore, the condition of the first. Unless they so subject themselves to the law, they can not live together ; and hence the only ground why the philosopher assumes such a law is, because he presupposes that they are to live together.

Now, we have already shown that, by reason of this very conditionedness of the law, each free being can adopt it only as a conditioned law, that is, can adopt it only to attain the end which conditions it. The end of the law is to make a common intercourse of free beings possible. But this is possible only if the person with whom I thus enter into a community has subjected himself to this law, if he has resolved to respect my freedom or my original rights. The law is not at all applicable, however, to a person who has not subjected himself to it, since the end no longer exists for which I adopted that law. Hence, although I have *generally* subjected myself to that law, I have not done so in regard to the particular person, who, for his person, has not adopted it. In other words, I have adopted that law, and have not adopted it ; I have adopted it in general, and have not adopted it in this particular case. Because I have adopted it in general, and have placed myself under the conception of Rights, I act rightfully, and have, therefore, a *Right ;* and because I do not adopt it in this particular case, I have a right to compel that other individual by attacking his freedom and personality. My right is, therefore, a *Right of Compulsion.*

The law being conditioned, and adoptable only in this its conditionedness, each person has the right to *judge* whether the case of its applicability exists or not. Each is necessarily his own *judge ;* and where the right of compulsion exists, the one who has the right is, at the same time, the judge of the other, against whom he has this right ; for the right of compulsion is possible only through the adoption of the Conception of Rights. Where this condition does not exist, no one is, or can be, the judge of the other.

No right of compulsion without a right of judgment, is the result of this investigation.

It is necessary, as we have shown, that the person who is to have the right of compulsion must have subjected himself to that law ; for otherwise he may well have the physical power of compulsion, but can never obtain a *right* to it, since the right only follows from the law.

Again : The right of compulsion results from the silence or the non-applicability of the law, but is by no means positively commanded by that law. Hence, there is only a *right* of compulsion, not a *duty* to compel.

From this deduction of the right of compulsion, it is clear that this right is applicable when one person violates the original rights of another person.

The first division of the Science of Rights having, therefore, established the original rights of man, the second division, which treats of the *Right of Compulsion*, (Penal Law,) has only to establish the various cases to which the right of compulsion *applies*.

C.

1. The right of compulsion, as well as each of its applications, has a ground ; but all that is grounded is necessarily finite, and reaches no further than its ground. If, therefore, the limit of the applicability of the ground can be fixed, the limit of the grounded also can be fixed. The ground of my law of compulsion is, that the other person did not adopt the rule of law, did not subject himself to the conception of Rights. By appealing to this ground, therefore I assume that I should have no right of compulsion, if the other did adopt that law, and—quantitatively expressed—that my right of compulsion extends only so far as the other does not submit to that law. The right of compulsion

has its limit, and this limit is the voluntary subjection of the other to the law ; all compulsion beyond this limit is unrightful, (illegal.)   As a general principle, this is immediately clear.   The only question in our case—we teaching a real, and not a merely formal Science of Rights—is this, whether and how this limit can be discovered and determined in its application.

A right of compulsion is incurred only when an *original right* has been violated ; but then it follows necessarily ; and hence the general right can be proved in each specific case.   It is also clear that he, who desires that right to be valid, does not desire the violation of the original rights, or, if the violation has taken place, desires it to be annulled. Hence the *quantity* of that right seems also *provable in each specific case;* that is, in each case the limit of the legal compulsion (punishment) can be accurately defined ; it extends to complete satisfaction and restitution ; both parties must be placed back in the same condition which they occupied before such violation took place.

But—and this is a circumstance which, in recent treatises on Law, seems to have been generally overlooked—the right of compulsion is grounded not only upon the present fact, that a person did not respect the law in this present case, but upon the fact that he thereby acknowledges not to have made that law his general rule of action.   One single unlawful act—even after a series of lawful acts— proves that the rule of law is not his irrevocable rule of action, and that his previous lawful acts were induced, not by respect for the law, but by other possible motives. It is this inference which warrants the conclusion that no free being can in safety live together with him, since safety can be grounded only upon a law. The person whose original rights have been violated, thus becomes justified in completely annihilating the freedom of the violator, and in canceling the possibility of ever again coming into contact with him in the sensuous world. The right of compulsion in so far is *infinite*, and has no limit at all—a proposition which the writers on Law have partly asserted one-sidedly and partly denied one-sidedly—unless, indeed, the violator subjects himself to the law. As soon as he so subjects himself, the right of compulsion ceases, since its continuance was grounded only upon the continuance of the lawlessness of the other ; and all further compulsion is now unlawful. In this respect the limit of compulsion is *conditioned.*

But how shall the *condition*, the true subjection of the other to the law, be given ?

Not through signs of repentance, promises of future better behavior, offers of damages, etc. ; for there is no ground to believe his sincerity. It is quite as possible that he has been forced by his present weakness into this repentance, and is only awaiting a better opportunity to renew the attack. This uncertainty does not warrant the other in laying down his arms and thus again exposing all his safety. He will, therefore, continue to exercise his compulsion ; but since the condition of the right is problematical, his exercise also will be problematical.

It is the same with the violator. If he has offered the complete restitution which the law inevitably requires, and it being possible that he may now have voluntarily subjected himself in all sincerity to the law, it is also likely that he will oppose any further restriction of his freedom, (any further compulsion by the other,) but *his* right to make this opposition is also problematical.

It seems, therefore, that the decisive point can not be ascertained, since it rests in the ascertainment of inner sincerity, which can not be proved, but is a matter of conscience for each. The ground of decision, indeed, could be given only, if it were possible to ascertain the whole future life of the violator.

If, of the original violator it could be known that, after having been liberated from the compulsion, he would not, in his whole future life, ever violate the law again ; and if, on the other hand, it could be known of the attacked party that, after having received restitution, he would, in his whole future life, refrain from all further exercise of his right of compulsion, then it might be believed that the former had sincerely subjected himself to the law, and that the latter had asserted his right of compulsion only with a view to assert his original rights. But such a knowledge of the future is impossible ; because, to make the future possible, the one must first lib

erate the other from his compulsion; and this we
have shown he can not do unless he has that knowledge of the future, since no one can abandon his
acquired superiority merely because the other protests that he is sincere.   There is a circle here.
The grounded is not possible without the ground;
and *vice versa.*   Before we see how the synthetical
method shall get us out of this circle, let us examine it a little closer.

A right of compulsion, as a general conception, has
been easily enough deduced from the Conception
of Rights; but as soon as that right was to be applied, we found ourselves wrapped up in an unsolvable contradiction; because the ground of decision
of such an application could not be given in the sensuous world, resting, as it does, in the conscience
of each individual.   The right of compulsion, as an
applicable right, is in evident contradiction with itself, since it can never be decided whether, in a
given case, the compulsion is lawful or not.

But the final decision of the question whether
the right of compulsion can be exercised by the
offended party himself or not, will also decide the
question whether a real Science of Rights is possible in so far as such a science is to designate a
science of the legal relation between persons outside of an established state organization and without positive laws.   As most of the previous teachers of the Science of Rights were content to philosophize *formaliter* about the Conception of Rights,

and were satisfied if their conceptions were think-able—little caring about their applicability—they easily avoided this question.

We have here answered the first question in the negative, and hence also the second question ; and in order to become convinced of our science, it is necessary to attain a complete insight into the im-possibility, which we have here demonstrated, of having the right of compulsion exercised by the offended party himself. Hence, this result is im-portant for our whole Science of Rights.

The circle was this : The possibility of mutually liberating each other on the part of the offended and the offender is conditioned by the knowledge of their whole future ; but this knowledge, again, is impossible, unless they mutually liberate each oth-er. The method, which has been prescribed by the Science of Knowledge, tells us synthetically to unite both opposites, and thus to get rid of the con-tradiction.

A synthesis of this kind would be, in our case: *the mutual liberation of both parties and the know-ledge of the whole future must be one and the same ;* or, in other words, this mutual liberation must in-volve of itself and guarantee the whole future, whereof knowledge is desired.

There is no question that such must be the re-sult ; the only problem is, how is it possible ?

The whole future experience, and the conviction of the perfect safety of both persons, is to be expressed in the one moment of liberation, and to be so expressed valid for *external* conviction, since no one can know the inner sentiments of the other. Both parties must, therefore, make it physically impossible for each other thereafter to attack each other ; and each must become externally convinced of this impossibility. Such a security for the future is called a guarantee.

Hence, the above synthetical result requires that both persons must mutually guarantee their safety ; otherwise, they can not live together, and one of them must be destroyed.

How is this guarantee possible ? We found that neither could put down the arms, because neither could trust the other. They must, therefore, place their arms, that is, their whole power, in the hands of a *third party* in whom both trust. Both must enjoin this third party immediately to repress that one of them who may in the future attack the other. The third party must have the power to do this, and must, therefore, be *the more powerful.* This third party would thus exercise the right of compulsion for both.

If he is to exercise this right for both, both must transfer to him the right of deciding not only their present dispute but all future disputes between them ; that is, they must confer upon the third party the power of judging, or the *judicial power.* They must confer this power upon the third party without reserve ; there must be no appeal from it. *Both parties must, therefore, unconditionally transfer*

*their physical power and their power of judgment,
that is to say, all their rights, to that third party.*

2. THESIS. The freedom of the person, according
to the Conception of Rights, is limited only by the
possibility that other persons are also to live with
him as free persons, and hence as also having rights.
Whatsoever does not violate the rights of another,
each person has the right to do, and this, indeed,
constitutes each person's *right.* Each one, moreover, has the right to judge for himself what is,
and to defend, by his own powers, what he so
judges to be, the limit of his free actions.

ANTITHESIS. According to a correct conclusion
drawn from the same Conception of Rights, each
person must utterly and unconditionally transfer all
his power and judgment to a third party, if a legal
relation between free persons is to be possible. By
this transfer each person loses altogether the right
to judge the limits of his own right and to defend
those limits. He makes himself completely dependent upon the knowledge and good-will of the third
party, to whom he has made the transfer, and ceases
to be a free being.

The antithesis contradicts the thesis. The thesis is the Conception of Rights itself; the antithesis is a correct result obtained from that conception. The Conception of Rights is, therefore, involved in a self-contradiction. This contradiction
must be canceled. The root of this contradiction

lies here : Under the Conception of Rights I can surrender only that portion of my freedom which is requisite for the coexistence of other free beings with whom I come in contact in the sensuous world. But now I am to transfer all my rights to the arbitrary power of a third party. This is impossible and contradictory, unless in this transfer I nevertheless remain secured in the possession of my proper sphere of freedom. Rationally, I can not transfer all my rights, and no one can demand that I should transfer them except upon this condition.

I must be able, therefore, to decide in my own person whether I have that security or not. My transfer is conditioned by the possibility of my being able to decide and of my deciding upon the sufficiency of this guarantee. When I do not decide upon it, my transfer of all my rights to a third party is impossible and illegal. When I do transfer my rights thus, it must be done with my own perfect free-will.

After I have once transferred my rights, I have, as has been clearly shown, no further right to decide upon the sphere of my freedom. My expressed decision on the sufficiency of the guarantee must, therefore, be possible, and be given before I make the transfer.

In this decision, that the guarantee is sufficient for me, I virtually say: "I am sure that, after I have thus transferred all my rights and made myself subject to a third party, my lawful freedom will not be in the least abrogated; I am sure that I shall never have to sacrifice any more of it than I should have been compelled to do in my own judgment by the mere Conception of Rights." In making this decision, I must overlook, therefore, the whole future experience of my state of subjection to a third party, and then judge whether the guarantee of my perfect security within the limits of Law will be sufficient.

What is it which is to be guaranteed to me? Perfect security of all my rights, as well against the third party to whom I have transferred my rights, as also through it against all individuals with whom I may come in contact. I must be convinced that all possible future law decisions, which may be pronounced in affairs of mine, will always be precisely as I should myself be compelled to pronounce them under the Conception of Rights. *Rules* of these future law decisions must, therefore, be submitted to my examination, according to which rules the Conception of Rights is to be applied to all possible future cases which may occur. Such rules are called *positive laws.*

All positive laws are, in a greater or less degree, deduced from the Conception of Rights. There is and can be no arbitrariness in them. They must be such as every rational being would necessarily make them.

In these positive laws the rule of Rights is applied to the specific objects which the rule comprises. Positive law floats in the midst between the Conception of Rights and the Decision of Law In positive law, the rule of Rights is applied to particular objects ; in the decisions of law, the positive law is applied to particular persons. The civil judge has to decide only what has occurred, and then to state the law which applies to the occurrence. If the law is clear and complete, the decision or sentence should already be contained in it.

The contradiction has been in part canceled. If I subject myself to a law which I have examined and approved, (such approval being the exclusive condition of a lawful possibility of my subjection,) then I have not subjected myself to the arbitrary will of a man, but to an unchangeable, determined will, in fact, to the will of Reason in general, or to my own will, as that will must be, if determined by the Conception of Rights ; and unless my will is so determined, I have no rights at all, as has been shown. Hence, far from losing my rights by such subjection, I rather first obtain them through it, since only by this subjection have I fulfilled the condition under which alone man obtains rights. Although I am subject, I am subject only to *my own* will. I have once really exercised my right of judgment, and that once was for my whole life and for all possible cases. All that has been taken from me is the care to carry out my own law decisions by physical force.

RESULT.

Man can transfer his physical power and right of judgment only to the necessary and unchangeable will of the Law, but not to the free and arbitrary will of a man. The former alone is required by the Conception of Rights, is alone the condition of all rights. The latter is not precisely against the Conception of Rights—simply because a right is not a duty, and because any one may therefore abandon a right if he chooses to do so—but neither is it a result of that conception.

3. But the contradiction has been solved only in part. The *law* is to give me the guarantee that, after I transfer my rights to it I shall still be protected in all my rights for the future. But what is the law? A mere conception. How, then, can this mere conception be realized in the sensuous world?

Again: I am to become convinced before the transfer of my rights of the utter impossibility that my rights can ever be violated hereafter. How can I become thus convinced? or, in other words, even after the mere will of the law pronounces that impossibility, who will guarantee me that the will of the law, and only of the law, will always rule?

I am to be secured against the law itself; hence it must be made impossible to turn the power of the law against me, except in the cases provided by the law. The law is to secure me against all others ; hence the law must always act where it is intended to act. It must never sleep where it is called upon to act.

In short, *the law must be a power.* The Conception of Law, which we obtained from the last part of our investigation, and the conception of a supreme power, which we had obtained previously, must be synthetically united. The law itself must be the supreme power, and the supreme power must be the law. Both must be one and the same ; and in subjecting myself to the law, I must convince myself that it is so ; that it is completely impossible that any power except that of the law can ever be turned against me.

The question is, therefore, *How does the law become a power ?* The power we seek is not a force of nature, is not a mechanical force, as we have already shown ; and hence men have the physical power of inflicting wrongs upon each other. The required power must, therefore, be a power dependent upon a will. This will, however, must not be free, but unalterably and necessarily determined through the law. Such a will can not exist, therefore, as the will of an individual. We are in search of a will which shall have power only where the law wills, and which shall have no power whatever where the law does not will ; *a will,* in short, *which is an infallible power, but only when in conformity with the will of the law.*

Superior power over a free being can only be realized by the union of *many* free beings, since the sen-

suous world holds nothing so powerful as a free being—for the very reason that it is free and can direct its forces with matured consideration—and
nothing more powerful than a single free being, except many. Their strength would, therefore, consist only in their union. In the present case, their
power is to depend upon the fact whether or not
they will the will of the law. Their *union*, therefore,
as the basis of their power, must depend upon that
fact; the only bond of their union must be that
fact. The moment their will should differ from the
will of the law, their union also, and hence their
whole power, must come to an end.

Now, this fact, that the desire to commit injustice
necessarily destroys their union, is the case in every
community of free beings. A number of free beings unite themselves, signifies: they desire to live
together. But this they can not do, unless each
restricts his freedom by the freedom of all others.
If a million of men live together, it is very possible
for each to desire as much freedom as possible. But
if you unite the will of all of them in one conception,
as one will, then that one will divides the amount of
possible freedom in equal parts amongst all; desires
all to be free, and hence desires the freedom of each
to be restricted by the freedom of all others. The
only possible point of union for their will is, therefore, the Law, and, in our case—where a fixed number of men of various inclinations and occupations
live together—the Law, *in its application to them*, or
their *Positive Law.* As sure as they are united,

L

they must will the law.   If but one of them is wrongly treated, this one certainly protests, and they are no longer united.

That, wherein they agree, we have stated to be their positive law, which fixes the rights of freedom of each.   It is not expressly necessary that they should all give utterance to it, or, perhaps, vote upon it.   Each rational being who has a knowledge of their number, occupation, etc., can tell them wherein they all agree.   Their positive law has been given to them by the Conception of Rights and by their physical *status*, just as two factors give the product.   The *content* of the law, therefore, does not depend at all upon arbitrariness ; indeed, the least influence thereof upon the law would involve the seed of dissension and future dissolution.

But the *form* of the law, its obligatory power, it only receives from the consent of the several individuals who unite thus into a commonwealth.

Concerning justice and law, therefore, all are agreed ; and all who are agreed necessarily desire law and justice.   There can not be a community, whereof one member has another will than the other member.   But as soon as two individuals are no longer united in their will, at least one of the two is also at variance with all the others ; his will is an individual, and hence an unjust will.   If the will of the other, with whom he is in conflict, agrees with the will of all the others, then this other is necessarily in the right.

There is no question as to the fact that, in such a commonwealth, the just will, if rallying into action, will be always able to overpower the unjust will, since the latter will is only that of an individual, whereas the former is that of all others.

The only question is, How can it be arranged that this will of all the others will be active and effective, wherever an individual will is to be repressed ; how, therefore, the physical powers of the individuals may be united with the power of the commonwealth into one, just as the wills of these individuals were united into one conception ? There must be a necessary and strict rule, whereby this union of all individual forces into one will result infallibly ; for each one who subjects himself to the law is to have a convincing guarantee that it will be impossible throughout the whole future for any other force than the power of the law to be active against him ; and that his security does not depend upon chance or the good-will of his neighbors, but is absolutely secured by the organization of the whole.

The strictest and only sufficient guarantee which each individual can justly demand is this, that the existence of the commonwealth itself be made to depend upon the effectiveness of the law.

(True, as a general thing this is already so. If injustice should become universal, society would necessarily dissolve itself, and thus perish. Often, it is true, law steps beyond its limits, and often, again, remains inactive; but these isolated cases do not necessarily dissolve the connection in actuality. For the individual there is, of course, little guarantee in the reflection that the whole commonwealth can not well perish unless each member thereof suffers injustice, and that he or other persons may well suffer violence at times without the protection of the law.)

The relation between each member and the commonwealth must, therefore, be thus, that, from each however apparently petty an injustice against the individual, there also results, necessarily, injustice against all. How is this to be attained? The law is to be, necessarily, Deed. · Now, the law can not fail to be deed if, on the other hand, the *deed is always law;* that is to say, if each act which is once permitted by the law does, by that one permission, become lawful,* and may be done by all others; in other words, if each act of each individual results in a universally valid law. If this has been recognized, then each injustice necessarily falls upon all; each offense is a public misfortune; what was allowable against me is now also allowable against every member of the commonwealth; and if a single one of them is to be secure, it is the first interest of *all*, first to protect me, and to secure me my right, and to punish the unlawful deed. It is clear that this guarantee is sufficient, and that, if this rule is established, the law must always be effectual,

* Law of Precedents.—TRANSLATOR.

though it can also never transgress its limit, because, if it did, transgression would become lawful for all.

It is clear that the individual who enters such an agreement receives his freedom, although he renounces it, and receives it *because* he renounces it; it is clear, that through it all contradictions are solved, and through its realization the supreme rule of law can be secured; it is clear, that every one who desires the supremacy of the law must necessarily desire such a commonwealth; and that through the conception thereof, our investigation has therefore been brought to a close. The analysis of this conception will lead us from the First Part of the Science of Rights, as the Science of Natural Rights, to its Second Part, or to the *Science of Rights in a Commonwealth.*

§ 2.

CONCERNING THE ORIGINAL RIGHTS OF MEN.

Rights can be spoken of only on the condition that a person is thought *as* a person, that is, as an individual, or, in other words, as occupying a relation to other individuals, between whom and him a community, though not actually posited, perhaps, is at least fictitiously assumed. For those things which, through speculative philosophy, we discovered to be conditions of personality, become rights only if other persons are added in thought, who dare not violate those conditions. Free beings can not, however, be thought as coexisting at all, unless their rights reciprocally limit each other, that is, unless the sphere of their *original rights* changes into the sphere of *rights in a commonwealth.* It would seem, therefore, impossible to reflect upon rights as original rights, that is, without regard to their necessary limitations through the rights of others. Nevertheless, such a reflection must occur and furnish the ground for an investigation of rights in a commonwealth. All limitations must, therefore, be abstracted from, and this is, indeed, so easy a matter for speculation, that it rather makes this abstraction involuntary, and needs only be reminded of having made it. The possibility of the abstraction offers no difficulty.

But it must be well remembered at all times, THAT the abstraction has been made, and that the conception produced by it, though it have ideal possibility, (for thinking,) has no real significance. If this is forgotten, a purely formal Science of Rights will be the result.

There is no status of original rights for *Man.* Man attains rights only in a community with others as indeed he only becomes man—whereof we have shown the grounds heretofore—through intercourse with others. Man, indeed, can not be thought as *one* individual. Original Rights are, therefore, a pure *fiction*, but a fiction necessary for the purpose of Science. It must also be always remembered, that the conditions of personality should be thought as rights only in so far as they appear in the sensuous world, and as they can be checked or disturbed by other free beings. It is proper, therefore, to speak, for instance, of a right of sensuous self-preservation, that is, of preserving my body as such ; but it is improper to speak of a right to freely *think* or *will.* I have a right of compulsion against the man who attacks my body, but not against the man who, perhaps, disturbs me in my peaceful convictions, or who annoys me by his immoral behavior.

The fundamental principle of all rules of law we have found to be this : Let each one restrict his freedom or the sphere of his free acts through the conception of the freedom of the other, (that is, so that the other may also exist as generally free.)

The conception of freedom as applied here to the other, namely, in its merely formal significance, furnishes the conception of the Original Rights, that is, those rights which absolutely belong to a person as such. Let us analyze that conception.

It is, in regard to its quality, the conception of a power to be absolute first cause. In regard to its *quantity*, it is the conception of an unlimited or infinite power, since it merely states that the person is to be free, but not how far he is to be free. Hence, the Conception of Quantity is opposed to the Conception of Original Rights as here expressed in its formal significance. In regard to its *relation*, this conception speaks of the freedom of the person only in so far as the sphere of the free actions of others is to be limited by it, because those others might make the required formal freedom impossible. Through its relation, therefore, the quantity is determined ; namely, the conception refers only to *causality* in the sensuous world, since in it alone can freedom be limited by freedom. In regard to its *modality*, finally, this conception has apodictical certainty. Each person is to be absolutely free.

The Original Right of a person is, therefore, his absolute right to be *only cause* (never effect) in the sensuous world.

The conception of a cause and here of an absolute cause, involves, first, that the quality and quantity of the act shall be completely determined by the cause itself ; and, secondly, that, as soon as the quality and quantity of the act is determined, the quality and quantity of the effect in the object of the act is also immediately given. You can proceed from the one to the other, you can determine immediately the one through the other ; as soon as you know one, you necessarily know both.

In so far as the person is the absolute and final ground of the conception of his causality, or of his purpose, the freedom manifested therein does not come within the limits of this investigation, since it never enters the sensuous world, and can, therefore, not be checked in it. The will of the person enters the sensuous world only in so far as it is expressed in the determination of the body. On this sphere of the sensuous world the body itself of a free being is, therefore, to be regarded as itself the final ground of its own determination ; and the free being, as appearance is here identical with its body. The body is the representative of the Ego in the sensuous world, and where the sensuous world alone enters into consideration, the body itself is the Ego. Hence, we use every day such phrases as, " *I* was not there," " He has seen *me*," " *He* is born, *he* died, *he* was buried," etc.

The body, therefore, considered as a person, must be absolute and final cause of its determining itself to have causality.   In what limits and under what laws the body is placed by its own organization, does not concern us here.   Whatsoever the body is not originally, does not appertain to it, or, that the body is not ; and hence that is not taken into account here.   Only that which is physically possible for the body, must also be possible of being actualized in the body, whenever the person so wills, and only when the person so wills.   An external cause must neither induce the body's motion, nor check its motion ; in fact, no external influence must immediately affect it.

Again : From this movement of the body, the effect made *possible* by it must infallibly result in the sensuous world.   Not exactly the result intended ; for if the person did not know well the nature of the things he operated upon, or did not properly calculate his force and their power of resistance, then the fault was his own, and he has no right to complain of the sensuous world. But the sensuous world must not be determined by a foreign free power outside of it, in opposition to that person's will; for if it is so determined, then he ceases to be free cause.

But the intentional determination of the body for the purpose of producing a certain effect upon the object, follows upon and from a preceding knowledge of the object to be effected; and hence the free being is, after all, dependent.

In a general way, we have already acknowledged this, and excluded it from our present investigation. Causality and definite knowledge mutually condition each other, and fill up the same sphere, as has been shown and explained before. A person *can not will* to have causality previous to and beyond the given, factical existence of the objects; for to have such a will would be self-contradictory; it is only within the sphere of the factical existence of the objects that the person is free. Within that sphere the person is free to leave things as they are or to change them in accordance with his purpose. He is free to reciprocally relate the various manifolds given to him, to determine them through each other, and to unite them into a whole as may best suit his purpose. If he is not free to do either of these, he is no longer dependent solely upon his will.

It is, therefore, required that every thing should

remain precisely as it has once been gathered into the conception of the rational being, whether it be already modified through it or not. Indeed, that which is not so modified in nature, becomes—by the very thinking of it, *as* not modified, and by joining it in thought to the modified—modified itself. The person has not modified it because it suited better to the modified things in its natural shape ; and the person would have modified it if it had so suited better. In refraining from a specific activity, he was, therefore, also active, and modified —if not the specific thing, at least—the whole, to which this specific thing was to be conformed.

Now, nature, obeying her mechanical laws, can not really change. All change in nature contradicts the conception of nature. That which appears to us self-alteration of nature, occurs in virtue of those mechanical laws, and could not appear to us as a change, but would appear to us as a permanent, if we sufficiently knew those laws. Hence, if those laws work any change in the world which we have proposed to form to our conception, it is our own fault ; for either those laws are too powerful for us, and then we should have considered that beforehand, or they are not too powerful, and then we should have controlled them through art and inventive ability. It is only through other free beings that unforeseen and unpreventable changes can be produced in our world—that is, in the system of that which we have received into our knowledge and related to our purpose—and that our free causality can, therefore, be disturbed. Now, a person has the right to demand that, in the whole sphere of this, his known world, every thing should remain as he has known it from the first, because in exercising his causality upon this his known world, he is regulated by that knowledge of it, and will be led astray, will find his causality checked, or will obtain other results than those he has desired, if his knowledge should turn out meanwhile to have been incorrect because a change had taken place in his world.

Here lies the ground of all *right of property.* That part of the sensuous world which is known to me, and has been subjected by me, though only in thought, to my purposes, is *originally* my property, (originally, I say, not in a *community.*) And being thus my property, no other person can have causality upon it without checking the freedom of my causality.

The old dispute, whether the right of property to a thing is obtained only through my *forming* it— modifying it in some way—or also through my mere will to take possession of it, is thus settled. It is settled by the synthetical union of both these determinations, as could not be expected otherwise in a strictly synthetical system, or by showing that the mere subjection of a thing to my will is equally a positive modification of that thing, since it presupposes my free resolve to abstain from a possible

activity for a certain end or purpose ; and by showing, moreover, as will appear directly, that the modification of a thing gives a right of property to it
only in so far as something is and remains thereby
subjected to our end.   The final ground of the
right of property is, therefore, the subjection of
that property to our purposes or ends.

A person desires his activity in the sensuous
world to be cause, signifies, therefore : a person desires a perception to result from it, which perception shall correspond to his conception of the end
and purpose of his activity.

It has already been remarked that, if this is to be
possible at all, the object of his activity must not
be disturbed by other influences ; and that the person, in willing his activity to be cause, must also
necessarily will the latter.

But it is equally clear, that the person who desires that future perception to result, must also
necessarily will the continuance of his own body
and of its present relation to himself as a willing
and knowing being ; or, more definitely expressed,
the person must also will a future state to exist,
which shall have resulted from the present state,
in consequence of the rule which he followed when
he resolved upon his act of causality.

Through the will, therefore, and only through the
will, is the future embraced in the present ; though
the will alone is the conception of the future, as
such, made possible, and the will not only embraces,

but also determines the future. It is to be *such* a future, and in order that the future can be such a one, I must be such a one ; and if I am to be such a one, I must have existence in general.

The argument is here that, from the willing of a determined mode of existence in the future, the willing of a future in general and the wish of our continued existence is the result. The assertion is, here, that we have the will to continue to exist, not for the continuance in itself, but for the sake of a determined state in the future ; the continued existence is not absolute end itself at all, but merely the means for some specific end. This experience, indeed, fully confirms. All men desire to live, the nobler men to *do* something more, the less noble, at least to enjoy something more.

The person wills what we have just shown as sure as he wills at all, no matter what it is he wills. This determined willing is, therefore, the condition of all willing, and its realization, namely, the preservation of our body, which, in Natural Law, is as much as *self-preservation*, is a condition of all other acting and of all manifestation of freedom.

If we unite all our results into one, the person, in demanding his original rights, demands *a continued reciprocal causality between his body and the sensuous world, determined and determinable solely through his freely formed conception of that world.*

The conception of an absolute causality in the sensuous world, or, since this conception was found to be equivalent to that of Original Rights, the conception of Original Rights itself, is thus completely exhausted.

The Original Rights are, therefore, an absolute and closed Whole ; each partial violation whereof affects the Whole and influences the Whole. If it is desirable to make divisions in the conception of Original Rights, that division can be only the one which the conception of causality itself involves, and which we have already developed. This would give, as the Original Rights of Men :

1st. The right to the continuance of the absolute freedom and inviolability of the body.

2d. The right to the continuance of our free influence upon the whole sensuous world.*

---

* Our Declaration of Independence, wherein the original rights of men, which have here been philosophically deduced, are expressed in their results, or simply asserted, specifies the right to the continuance of the absolute freedom of the body as the *Right to Life ;* the right to the inviolability of the body as the *Right to Freedom ;* and the right to the continuance of our free influence upon the whole sensuous world, as the *Right to the Pursuit of Happiness.* The latter right is also often called the Right to Property. Our Declaration of Independence, therefore, completely exhausts the conception of original rights. By proceeding "and in order to have these rights," etc., the Declaration of Independence further asserts, by inferring the right of compulsion, that original rights can only be secured as rights by the establishment of a commonwealth. In that one immortal sentence from the Declaration of Independence, therefore, the whole Science of Rights is involved, and can be deduced from it in its application to the least of possible law-cases.—TRANSLATOR'S REMARK.

There is no particular right of self-preservation ; for that the use of the body as a tool, or of the things as means, should have, in a certain case, the immediate purpose of preserving our body, as such, is accidental. Even if we have a lesser purpose, our freedom must not be disturbed ; for it must not be disturbed at all.

But it is well to be remarked, that our Original Rights are valid not only for present purposes, but extend as far into the future as we can embrace the future in our minds or plans ; and that, hence, they immediately and naturally involve the right *to secure those rights for all future.*

The Original Rights return in themselves, justify themselves, and constitute themselves as Right ; that is to say, they become an absolute Right ; and this proves that the circle of our investigation, as far as these rights are concerned, is completely closed, since a complete synthesis has now been established. I have the right to will the exercise of my rights throughout all the future, so far as I posit myself, simply because I have these rights ; and I have these rights because I have the right to will them. The right to be free cause, and the conception of an absolute will are the same. He who denies the freedom of the will must also necessarily deny the reality of the Conception of Rights, as *Spinoza* indeed does, whose right signifies merely the power of the *determined* individual, limited by the All.

§ 3.

CONCERNING THE RIGHT OF COMPULSION.

I.

PRELIMINARY.—The right of compulsion, according to the above, is to have its ground in a violation of the original rights, that is, when one free being extends the sphere of its free actions so far as to violate thereby the rights of another free being. But that first free being, being free, has assuredly also its original rights, which are infinite, as we have shown. How then can it, by the free exercise of those rights, violate the rights of another? It seems as if the original rights must, after all, have a determined quantity, fixed by the law, if, by their exercise, the violation of a right is to be possible. The answer to the question, In what case is a right violated and does the law of compulsion therefore apply? depends, therefore, upon the answer to another question, namely: what quantity of freedom does the Conception of Rights determine for each free being?

In other words, if any exercise of freedom is to be *illegal*, and may thus authorize compulsion, then the *legal* use of freedom, that is, of the original rights, must be limited by definite boundaries; and the illegal use can not be determined unless the legal use is known; both are determinable only through opposition. If these limits can be ascer-

M

tained, and if each person keeps within them, then a right of compulsion does not arise at all ; *an equilibrium of rights* is the result, which it must now be our task to determine, for only where this equilibrium of rights is disturbed, may the law of compulsion become applicable. After we have determined this equilibrium of rights, we can proceed to a consideration of the right of compulsion, but not before.

II.

DEDUCTION OF AN EQUILIBRIUM OF RIGHTS. —All law relations are determined by this principle : each one must restrict his freedom by the possibility of the freedom of the other. We have shown what the conception of freedom, or of original rights, involves. Such an infinite freedom would, however, cancel the freedom of all but a single person ; nay, would even cancel the physical existence of freedom ; and the conception of rights would therefore contradict itself. But this contradiction solves itself as soon as it is remembered that the law applies not to a single one free being, but is valid for all free beings. If A is to limit his freedom so that B can also be free, B, on the other hand, must also limit his freedom so that A can be free, etc., etc. Nay, A can not even self-limit his own freedom by the possibility of B's freedom, unless B also limits his own freedom by the possibility of A's, the principle of law being not applicable at all unless both take place. Unless both self-limit their freedom, neither does. This has indeed been shown already sufficiently. The only question is, how does this as yet empty conception become applicable? If one person says to the other, " Leave that alone, it limits my freedom!" why should not the other reply, " But it limits my freedom to leave it alone ?"

The question therefore is, *how far* shall each one limit the quantum of his free actions by the possibility of the other's freedom ; how far does the freedom extend which each may retain for himself, and only by respecting which the other can show himself also entitled to rights ; and how far does the freedom extend which he must resign to the others in his conception of their freedom, and only by respecting which he can show himself entitled to his own freedom ?

The law-relation is determined solely by the established principle of law. Our question can therefore be determined only by that law principle. But this we have discovered to be purely formal, and not at all determining any quantity. It fixes merely the *that*, not the *in how far*. The whole principle of law is, therefore, either not at all applicable, and results merely in a play of empty conceptions, or the *in how far* must result from the *that*, and by determining the latter the former must also be determined. In other words, the mere conception of the freedom of another being must also determine the quantity of limitation which I have to put upon my own freedom.

Let us see what this synthesis may involve, and what it may therefore signify.   It involves

A. The *actual* self-limitation of a free being is conditioned by the cognition of another free being. Whosoever has no such cognition can not self-limit his freedom ; and the possible free beings whom he does not know, do not bind him to limit his freedom.

(In the deduction of original rights a person is thought isolated in the sensuous world. Not knowing, therefore, any other person, he may extend his freedom as far as he chooses, and take possession of the whole world.   His right is really—if original rights ever could be *real* rights—infinite, for the condition which would limit it does not exist.)

B. The self-limitation of a free being is not only *posited* by the cognition of another free being, but also, at the same moment, completely *determined.* That it is so posited we have already shown.   But it must also be determined ; that is, the mere cognition of the other must determine the limit which the person has to put upon his own freedom.

C. My freedom is limited by the freedom of the other only on condition that he limits his freedom by the conception of mine.   Otherwise he is lawless. Hence, if a law-relation is to result from my cognition of the other, the cognition and the consequent limitation of freedom must have been mutual.   All law-relation between persons is, therefore, *conditioned* by their mutual cognition of each other, and is, at the same time, completely determined thereby.

We now proceed to apply our synthesis to the several cases determined by it ; and firstly to the right of the continuing freedom of the body.

1. We have shown that a rational being, when perceiving a body articulated for the representation of reason in the sensuous world, must posit that same as the body of a rational being. By positing that body, it determines it also as a certain quantity of matter in space, which fills this space and is impenetrable in it.

Now, the body of a rational being is necessarily free and inviolable in virtue of its original rights. Hence, the other person who takes a cognition of that body must, by virtue of this his cognition, be forced to restrict his freedom to causality in the sensuous world, by that body and by the space which it occupies. He can not posit that body as a thing to be influenced by him arbitrarily and subjected to his purposes, but solely as something whereby the sphere of his causality is limited. That causality may extend everywhere except to the space occupied by this body. As soon as I have seen the body and recognized it as that which it is, I have also recognized something which limits my causality in the sensuous world. My causality is excluded from the space occupied by that body at any time.

But since this self-limitation depends upon the fact that the other has also seen and recognized me in the same manner, and limited his freedom as I limited mine, my limitation and the right of the

other to it is, after all, only *problematical;* and it is
impossible to decide whether it has occurred or
not.

2. By positing the body of that other being as
absolutely free in its self-determination to have
causality, and by positing the being represented
by it, as a free cause in the sensuous world, I must
necessarily posit that this being desires to have
some effect in the sensuous world to correspond to
its conception, and hence that it has subsumed certain objects of the sensuous world to its ends, according to the conception of original rights. The
other being must assume the same of me.

These objects, subjected by each to his particular purposes, must be mutually inviolable to both
of us, if we know them. But since this subjection
remains within the consciousness of each, and does
not manifest itself in the sensuous world, the objects of this right and limitation remain also problematical.

3. The objects of this right are problematical,
and not only they, but the right itself is problematical, is uncertain, and depends upon the unknown
condition, whether both parties have mutually rights
upon each other. I am bound to respect the objects which the other has subordinated to his ends
only in so far as the other respects those which I
have subordinated to my ends. But he can not respect them until he knows them ; nor can I respect
his until I know them. This mutual ignorance

cancels even the possibility to approve each other
as beings who have rights. And since this ignorance extends even to the fact whether each intends to respect the freedom and inviolability of
the other's body, the result is, that no law-relation
at all is possible between them ; every thing is and
remains problematical.

In our deduction of the right of compulsion, we
discovered already that, as soon as that right is to
be applied, men can not live together without an
agreement. We now find that this impossibility
exists even before the right of compulsion is applied, and enters, indeed, as soon as mutual rights
are tried to be established.

That problematical state and uncertainty can not
remain permanent if a living together of individuals under the conception of rights is to be possible ;
for if it does, no one can subject objects to his ends
without fearing that the other may already have
subjected them to his own purposes, and without
fearing, therefore, to trespass upon the other's
rights. Nay, neither can be secure of his previous
possessions, since it is always possible that the
other may take possession of it under the presumption that it has as yet no owner, and since in
that case it would be impossible for the previous
owner to prove his title ; which title again might
also be *illegal,* however *honestly* supposed to be
legal, since the other may previously have subjected the object of it to his purposes. How is this to

be decided? It is quite possible that neither of the parties know which of them has the previous title ; or, if they could know it, their ground of decision would always remain a matter of internal conscience, and could, therefore, not attain external right. A law-dispute arises between them, which can not be decided, and a dispute of physical powers, which can only end with the physical annihilation of one of them. Only by pure chance, namely, if it should happen that neither has a desire for what the other has, could they possibly live together in peace. But they can not possibly allow all their right and security to depend upon pure chance.

Unless this uncertainty is removed, a legal relation between both is impossible.

If it is problematical, moreover, what the objects of the rights of both parties and of their mutual obligation are, it is also problematical whether a condition of rights and whether obligation do at all exist. He who desires the conception of rights to be realized, desires this problematical condition to cease. This condition must be removed ; and the Conception of Rights itself desiring that removal, there must be a right to remove it. The person, who does not desire to remove that condition of uncertainty, testifies by that very fact that he does not desire Law to rule. He becomes, therefore, lawless, and justifies, on the part of the other, an infinite compulsion.

But how shall their ignorance be removed? It has been shown, that the conception of a person involves the assumption that he has subjected something in the sensuous world to his purposes. It would thus seem necessary that each person, when obtaining cognizance of the existence of another person, must limit his possession of the sensuous world to some *finite quantum ;* for otherwise, the other person could not exist as a free being ; but *what* particular finite quantum each person so chooses as his own, must depend altogether upon his freedom. Again : This choice remains a matter of the person's own consciousness, and does not manifest itself in the sensuous world. Each must, therefore, state to the other what he has thus appropriated as his own, since such is the only way to remove the uncertainty which threatened to cancel the Conception of Rights. Each is legally bound to *determine himself internally* as to what he desires to appropriate for his exclusive use ; and each has the right to compel an undetermined person to thus determine himself, since the establishment of Right requires that the determination of each in this respect should be made known. Each is, therefore, moreover, legally bound to *express himself externally* concerning this his self-determination, and the other has a right to compel him to this expression, that is, to compel him to make a *declaration of his possessions.*

All lawful relation between persons is thus conditioned by the reciprocal declaration of what each desires exclusively to possess, and becomes possible only through such a declaration.

These declarations of several parties may agree or may conflict with each other ; agree, if no one declares a wish to possess what the others have appropriated, and conflict if both claim the same object. In the first case they are already united ; but in the latter case their dispute can not be settled by grounds of law at all. For as to the claim of previous possession, this neither of the parties can prove externally, and hence neither can furnish a legal proof. For since the law declares the expression of the will to possess something to be the ground of all property, and since both parties express that will at the same time, both parties have an equal right before the law.

Two solutions of this difficulty are possible.

Firstly. Both parties may mutually compromise as to their respective claims, and may thus enter the required condition of harmony. It must be remembered, however, that neither has the right to compel the other to compromise ; for the other's refusal to cede part of his claims does not prove his unwillingness to recognize law in general. He has chosen a particular possession and thus has fulfilled the requirement of the law. He is, moreover, willing to subject himself to the rule of the law hereafter, provided his claim to his choice possession be granted. But he has no notion of of ceding that claim merely in obedience to my will, and because I also desired that same piece of possessions. He holds my will to be a particular, individual will, and not the common will of the law, which we both ought to acknowledge, but which does not decide in this case as to whose claim is the right one.

Or, secondly, if they can not agree, a quarrel or war will ensue, which can end only with the complete extermination of one of the parties. Now, since such a war—as, indeed, all war—is against the law, or is absolutely unlawful, they are bound, in order to prevent the war, to transfer the decision of their dispute to a third party, and hence to transfer their whole right of deciding questions at law and their physical power to enforce such decision to this third party. Or, as we expressed it before, they must both join a commonwealth ; and each has the right to compel the other to join a commonwealth with him, since only thus the maintenance of law and a legal relation between men is made possible.

How the rights of property are settled, if the parties thus enter a commonwealth, we shall see hereafter, when we come to speak of the Conception of Rights as applied in a commonwealth. At present the only question which concerns us is this : Supposing, therefore, all parties to be agreed from the start, or to have agreed by a compromise as to their exclusive possessions, and supposing each one to have now lawful possession only of what has thus been ceded to him by the general declaration of property, upon what ground is his right of property to the *particular and fixed* objects based, which the general division has assigned to him ?

Evidently, altogether upon the fact that their wills were agreed and not in conflict, or that the one has ceded what the other claimed. Each one, by saying, " This only shall be my possession," says, at the same time, " Every thing else may be thine," and *vice versa.* Their right of property, that is, the right of exclusive possession, is therefore completed and conditioned by *mutual recognition,* and does not exist without it. All property is based upon the union of many wills into one will. Through this mutual recognition, indeed, does a *possession* change into *property.*

I am excluded from the possession of a determined object, not through the will of the other, but only through my own free-will. If I had not excluded myself, I should not be excluded. But I must exclude myself from something in virtue of the Conception of Rights.

Another result could, indeed, not have been expected. If each person is to have original right of property to the whole sensuous world, but not to retain that right in actuality, and yet is to be and remain absolutely free, this is the only possible solution.

My right of property to a *particular* object (not the right of property in general) is, therefore, valid only for those who have recognized this right of property amongst each other, and no further. It always remains possible, that all the rest of mankind will come and dispute my right of property to something recognized as mine by the few with whom I have entered into a legal relation. There is, hence, no sure and absolute title to property except a title recognized by the whole human race. To obtain this recognition seems an infinite task, and yet it is easy of solution, and has, indeed, been solved long ago by men. To wit, each citizen of a commonwealth guarantees to each other citizen thereof his right of property to his selected possession. Now, the adjoining commonwealths acknowledge and guarantee the right of property of this commonwealth, and hence of each citizen thereof. The commonwealths adjoining *those* again acknowledge *their* property, etc., etc. Even the remote commonwealths, therefore, which have not directly recognized my right of property in my commonwealth, have done so implicitly, since they have recognized the right of property in adjoining states, and can therefore not trespass upon the property of those states, which adjoining states again have acknowledged the same rights in the states next to *them*, etc., etc. As our earth is an absolutely closed and connected whole, each piece of property is, therefore, mediately recognized by all mankind, through the immediate mutual recognition of adjoining commonwealths. True, in a state of war all law relation ceases, and the property of all the states at war becomes insecure ; but a state of war is not a lawful condition.

When this general declaration of property occurs, if some objects of the sensuous world should remain unappropriated, these unappropriated objects are property of none, *(res neutrius.)* It needs no special declaration to fix these objects, since all objects not expressly declared to be appropriated are unappropriated. Now, in regard to these unappropriated objects the same difficulty may arise, which we met at the first start, when attempting to fix the right of property in general. After this general declaration, two persons may desire to possess themselves also of this unappropriated property, and, as each one has the same right to it, a state of uncertainty will again result, which can not be allowed to remain if the Conception of Rights is to rule. That uncertainty must be removed. In the first general establishment of a state of law, therefore, a rule regarding this future appropriation of unappropriated possessions must be fixed. It is not only advisable to do so, but such a rule *must* be fixed and agreed upon, or a complete and secure state of law is impossible. Each person has, therefore, the right to compel the other to agree to some rule, generally valid, for those future appropriations.

What sort of a rule may this be? The *declaration* of property determines the object taken possession of ; the *recognition* secures to the proprietor the guarantee and consent necessary to make it his property. Now, this recognition may precede the declaration; that is, at the moment of the first agreement, a rule of recognition may be fixed for all future time ; but the declaration can not precede the recognition, if it is to refer to *future* appropriations. To make such a rule possible, therefore, it would be necessary to mutually agree, that each will hereafter recognize each declared possession of the other in the region of the unappropriated objects to be that other's property the moment such a declaration is made.

In virtue of such an agreement, the one who would first make public his declaration would thereby secure a complete right of property and title to it, since all others would have agreed in advance to respect such a title. Hence, there arises here for the first time, and solely in consequence of a voluntary but legally necessary agreement, a *rule of law from priority of time ;* and the law formula : *Qui prior tempore, potior jure,* which had hitherto no legal validity for an external court of law, has now been grounded. Another law formula, *Res nullius cedit primo occupanti,* is at the same time more particularly determined and limited. There are no absolutely *res nullius* in the eye of external law. Things are ownerless only through a mutual declaration and exclusion from them, (*res neutrius.*)

The possibility of an endless law dispute has not been removed, and the proper law relation has not been completely secured, unless it can be

so arranged that the declaration follows immediately the taking possession of an object. For
unless I do immediately declare my possessions,
another person may come to declare his possession of the same object, (not having known of mine,)
and the law dispute will again be interminable.

Possession and declaration must therefore be
synthetically united, or the occupied object must, at
the occupation, be so determined that the other
can not perceive the object without perceiving that
it has been taken possession of. The object itself
must express the declaration ; hence, both parties
must have agreed upon certain signs of occupation ;
and since it is necessary to have these signs in order to make possible the rule of law, there is a right
to compel the other to make and respect these
signs. These signs are signs only in so far as they
have been agreed upon. Hence, they may be of
any possible nature. The signs used in landed
property are usually fences or ditches. Animals
are thereby prevented from entering such property,
and rational beings are thereby reminded that they
are not to make use of their power to enter it.

Concerning the abandonment of property, *(dere-
lictio dominii,)* in regard to which law disputes
might also be possible, it is at once clear, that the
first property which was acquired through mutual
declaration and recognition, can be abandoned only
by the express declaration of the possessor, that he
no longer desires to possess it. For the grounded

reaches as far as the ground. Now, the declaration is the sole ground of this kind of property, hence the property can not be deemed abandoned until the declaration is annulled. When it is annulled, the property becomes ownerless, and belongs to the class of ownerless objects already alluded to.

As far as the afterward acquired property (*dominium acquisitum*) is concerned, the title to which is obtained through the sign of occupation, it can, of course, be abandoned only by the removal of the sign ; and, by the removal of the sign the title to this property is abandoned in virtue of the same rule ; the grounded extends no further than the ground. It might be maintained, that the sign having once been fixed upon the property, every body now ought to know that it has been taken possession of, and that the removal or destruction of the sign ought not to invalidate the title. But you never can prove that others have seen the sign. They may never have seen the property, or if they have seen it, may never have noticed the sign. Hence the sign is not superfluous, but is the necessary and continuing ground of right to the property ; and if the owner takes it away or allows it to be destroyed, he is to be considered as one who has abandoned his property.

By making this fixed agreement concerning their property, the persons who make it reciprocally prove to each other that they have subjected themselves to the law, and hence, that they are beings who have

N

rights. By means of this property covenant, therefore, do the freedom and inviolability of their bodies, which before remained problematical, also receive sanction, and now become a categorical right. Of course, to secure it in a particular agreement is not necessary, since the *in how far* of that freedom is not at all disputable, but is given in the mere cognition. The *that* of those rights of the body, however, is decided by the property covenant.

Our investigation has thus returned into itself. What was first problematical, has become in its simple self-development categorical ; and our investigation is, therefore, completely exhausted.

The free beings have now been completely determined in regard to the limits of their free acts in relation to each other. Each has its determined stand-point in the sensuous world, and they can not get at all into a law dispute, if they keep on that stand-point. An equilibrium of rights has been established between them.

The synthetical proposition, that the in itself *formal* principle of law does also determine the material extent of the rights of each person, has approved itself as true by its universal applicability. Through the mere cognition of a free being my law relation to it is immediately determined for me, that is, is posited as necessarily to be determined.

Either I must determine it myself freely, or the state determines it for me.

We have thus answered the most important question of the Science of Rights: How can a purely formal rule of law be applied to determined objects?

III.

THE PRINCIPLE OF ALL LAWS OF COMPULSION OR OF PENAL LAW.

Our whole argumentation in the deduction of an equilibrium of rights turns around in a circle; and if we reflect upon this circle, the lawful condition, which was to be made possible through the establishment of an equilibrium of rights, again becomes impossible, and the Conception of Rights appears still empty and without an applicability.

The rational beings, which we posited as reciprocally recognizing each other as such, were all uncertain whether the one could depend upon its rights being secured against the attacks of the other; and hence whether the other one had any rights at all, or ought not rather to be driven away by physical force from the sphere of causality of the first one. This uncertainty we claimed to have removed in causing both to mutually recognize and determine the sphere of their rights, since this recognition and determining was evidence that both had subjected themselves to the Conception of Rights.

But their mutual security is so far from being

based upon their agreement to live together in a
lawful condition, that it rather is based altogether
upon the fact, whether in all their future acts they
will conform to this agreement.   Hence, the agreement presupposes mutual confidence of the one in
the other, that he will make that agreement his
irrevocable rule of action.   But the adoption of such
a rule presupposes in each party the will to establish and maintain a lawful condition between them ;
presupposes, therefore, their subjection to the Conception of Rights ; and thus that which was to prove
the honesty and lawfulness of each party, namely,
his subjection to the law, proves it only if that
which is to be proved is presupposed, and has no
validity or significance unless such presupposition
is made.

Our whole subsequent investigation depends upon
the correct and strict comprehension of this point.
The security of both parties is to depend, not upon
chance, but upon a necessity, equal to a mechanical
necessity, and one from which there is no exception possible.   Now, such a security is possible only
if the Conception of Rights has been made the irrevocable rule of action of each party ; and unless
both are convinced that each has thus adopted it,
the agreement to respect each other's property and
personal liberty affords no security at all, since it
rests upon this very subjection to the Conception of
Rights and has no effect otherwise.   There are many
reasons which might induce either party to enter
an agreement without having the slightest inten-

tion to keep up to it. Or they may have made the agreement with sincere intention to keep it and to live together in a legal state, and yet may have since changed their minds. The moment one party can suppose this possible of the other, he has no security any longer, but must always be prepared for disturbance and war, and thus can lead the other party, who may still be honest and sincere in his submission to the law, to entertain the same distrust. Each party thus obtains the right to annul the agreement and to get rid of the other party, since the possibility of both parties living together as free beings has been canceled. Their agreement is annulled, because that upon which it was based, mutual confidence, has been annulled.

Result : *The possibility of a legal relation between persons is conditioned by mutual fidelity and confidence.* But mutual fidelity and confidence are not dependent upon the Conception of Rights, and can not be compelled by law, nor is there a right to compel confidence and fidelity, since confidence and fidelity can not be externally manifested, and hence do not appertain to the sphere of the Conception of Rights. Nor can I even compel any body not to manifest his distrust in me ; for if I had that right of compulsion, it would force him to abandon all care for his own security, and hence all care for his freedom and his rights. Such a right on my part would make him subject to my arbitrary law decisions and to my power; in other words, would enslave him, and no one has the right to enslave another.

Whenever fidelity and confidence between persons living together have been lost, mutual security and legal relation between them have become impossible, as we have seen. The parties can not become convinced of the groundlessness of their distrust, simply because such a conviction can be based only upon a fixed, unchangeable good will—a will which each person can scarcely presuppose in himself, much less in others. Fidelity and confidence, therefore, when once lost, can not be restored ; either the distrust continues and spreads, or a war finally breaks out, which is an unlawful state, and, moreover, can not restore confidence.

Now, none of the parties care about the good will of the other in itself, in its *form ;* for, as far as the good will is concerned, each is accountable only to his conscience. It is the results, or the *material* of the will, which they care for. Each wills and has the right to will that the other party's *acts* shall always be such as would result if he had a good will. Whether this good will really is the incentive of those acts or not, is all the same to him. Each has claim only to the *Legality* of the other, not to his *Morality.*

Nevertheless, the provision to be made to repress acts which ought not to occur, must not operate through means of a mechanical power of nature ; firstly, because this can not be done,

man being free, and hence able to resist and
overcome any power of nature; and secondly, because such a procedure would be unlawful; for
man would thus be changed into a mere machine
in his legal state, and would not be supposed to
have any freedom of will, to secure which, alone,
the whole legal relation is established. Hence, the
arrangement to be established must be of such a
character as to relate *to the will itself*, as to induce
and compel the will to determine itself never to
will any thing inconsistent with lawful freedom.

It is easy to see, that such must be the solution
of the problem; but it is far more difficult to determine what this solution may really signify and involve.

The free being with absolute freedom proposes
to itself certain ends. It wills because it wills, and
the willing of an object is itself the last ground of
such willing. Thus we have previously determined
a free being, and any other determination would destroy the conception of an Ego, or of a free being.

Now, if it could be so arranged *that the willing
of an unlawful end would necessarily—in virtue of
an always effective law—result in the very reverse of
that end*, THEN THE UNLAWFUL WILL WOULD AL-
WAYS ANNIHILATE ITSELF. A person could not
will that end for the very reason because he did
will it; his unlawful will would become the ground
of its own annihilation, as the will is indeed always
its own last ground.

It was necessary to establish this principle in all its synthetic fullness, since upon it all laws of compulsion (the whole Penal Law) are grounded. We shall now proceed to analyze it.

The free being proposes to itself an end. Let this end be called A. Now, it is very possible that this A may be related to other ends as a means, and that these other ends are again so related to still others, etc. But no matter how far this relation extends, at the end there must be an absolute end which is willed simply because it is willed. All possible mediating ends are related to this absolute and total end as its parts, and in so far are also to be regarded as absolute end. I will A, signifies, I demand that something corresponding to the conception of A be given in perception as existing. Hence, the conception of the real existence of A, or the will that A shall exist, is the real motive power of the will A. As sure as I desire A and its real existence, I must detest its opposite as the greatest evil possible to me.

Hence, if I can foresee that an act which I undertake to realize A must necessarily result in the opposite of A, I can not wish to realize A, for the very reason that I do desire it and do not desire its opposite; I can not will A because I will it. Our problem is therefore solved. The lawless will annihilates itself and keeps itself in its own limits.

Hence, if a contrivance could be secured which would operate with mechanical necessity so as to cause each lawless act to result in the very opposite ıt was intended to produce, then such a contrivance would compel the will to desire only what is lawful ; and would restore the security which must be restored, after fidelity and confidence have been lost. The good will would be rendered superfluous for the external realization of right, since the bad will would be forced by its very badness to effect the same end. A contrivance of this kind is called a *Law of Compulsion.*

There exists a general right to establish such a contrivance, since reciprocal legal freedom and security can only exist, as we have discovered, by means of it. Hence, the problem to establish it is involved in the Conception of Rights.

The freedom of the lawful will remains unviolated by this contrivance, and retains all its dignity. So long as a person desires that which is lawful only for the sake of lawfulness, he experiences no longing for the unlawful ; and since the law of compulsion operates only where this longing exists, it never effects the just person at all. His own good will places him above all external law, and he is utterly freed from it.

But a person may trespass upon another person's right without being thereunto impelled by a bad will. It may be done through carelessness. The law of compulsion, however, is operative only when a bad will exists ; and hence, through its means the rights of persons are not yet sufficiently protected.   Let us examine this.

All carelessness can be reduced to this, that the careless person *has no will at all* in cases when he ought to have a will and when he must be assumed to have had one as sure as he claims to be a free and rational being.   If in a certain case he has acted without a clear conception of his acting, if he has acted mechanically, obedient to chance impulses, it is impossible to live together with him in security as a rational being.   He ceases to be a rational being, and becomes a product of nature, which ought to be compelled to inactivity.   But this can not be done, both because he has, after all, a free-will, and because his general freedom must be respected.

The following rule applies to such cases : Each person must take as much care not to violate the rights of others as he takes care that his own are not violated.   The proof of the validity of this rule is as follows : the final end required of me by law is, *mutual security.*   This involves the end, that the rights of the other shall not be violated by me, in the same degree as the end, that mine shall not be violated by him.   Both these ends, the inviolability of mine as well as that of the other's rights, must be equally ends of my will, and until they are so, my will is not a lawful will.

The question is : How is it to be so contrived that a person will have a will when he ought to have it, or, as we have just now determined the proposition, that he will take as much care not to violate the right of the other, as he takes care to protect his own right against the other ?

Let us first examine the rule as we determined it at the outset, because it is the most difficult, and hence makes the investigation most interesting. How then is it to be contrived to produce a will where it ought to be ?

That which has no will at all is not a free or a rational being. The free persons, whom we have posited here, have a will ; the direction of that will is also known, for they have announced the objects which they have subjected to their ends, (their property.) This will, which is known to exist, must be so worked upon by the contrivance postulated, as to produce of itself the will which is lacking, and which, nevertheless, is necessary for mutual security ; that is to say, the gratification of the will, which they have, must be conditioned by their having the other will, which they ought to have but perhaps have not.

To illustrate : I am known to have the end A. Now the law relation I have entered into with other free beings, demands that I also must have the end B ; but it is not known whether I will always entertain the end B. The way to force me to entertain B at all times, is to make it the condition of A. For in that case I am compelled to will B, since A is not possible without it. A is the end to assert my own right, B the end not to violate those of the other. Hence, if a law of compulsion can be contrived, which with mechanical necessity will make the violation of the rights of the other a violation of my own rights, then I will certainly take as much care to protect his as to protect my own. In short, each loss which the other suffers through my carelessness, must become my own loss.

The distinction between the former and the latter application of the law of compulsion is clear : In the first case, my will went beyond its limits, and attacked the exclusive rights of the other, with a view to use them for my own advantage. The law of compulsion addressed itself to this going beyond of my will, in order to drive it back within its limits.

But in the second case, my will did not go far enough ; for it did not notice at all the rights of the other, as it should have done. Here, therefore, the law addressed itself to the care I take of my own rights, in order to impel my will to go far enough. Regard for my own security has, therefore, under the law of compulsion, the contrary effect intended by my own will, namely, to induce regard for the other's security. Thus the equilibrium of rights is fully secured, and the conception of a law of compulsion, which is to secure those rights, has been completely exhausted.

IV.

The Establishment of a Law of Compulsion.

The law of compulsion is to work in such a manner that every violation of the rights of the other is to result for the violator in the same violation of his own rights. The question is, How can such an order of things be established ?

A compulsory power is evidently required which shall irresistibly punish the violator. Who is to establish such a power ?

This power is posited as a means to realize reciprocal security, whenever fidelity and confidence have been lost ; and is posited in no other respect. Hence, it can be desired only by a person who has that object in view ; such a person, however, must *necessarily* desire its establishment. The persons posited by us as making the agreement, have that object in view ; hence they, and they alone, can desire the means to realize it. Their will is united in the object in view, and hence must also be united in the only means to realize it ; that is, they must will to make an agreement concerning the establishment of a law of compulsion and of a compulsory power.

What sort of a power is this to be ? As a power operative under a conception, and under a conception of absolute freedom—namely, of the limits posited by the contracting parties to their causality in the sensuous world—this power can not be a mechanical power, but must be a free power. Such a power, however, is not posited beyond their own common power. Their agreement to establish a law of compulsion will thus have to contain the provision : *that both parties agree to treat, with united strength, that one of them who shall violate the rights of the other, in accordance with the provisions of the law of compulsion.*

But if the law of compulsion becomes applicable, one of these parties must be the violator, and it is contradictory that this one should lend his own strength to repel his own attack. He can, therefore, only promise that he will not resist the compulsion of the other, but will voluntarily submit to the punishment of the other. This, however, is also contradictory, since his original violation presupposes that he intended to deprive the other person of his rights, and if he did, he will not now voluntarily give them up.

Nevertheless, it must be so. For how else can a superior power of right be realized ? since we must ascribe to both parties equal physical strength. Thus it seems that the same party whom I could not trust to refrain from violating my rights, and who, moreover, has since shown that this my distrust was justified, must now be trusted by me voluntarily to submit to the punishment provided by the law of compulsion. But this same difficulty remains if that party does so submit. For if the aggrieved party himself inflicts the punishment provided by the law of compulsion, who is to guarantee to the aggressor that the aggrieved party will not purposely step beyond the provisions of the law of compulsion, or that he has not made a mistake in applying it? The aggressor also must, therefore, have an impossible confidence in the justice and wisdom of the other, after first having lost that confidence ; all of which is contradictory.

An agreement such as we have found necessary is, therefore, contradictory, and can not be realized.

It could be realized only if the aggrieved party had always superior power, extending, however, only to the limit provided by the law of compulsion, and if he lost all that power as soon as he had reached that limit ; in other words, *if each party had precisely as much power as right.*

This condition is, as we have seen before, possible only in a commonwealth. Hence, an application of the law of compulsion is not possible except in a commonwealth ; outside of a commonwealth compulsion is only problematically lawful, and for that very reason is always unlawful if really applied.

Hence, *Natural Law,* or a legal relation between men, is not possible at all except in a commonwealth and under positive laws.

Either general morality, and universal faith in this morality, prevails—and even in that case it would be the most marvellous of all chances if men could agree upon their claims ; and if morality so rules, law does not exist at all ; for that which law should enforce occurs without its application, and that which it prohibits is never done. For a race of perfect moral beings there is no law. That mankind can not be this race is clear from the simple fact that man must first be educated, or must *first educate himself*, to become a moral being.

Or there is no such general morality, or, at least, no universal confidence in it. In that case, the external rule of law certainly becomes applicable but it can be applied only in a commonwealth. Natural law, therefore, becomes inoperative.

But what we thus lose on the one hand, we get back with profit on the other hand ; for the commonwealth now becomes the natural condition of man, and its laws will, after all, be only Natural Law realized.

SECOND PART OF THE SCIENCE OF RIGHTS.

———◆———

Book One.

CONCERNING STATE ORGANIZATION.

§ 1.

SYSTEMATIC DIVISION OF THIS SECOND PART.

THE problem which we were unable to solve, and which we hoped to solve through the conception of a commonwealth, was this : to realize a power which might enforce the Conception of Rights (or that which all persons necessarily will) amongst persons who live together in a community.

The object of their common will is *common security* ; but since only self-love, and not morality, is supposed to exist—the willing of the security of the other emanates from the willing of the security of himself in each person. The former is subordinated to the latter. No one is supposed to care that the rights of the other are secure against his attacks, except in so far as his own security is conditioned by this security of the others. We may express this in the following formula : *each one subordinates the common end to his private end.*

The law of compulsion is intended to produce this reciprocity or this necessary connection of both ends in the will of each, by combining the welfare of each with the security and the welfare of all others.

But the will of a power which is to execute the

law of compulsion can not be of this character ; for the subordination of the private to the common will being produced only by this power, which must be superior to all other power, that subordination could be produced in the supreme power only by its own power, which is a contradiction.   Hence, that subordination and harmony of private and public will must not wait to be produced, but must exist from the very beginning in the power which is to carry out the law of compulsion ; in other words, the private will of that power and the common will of all persons must be one and the same will ; the common will itself, and none other, must be the private will of this power, and the power must have no other particular will of its own at all.

II. The problem of the Science of Rights is, therefore, *to discover a will, which can not possibly be other than the common will.*

Or, to use our previous formula, which is better suited for our investigation, *to discover a will, wherein private and common will are synthetically united.*

Let this will, which is to be discovered, be called X.

A. Each will has itself (in the future) for its own object.   The ultimate end of each willing person is his own preservation.   This applies to X also ; and hence this is the *private will* of X.   This private will is in X to be the same as the common will. The common will is the security of the rights of all.   Hence X, as much as it wills *itself*, must will the security of the rights of all.

B. The security of the rights of all is willed only through the harmonious will of all. *Only in this* are the wills of *all* harmonious ; for in all other matters their willing is particular and has individual purposes. No individual singly has this for his object, but only *all* in common will it.

C. X is therefore itself this agreement (harmony) of all. As sure as this harmony wills itself, it must will the security of all, since it is itself this very security of all.

III. But a harmony like this is a mere conception. Such it is not to remain ; but to be realized in the sensuous world, that is, to be established in a determined utterance and to have effect as a physical power.

All willing beings in the sensuous world are men to us. Hence, that conception must be realized by men. This requires :

A. The will of a *certain* number of men in some particular time-moment must become really harmonious, and must declare itself as thus harmonious.

It is important here, to show that this required harmony does not occur of itself, but is grounded *in an express act in the sensuous world, perceptible at any time and possible only through free self-determination.* The proof of this act has already been given, when it was shown that the applicability of the Conception of Rights is not possible, unless each person has made an express declaration of the extent to which he has subjected objects of the sensuous world to his end, or to which he has taken possession of them.

The further development of this act is undertaken in our first book : CONCERNING STATE ORGANIZATION.

B. This common will must be clothed with a power, and with a supreme power, so that it may maintain itself and its decisions by compulsion. This power involves both the right to decide law disputes and to execute these decisions : Judicial and Executive power.

The manner of its establishment is developed in our second book : CONCERNING THE STATE CONSTITUTION.

C. This common will must be established as the unchangeable and permanent will of all, which each agrees to recognize so long as he remains in the commonwealth ; a fact which must always be borne in mind. The whole future will of each individual is concentrated into the one moment when he declares his willingness to participate in the commonwealth ; and this extending the present will so as to embrace the whole future, changes the expressed common will into LAW. In so far as the common will determines how far the rights of each person shall extend, the law is called *Civil Law ;* and in so far as it determines the punishment which shall follow a violation of the law, it is called *Penal* or *Criminal Law.*

The further development of these conceptions is

undertaken in our third book : Concerning Municipal Law.

§ 2.

CONCERNING STATE ORGANIZATION.

Preliminary.—Let us analyze more thoroughly
than we have done heretofore the conception of
the fundamental agreement upon which a commonwealth is established.

An agreement presupposes two persons who are
posited as each desiring the same object to be his
exclusive property. The object upon which they
are to agree must, therefore, first, be of a nature
which will allow it to become exclusive property,
that is, which will allow the object to remain the
same as conceived by either person when subjected
to his end ; and, second, of a nature which will allow it to be subjected to an end only as exclusive
property. (See the deduction of the right of property in the paragraph on Original Rights.) If the
former is not the case, then no agreement is possible ; if the latter is not the case, no agreement is
necessary. Hence a certain amount of light or of
air is not a legitimate object of an agreement.

Again : Both parties must have the same right to
the object, otherwise there exists no law dispute between them to be settled by an agreement. This
is, indeed, the case as far as all objects and all free
beings, who claim those objects, are concerned.

Previous to the agreement, the only legal ground which a person can make valid for the possession of a disputed object is his freedom and rationality ; but all free beings can make the same ground valid. A dispute concerning the possession of their bodies is not possible amongst persons, since the natural end of each body, to be moved through free-will, is physically impossible to all but one. But to the rest of the sensuous world, all persons have the same claim.

It is not necessary, however, that both parties need claim the same property at the *present* moment ; the fear that such a claim may be raised in the *future* is sufficient to make an agreement necessary. But unless either case occurs, an agreement is altogether unnecessary, since then the sphere of freedom for both parties is so separated that a collision of wills is considered impossible. So long, for instance, as their possessions are separated by a river, which both parties consider impassable, it is useless for them to promise each other that they will not cross the river and attack each other's property. Nature has made the river the limit of our physical power. It is only when the river becomes fordable, or when we invent ships, that it becomes necessary to fix the river as the limit of our possessions by agreement.

This will of each party, to have exclusive possession of this or that piece of property, is the private will of each party. Hence, in the agreement there are, firstly, *two private wills*, which may be called *material wills*, since they are directed upon an object.

The possibility of an agreement requires, moreover, that both parties have the will to come to an agreement concerning their disputed claims, or to relinquish each a part of his claim until both claims can coexist together. If one or both of the parties have not this will, an agreement becomes impossible, and war is the result. The Conception of Rights requires each rational being to have this will, and there is a law of compulsion to force each person to enter an agreement, (which, it is true, has no applicability, since it is impossible to determine to what extent a person should relinquish his claim,) all of which has already been proved.

This will of both parties to compromise their law dispute peaceably, we shall call, since it refers to the form of the agreement, their *formal common will.*

Their will to restrict their two private wills so far that they may no longer conflict with each other, and hence to relinquish each a part of his claims for now and ever, we shall call their *material common will.*

By this agreement of both contracting parties, the will of each now extends also to the property of the other, which, perhaps, it did not previously, since the other party may not even have known it ; but it does so only *negatively.* The will of each party extends beyond its own private end, but merely as a negative will. Each one does *not* will what the other wills ; that is all. Whether a third party wills the possessions of the other, is to each a matter of indifference. The material will of both parties, in so far as it is a common will, is purely negative.

The conception of an agreement requires, moreover, that this common will be established as a permanent will, determining all future free acts of both parties, as the rule of law which fixes their whole future legal relation to each other. As soon as one of the parties transcends the limits of this agreement in the least, the agreement and the whole legal relation established by it is annulled.

It might be supposed that, in case of such a violation of the agreement, the aggrieved party had only a claim to demand damages, and that a restitution would place all things back in their original position. This is true, if the aggrieved party is satisfied with the restitution and is willing to renew the agreement with the other party. But it is very important, for the sake of our future results, that it should clearly appear, that the offended party is *not* legally bound to be satisfied with damages ; the one violation of the agreement strictly annulling the whole legal relation between them.

For this reason : Previous to the agreement each of the parties had the most perfect title to the possessions demanded by the other party and ceded to that other party in the agreement. Though the first party may not even have had knowledge of the existence of those possessions, he might have obtained that knowledge at some future time. His right to those possessions he lost only by the agreement, by his voluntary cession. The agreement, however, exists only in so far as it is always maintained ; its violation annuls it. When the ground is annulled, the grounded is also annulled ; and since the contract was the only ground of the cession of those possessions to the other, with the contract that cession also is abrogated. Both parties are again in the same relation to each other which they occupied before the agreement.

A.

No legal relation is possible without a positive determination of the limit to which the freedom of each individual is to extend ; or, which is the same, without defining their property in the widest sense of that word, namely, in so far as it signifies not only the possession of real estate, but the *rights to free acts in the sensuous world generally.*

In the organization of a state or commonwealth, therefore, if that organization is to establish a general legal relation between individuals, *each individual must agree with all others concerning the property, rights, and liberties which he is to have, and which he is to cede to the others.** Each must

* " *The Declaration of Independence was a social compact by which the whole people covenanted with* EACH *citizen of the United States, and each citizen with the whole people,* that the United Colonies were,

make this agreement with all the others *in person.* *Each,* is the one party, and all the others, *as individuals*—for only as individual free beings does he agree with them—are the other party. Each one has said to all : I wish to possess this, and demand that you shall release all your legal claims to it. All have responded to each : We do release our claims to it, provided you release your claims to our possessions.

All the requirements of an agreement are contained in this one. Firstly, the private will of each individual to possess something as exclusive property, for otherwise he would not have entered the agreement. Each citizen of a state has, therefore, necessarily a property ; for if the other had not guaranteed him his property, he would not have guaranteed theirs. Secondly, the formal will to make the agreement. Thirdly, it is necessary that each shall have agreed with the other concerning the *matter* of his possessions ; otherwise the agreement could not have been effected. Fourthly, the will of each is positive only in so far as his own possessions are concerned, and negative in regard to the possessions of all others. Again,

and of right ought to be, free and independent States." (John Quincy Adams, *July Oration,* 1831.) But they covenanted more. Each citizen also covenanted with the whole people, and the whole people with each citizen, that all men are endowed with the rights of life, liberty, and the pursuit of happiness. These rights they guaranteed to each other in that compact ; and hence the Declaration of Independence is the Property Compact of the citizens of the United States.—TRANSLATOR.

the possessions of each are recognized by the others only so long as the former recognizes their possessions. The least violation cancels the whole agreement, and justifies the offended party, if he has the power, to take away from the aggressor all his possessions. *Each, therefore, pledges all his property as security that he will not violate the property of all others.*

I call this first part of a state organization the *Property Compact* of the citizens.

Each individual has at one time actually thus declared his possessions, whether by word or by deed, in choosing publicly a profession, which all the others, at least tacitly, have consented to, and thus guaranteed.

We have assumed that in a commonwealth all make the agreement with all. Some one might object that this is not necessary, and that, since men do business necessarily in a limited sphere, it would be sufficient if each individual made such an agreement with three or four of his next adjoining neighbors. According to our presupposition, however, this would not be sufficient. Our presupposition must therefore assume that each person can come in conflict with each other ; that hence, each is not limited to his chosen sphere in space, but has the right to traverse the whole sphere of the commonwealth.* It will appear, hereafter, that this

* TRANSLATOR'S REMARK. — Fichte does not touch the real point of difficulty here. The objection, as raised by himself, in-

is really the case.   At present we only wish to show
from this requirement that, in a commonwealth, the
agreement should be one of all with all, and that,

volves this question : Why may not each two or three persons on
the earth make such an agreement ? why must the state be a *large*
commonwealth ?   The solution suggested is the true one, though it
is not expressed clearly and not at all deduced ; namely, the possibility is to remain " that each person may come in conflict with each
other " *on the face of the whole globe,* or rather, *with each individual
member of the whole human race.*   I say, Fichte has merely suggested
this solution, and has not at all attempted its deduction.   Of course,
as a principle of law, it must be involved in the conception of rights
*that each person shall restrict his freedom by the conception of the free-
dom of all others ;* and the deduction may be thus sketched in its
leading features :

It has been shown that the consent of all human individuals must
be obtained in order to render the title to any property (or rights in
general) perfect.   It has also been empirically stated by Fichte that
this universal consent exists in the treaties of adjoining states,
recognizing each other's possessions.   This is not correct as an
empirical statement ; if it were, we should have no wars.   As a
matter of fact, not a single state (our Republic excepted, for reasons
which will clearly appear) recognizes the possessions of the other,
but only awaits an opportunity to appropriate them ; and the ground
of this is, that a legal relation is possible only between individuals,
but not between states, when such states assume to be absolute
bodies.   From this universal uncertainty of property in all countries,
which uncertainty increases with the number of small absolute
states, (and hence was never greater than in Germany during the
feudal times,) arises the unlawfulness of all states which do not
embrace the possibility of annexing the whole globe, or of uniting
the whole human race under one form of government.   A small
state of two or three persons, therefore, would be in contradiction
to the conception of rights.   There is not perfect security—and perfect security that conception demands—possible in it.   Nor is such
security possible in any absolutely limited state.   A commonwealth
which is to afford perfect security must embrace the whole globe,

although the possessions of all on the surface of the earth may be in part, that is, in a certain respect, divided amongst the individuals, still in another respect, which the agreement must also determine, there must be a sphere of action for all; the merchant, for instance, retaining the privilege to travel and to sell his goods, the cattle-raiser to drive his cattle over the high-roads, the fisher to walk upon the property of the agriculturist along the rivers, etc., etc.

Now, since the Conception of Rights can not be realized except through a universal commonwealth of all mankind, the right to realize it must always remain a right of each individual; and it is this

or at least, in order to be conformable to the conception of rights, must contain the *possibility* of uniting all mankind. We shall show in another place, that the only commonwealth which contains this possibility is that of the United States, and that hence the United States, with its form of government of a Confederate Republic, is the only lawful commonwealth on the face of the globe.

For only a Confederate Republic furnishes really those states which Fichte wrongly asserted empirically to exist, namely, states which guarantee each other's possessions. None of its states being absolute, there is no cause for a war between them; only riots (our late war was merely an organized gigantic riot)* are possible in a confederation. No state would be bettered by being enlarged, nor even lose by being made smaller.

---

* The distinction between war and riot may be held to be either quantitative or qualitative. If held to be only quantitative, our late war, of course, was a war, and every large riot must then be called a war. But if we wish to make a qualitative distinction, a war can only be waged between separate absolute states, with a view to conquer each other's possessions, directly or indirectly; and a riot or insurrection is a revolt against the law within a certain commonwealth. A riot is opposition to law; a war has no reference to law at all, but ignores it

right to realize a true lawful relation between mankind, which is the *legal* ground, why each individual, besides his particular limited sphere in space
selected as his exclusive possession, has a right to
claim all the rest of the world as sphere of causality.   Only, this latter right is neither exclusive nor
absolute.   It is defined in the separate commonwealths, but a universal determination of this right
is not possible until the object contemplated by it,
the establishment of a Universal *Confederacy*, has
been realized.

B.

But the object of state organization is, to protect
the rights guaranteed to each in the property-compact against all attacks whatever, and so to protect
them by compulsion or physical force, if necessary.

Such a protecting power has not been established
if the will of each party remains only negative so
far as regards the property of the other.   The property-compact must, therefore, embrace another
compact, in which each individual shall likewise
covenant with all the other individuals of the commonwealths that he will protect their specified property (or rights) to the extent of his physical power, provided they will protect his property in the
same manner.

This agreement we will call the *Protection-Compact.*

This second compact is in its matter conditioned by the first. Each can only agree to protect what he has recognized as the right of the other, whether it consist of present possessions or in the permission to obtain future possessions under a certain rule. But he can not promise to assist the other if the other should involve himself in quarrels not provided for in the agreement.

This second compact is distinguished from the first in this, that the negative will in respect to the other's property now becomes positive. Each promises not only to abstain from attacking the property of the other, but, moreover, to assist in defending it against the attacks of any possible third party.

Like every agreement, the protection-compact is conditioned. Each promises to the other protection on condition that the other will also protect him. The agreement is annulled if any party does not fulfill its conditions.

The protection-compact is distinguished from the property-compact remarkably in this, that in the former both parties agree merely *not to do* certain things, whereas in the latter both parties agree *to do* certain things. It can, therefore, be known at all times whether the property-compact has been complied with, since it only requires knowledge that certain things have not been done by the other party ; but it can not always be known whether the protection-compact has been complied with,

P

since it requires that the other party shall do cer
tain things which he can not do at all times, and
which he really is never obliged to do.

Let us examine this important point more closely.

The protection-compact is a conditioned agreement concerning positive duties, and as such it can,
in strict law, have no effect whatever, but is null
and void.

The formula of such an agreement would be as
follows : On condition that you protect my rights,
I will protect your rights.   How, then, does some
party obtain the right to claim the protection of the
other ?   Evidently, by *actually protecting the rights
of the other.*

But if this is so, no party will ever obtain a strictly legal claim to the protection of the other.

It is important for our whole future investigation
that this be clearly comprehended, and this comprehension depends upon a thorough insight into
the nature of this compact.   I am legally bound to
protect you only on condition *that you protect me.*

Let it be clearly noted what this last clause signifies.   It does not mean, merely, "that you have
the good will to protect me."   For good intentions
can not be proved before a court of external law,
and, moreover, might change at any moment.   Indeed, it is the right of each party, never to be compelled to depend on the good intentions of the other
party.   Nor is that clause equivalent to saying, "On
condition that you have protected me at some past

occasion." For the past is past, and is of no moment to me at present. Morality, gratitude, and other internal or moral qualities may, it is true, induce me to recompense past services, but in a Science of Right we must not take morality into account at all. On the field of law there is no means to unite men except through this insight : whatever you do to the other party, whether of good or of evil, you do not unto him, but unto yourself.

Applying this to the present cases, it would be necessary to become convinced, that in protecting the other party I simply protect myself, either actually in the present or prospectively in the future, namely, if protection of my rights in the future is the necessary result of my affording protection to him now. The former is not possible ; for in protecting the other, I do not need and do not receive present protection. The second is equally impossible ; for I can not have absolute certainty that the other will protect me again in the future.

Our above exposition is the most stringent, but the matter may be viewed from various sides. For instance, either both parties are attacked at the same time, and in that case neither can afford protection to the other, or they are attacked at different times. In the latter case, the party called upon to protect the other, might say, Our agreement is a conditioned one ; only by affording protection to me do you get a claim to my protection. Now, since you have not actually fulfilled the condition, the conditioned, of course, is null and void. In the same manner the other party will argue, and thus the conditioned will never become realized, because the condition can never be realized. They may come into a relation of moral obligation, if one party assists the other, but never into a relation of legal obligation.

Let us compare this in itself null and void compact with the right based upon the property-compact. In the latter compact, the condition is only negative on either side, namely, that neither party shall attack the rights of the other ; and hence it can always be proved before external law, that its conditions have been complied with, and that a legal obligation exists. The condition in the property-compact is not a something, but a nothing ; not an affirmation, but a mere negation, continuously possible at all times ; and hence the conditioned is also possible at all times. I am always obliged to refrain from attacking the rights of the other, because thereby, and only thereby, do I legally restrain him from attacking my rights.

But if the protection-compact is null and void, then the security of the property-compact is also canceled, and the Conception of Rights can not be realized.

The difficulty must be removed, and the solution

of this problem completes the fundamental compact of every state organization.

The chief difficulty was, that it always remains problematical whether the obligation required by the protection-compact has been met or not, and hence, whether the other party has obligations or not. If this uncertainty can be removed, the difficulty is solved. It is removed, if the mere entrance into the agreement, the mere becoming a member of a state organization, carries along with it the fulfillment of the obligation demanded by the protection-compact ;* in other words, if promise and fulfillment are synthetically united, if *word and deed* become one and the same.

What we have just stated concerning the protection-compact, applies to all compacts involving positive obligations, since it has been deduced from the general character of such compacts. In establishing, therefore, the form whereby the protection-compact may become valid, that is, by making word and deed one, we have established the universal form of all such compacts.

C.

The protection-compact is to contain, at the same time, the fulfillment of its obligations. How is this to be realized? Evidently in the following manner:

---

* The protection-compact, therefore, forms part of the Constitution.—TRANSLATOR'S REMARK.

The compact, which is to establish the state organization, must at the same time provide for a protective power, to which each member of the organization must furnish his contribution. This contribution would at once be the fulfillment of his promise to protect the rights of all other members, and there could be no further uncertainty as to his affording that protection to the others upon which his own claim to protection is grounded.

But how is this protective power to be established, and what is actually established in establishing it?

To make clear the important conception we shall thus obtain, let us again place ourselves on the standpoint from which we saw the one person entering into an agreement with all the others. He is the one of the contracting parties. A contribution is demanded of him as the condition of his entering the state. By *whom* is this contribution demanded? Who is the second party to this agreement?

This second party demands a protective power— for what particular individual? For absolutely no particular individual, and yet for all; for each one who may be attacked in his rights. This each one may or may not be every single one of them. The conception of the individual to be protected is, therefore, an undetermined conception; and thus arises the conception of a Whole, which is not merely imaginery, (created by our thinking,) but which is *actual;* a Whole not merely of all individuals, but of a totality.

Let us describe this totality more at length. A mere abstract conception is created solely through the free act of the mind. Such was the conception of all persons together, which we established above. But the conception which we have now obtained is not created by an arbitrary act, but by something actual; which, however, is as yet unknown, and can be determined only in the future through the apprehended attack. No one knows upon whom this attack will be made, but it may be made upon all. Each can, therefore, believe that the whole contrivance has been established solely for his particular benefit, and hence will cheerfully furnish his contribution. But the attack may also be made upon another. The contribution, however, has already become part of the Whole and can not be withdrawn. This undeterminedness, this uncertainty as to which individual is to be attacked first, this suspension of the power of imagination, therefore, constitutes the real tie of union. It is it, by means of which all flow together into one, and are now united no longer in an abstract conception, as a *compositum,* but in *fact,* as a *totum.* Thus nature in the state unites again what she separated in the production of many individuals. Reason is only one, and its representation in the sensuous world is also only one; mankind is a single organized and organizing Whole of Reason. Reason was separated into many independent members; but even the natural institution of the commonwealth cancels this independence provisionally and unites separate numbers into a whole, until finally morality recreates the whole race into one.

The conception thus attained can be properly illustrated by the conception of an organized product of nature ; for instance, of a *tree*. If you give each separate part of the tree consciousness and a will, then each part, as it desires its own preservation, must also desire the preservation of the whole tree, because its own preservation is possible only on that condition. Now, what, then, is the tree ? The tree in general is nothing but a conception, and a conception can not be violated. But the part wills that *not a single* part of all the parts shall be violated, because that violation would inevitably be felt by it too. It is different with a mound of sand, where each part exists separately, and can, therefore, be careless as to what other parts are separated, trodden down, or scattered away.

The thus established totality is, therefore, that which is to be protected, and is the required second party to the compact.

The point of union of this totality has been shown. But how and through what determined act of the will has this whole become a Whole ?

We remain on our previous standpoint, from which we saw a single person enter the agreement ; and our question will soon be answered.

That single person expresses his will to protect, of course, the Whole. He, therefore, becomes a part of the Whole, and joins together with it; whether he become, as can not be foreseen, the protector or the protected. In this manner, through covenants of single persons with other single persons, the Whole has arisen; and when all single persons have covenanted with all other single persons, the Whole is completed.

We call this compact, which secures and protects the two previous compacts, and in union with them forms the fundamental compact of state organization, the *Union-Compact.**

---

* Our *Constitution*, (or State constitutions.) Those who do not like to have the Declaration of Independence considered as the fundamental property-compact of our Constitution will, perhaps, be better pleased if we call the Bill of Rights (the amendments) of our Constitution the property-compact; the sections, which constitute the government and provide for its efficacy, the protection-compact; and the preamble the union-eompact.

Our forefathers originally intended to keep the property-compact separate from the Constitution. They held that the Declaration of Independence specified the original and inalienable rights of men in sufficiently comprehensive terms, and that it would only be productive of harm to specify them in greater detail in the Constitution, since such specification must necessarily be imperfect and would leave room open to the interpretation, that rights *not* specified could be taken away by act of Congress. The Patrick Henry party, however, insisted on having this specification, and hence the original amendments to the Constitution, which are nothing more than an imperfect specification of the three fundamental original rights asserted in the Declaration of Independence.—TRANSLATOR'S REMARK.

D.

By virtue of this union-compact, each single person becomes part of an organized whole and melts into one with it.   Is he swallowed up into it in all his being and essence, or does he remain free and independent in a certain other respect?

Each gives to the protecting body his *contribution;* he gives his vote to the election of magistrates and to the constitution, and his fixed contribution of forces, services, natural products, or all of these changed into the common representative of value—money.   But he does not give himself and what belongs to him altogether.   If he did, what would remain his for the whole to protect? The compact would be a contradiction, established on the pretext of protection, and yet with nothing to protect.* Its fundamental principle would be: all promise to protect, although all promise that they will have nothing to protect.   Hence, the protecting body consists only of parts of that which belongs to the single individuals.   The whole embraces them all, but each of all only in part.   But in so far as they are thus embraced in it, they constitute the state and form the true sovereign.   Only in giving his contribution does each belong to the

---

* On such a contradiction the "right" of conscription is based. The citizens of the United States have formed their constitution and government solely to guarantee to each other "life, liberty, and the pursuit of happiness."   By ordering conscription, government takes away your freedom, in order to make you free ; takes away your life, in order to secure it.—TRANSLATOR'S REMARK.

sovereign. In a free state *the payment of taxes is an exercise of sovereignty.*

But that *which is to be protected* embraces *all* that each one possesses.

The totality thus established can not undertake to protect any thing which it has not recognized. *By undertaking to protect all the possessions of each citizen, it recognizes his title to those possessions;* and thus the property-compact—which it at first appeared was only concluded between all as single individuals—is confirmed by the actual totality of the commonwealth.

In so far as the Whole must regard all violation of any of the possessions or rights of the single citizens as *inflicted upon itself*, the Whole is *proprietor* of all; but in so far as it wishes *to have free use of any thing*, only that which each citizen contributes toward the Whole is property of the state.

That which the individual does not contribute to the Whole is his own, and in respect to it he remains individual, a free, independent person; and it is this very freedom which the state has secured to him, and to secure which he became member of a state. Man separates himself from his citizenship in order to elevate himself with absolute freedom to morality; but in order to be able to do so, he becomes a citizen.

In so far as the individual is limited by the law, he is a *subject*, subject to the protective power within its limited sphere. Again: The agreement was entered into with him only on condition of his furnishing his contribution, and hence the contract is canceled when he does not furnish it. Each one, therefore, guarantees with all his property that he will so contribute, and he loses his right to his property if he does not contribute. The Whole likewise, since he voluntarily resigns all participation in the decision of cases, becomes his *judge*, and he is in so far subject to it with all his property. If there is a penal law providing for such cases, as is to be supposed, he may buy off his fault by paying a penalty, and may thus save his property by losing only part of it.

Thus our investigation returns into itself, and the synthesis is closed.

The state-compact is, therefore, a compact which each single citizen enters into with the actual Whole, which Whole results from the agreements of the single individuals with each other, and whereby he becomes One with this Whole in regard to a certain part of his rights, receiving in return the rights of sovereignty.

The two parties of the contract are: the individual and the state as a whole. The compact is conditioned by the free, formal will of both parties to enter into an agreement. The material will, about which the parties must agree, is, on the one side, fixed property ; on the other side, relinquishment of title to all other property, and a fixed contribution to the protective power. Through this compact the citizen of the one party receives a *secured* property ; and the state of the other party receives both a quit-claim to all other property in the state, which is necessary to perfect the title of all the other citizens of the state, and a fixed contribution to the protecting power.

This compact guarantees itself, it contains in itself the sufficient ground that it will be kept, as indeed all organized bodies have in themselves the sufficient ground of their existence. Either this compact does not at all exist for a person, or, if it does, it completely binds him. But the person who does not belong to this compact stands, indeed, in no legal relation to other persons at all, and is rightfully excluded from a reciprocity with other beings of his kind in the sensuous world.

COROLLARIUM.

So far as I know, the conception of the state as a whole has heretofore been established only by an ideal gathering together of the individuals, and thus the true insight into the nature of this relation has been lost. By such a gathering together, all possible things may be collected into a whole. The uniting tie is always merely our thinking, and all the parts remain isolated as before, the moment we think differently.

A true union has not been comprehended until the uniting tie has been shown up *outside of the conception*—as we say, from the empirical standpoint

—or until *that which compels us in thinking to make
this union*, as we say, from the transcendental stand-
point, has been shown up.   We have shown up this
uniting tie of the state as a whole in the conception of the individual who is to be protected.   That
individual being necessarily undetermined, because
any one of all individuals may need the protection,
this very undeterminedness unites all individuals
into one.

The most proper illustration of this conception
is an organized product of nature.   Precisely as in
it, each part can be what it is only in its connection,
and out of it would not be this ; nay, out of all organic connection, would be absolutely nothing, since
without the reciprocal action of organic forces, holding each other reciprocally in equilibrium, there
would be no permanent form at all, but merely an
unthinkable eternal war between being and not being : so, also, does man receive only in the state
organization a determined position in the series of
things, a point of rest in nature ; and each receives
this determined position toward others and toward
nature only by living in *this determined* organization.   Through the union of all organic power does
nature constitute herself; through the union of
the arbitrariness of all men does mankind constitute itself.

It is the character of inorganic matter, which is
thinkable only in conjunction with and as a part of
the organized world, that in it no part can be found,
which has not the ground of its determinedness in

itself, which is not completely explainable in itself; whereas, in organized products no part can be found which has the ground of its determinedness in itself, and which does not refer to and presuppose a being outside of itself.

The same relation exists between the isolated man and the citizen. The former acts purely to satisfy his wants, and none of his wants are satisfied except through his own acts ; whatever he is exteriorly he is only through himself. The citizen, on the contrary, has much to do and to leave undone, not for his own sake, but for the sake of the other ; and, on the other hand, his highest wants are satisfied not by his own acts, but by the acts of others. In the organic body each part continually preserves the whole, and in preserving it preserves itself ; so also is the citizen related to the state. It is not necessary to have this preservation of the whole particularly in view ; each citizen, in *preserving himself* in his position as part of the whole, preserves the whole ; and again, the whole, by preserving each in his position, preserves itself, and returns into itself.*

* The deduction here undertaken lacks comprehensiveness *in its application.*

Firstly : An organized product of nature is not a completed whole. Not only do its parts point to an outside end, but the whole itself expresses this insufficiently, chiefly through the distinction of sex. A tree, as a whole, is not a complete organization. There is only one whole, one true, organized product of nature ; and that is the whole of nature itself.

Secondly : If within the whole of nature we draw a distinction between organized products of nature and inorganic matter, the line of that distinction is arbitrary. For if it is once clear that there is only one complete organization, embracing all nature, then every part of nature, as part of that organization, must also refer to it, and thus the distinction between organic and inorganic matter falls away. (That distinction has indeed been swept away long ago by LEIBNITZ, whose monad-theory is this very statement.) Every grain of sand is as much an organized product as the tree or the animal ; and its reference to the totality of nature is quite as clear, if we get to the inside of it. (Each monad, says LEIBNITZ, from this very character of referring to another, must express the whole universe.)

Thirdly : It is, therefore, possible to say both : all parts of matter are organic, or all parts of matter are inorganic. They are organic, if you consider that each atom must still be part of an organization, and as such express it ; it is inorganic, if you consider that even the most perfect animal does not describe a complete return into itself, and is no more perfect (qualitatively) a product of nature than a grain of sand or a piece of rock. Both statements are true, or neither is true ; for both are true only in their synthesis, under the higher conception of the whole of nature as the complete organization.

Fourthly : Hence, that which was to be illustrated by the conception of a product of nature, and which is equally taken from empirical observation, must be modified. The state, as an **organization**, is either the totality of mankind, or every two individuals may form a state. There is no ground why a state should be limited by another number than the totality of rational beings on earth, just as we found no ground why the conception of organized products of nature should be limited by only quantitative lines. I have already shown that FICHTE never touches this difficulty. But it follows from his speculative ascertainments clearly enough. If every fraction of individuals can form a state organization, then the smallness of the fraction can not be determined, and it is purely a matter of chance how states will shape themselves. Every two individuals have the right to form a different state. I have shown why no limited number of individuals has this right, namely, because they are not perfectly secure until they have agreed with *all* members of the human race. The only legitimate form of government is, therefore, one which embraces, or proposes ultimately to embrace, all mankind ; and a true state organization must embrace all members of the human race. Only then is it a Whole, a Totality.—TRANSLATOR.

Book Second.

CONCERNING THE STATE CONSTITUTION.

Q

THE ESTABLISHMENT OF A GOVERNMENT.

THROUGH the state organization the common will has manifested itself, and become the law of all. But it has not yet been established actually, nor has the power to protect all the individuals of the state been, as yet, conferred upon it. The common will is realized in the state organization as mere will ; but not as power to maintain itself, not as a *government*.

This is our present problem.

The individuals of the commonwealth, as physical persons in the sensuous world, necessarily are themselves possessed of power. Until some one transgresses the law, his will must be assumed to be in harmony with the common will, and hence his power is part of the common power. Thus each one, even if he has the desire to transgress the law, must always fear the power of all others, and all others must constantly fear his power ; simply because neither party can have a knowledge of the other's intentions. In short, the power of all keeps the power of each single individual in check ; and the most complete equilibrium of rights is thus established.

But as soon as the law has been transgressed, the matter changes. The transgressor is now excluded from the law, and his power from its power. His will is no longer in harmony with the common will, but is a private will.

So also is the offended party excluded from the execution of the common will; for the very fact that he is the offended party makes his will; that the transgressor shall be punished, a private will and not the common will. His private will, we have shown, is kept in check only by the power of the common will. If this power were intrusted into his hands for the purpose of executing what is clearly his private will, his private will would no longer be kept in check by the common power. Hence, only a *third party* can be judge, of which third party it is to be assumed that the whole dispute concerns him only in so far as the common security is endangered thereby, since he can have no private advantage in deciding in favor of this or the other party; and of which party it is, therefore, to be assumed that his will is the common will, utterly uninfluenced by his private will.

Nevertheless, the possibility remains that the third party, from some unexplainable preference in favor of one of the parties, or because he may be interested after all, or because he is liable to error, will pronounce an unjust decision and combine with the offender to carry it out. Both parties would thus be united in favor of injustice, and the supreme power would no longer be on the side of the law.

How is such a combination in favor of injustice to be made impossible?

The will of the common end or the rule of the law is, as we have shown, conditioned by the will of the private end of each; his desire of public security is conditioned by his desire of his own security. Hence, it would be necessary to effect a contrivance which would make it impossible for individuals to combine together against the security of others without infallibly losing their own security.

It is certainly true, that if such a combination has once been formed in a state, it thereby becomes possible a second and a third time, and hence that each member of the first combination must apprehend that the rule of his own conduct will at some future time be turned against him. But still it is possible that each one will think, It won't hit me; I shall be smart enough to be always on the winning side.

The possibility of such a thought must be utterly taken away. Each one must become convinced that the subjection and unlawful treatment of *one* member of the state will infallibly result in his own subjection and unlawful treatment.

Such a conviction can be produced only by a *law*. The unjust violence against an individual must, therefore, become *legalized* by its having occurred in one case. Because something has been allowed to occur once, each citizen must thereafter have a perfect right to do the same. In the words of a previously-used formula : Each deed must necessarily become law ; if it does, then every law is sure to become a deed.   (This proposition is, indeed, a matter of course ; for the law is the same for all men, and hence what the law allows to one it must allow to all.)

But this proposition can not be realized ; for through it right and justice are annulled for all time.   The Conception of Rights can not involve such a self-contradiction ; hence, it can only signify that no single case of a violation of law must ever be allowed to occur, since its occurrence would annul law for all time to come.   How this is to be actualized will appear directly, when we shall examine more closely the established conception of a *power* of the law.

We have said that the protective power must be one, the self-preservation whereof is conditioned by its continuous effectiveness, which will, therefore, be annihilated for ever if it remains inactive in one single case ; the *general existence* of which, indeed, depends upon *its manifesting itself in every single case ;* and since this order of things is not sure to be established of itself, it must be provided for through a fundamental law of the constitution.

It is established when the following provision is made : That a law shall have no validity for future cases until all previous cases have been decided according to it.   In other words, no one must be allowed the benefits of a law until all previous persons who have claims under the same law have had their claims settled; and no one must be punished under a certain law until all previous violations of this law have been discovered and punished. And since all laws are really only One Law, the provision must be : that the one general law can not be applied in any particular case until all previous cases have been decided according to it. A law, which in this manner prescribes a law to itself, such an in itself returning law, is called a *Constitutional Law*, or the *Constitution.*

If this order of things is made secure by a power of compulsion, then the security of all and the uninterrupted rule of law seems firmly established. But how is it to be thus secured ?

If, as is always presupposed here, the whole commonwealth holds the power of compulsion in its hands, what other power is there to force the commonwealth to see that the required order of things is always upheld ? Or, supposing that all members of the state should for a while observe their fundamental compact and the required constitution, but should in a certain case be unwilling or unable to redress at the moment the grievances of some party or another. In that case, the operations of the law would come to a stand-still, and the disorders arising therefrom would soon be so great as to compel the people to violate their constitutional provision and —leaving old offenses unpunished—to try and stop disorders by energetically punishing new offenses.

For such a stand-still of the law would be the punishment of their laziness, negligence, or partiality ; and why should the people inflict upon themselves a violence of this kind ?

In other words, the people would be their own judge of the administration of the law. Now, so long as insecurity had not become general, the people would probably allow many violations of the law to pass unpunished. Suddenly, when matters would grow intolerable, the people, in order to remedy past neglect, would pounce with unjust and passionate severity upon the criminals, whom previous laxity had rendered bolder, and who had been led to expect the same laxity in their own cases, but whose misfortune had brought them into the clutches of the law at the very epoch of the awaking of the people. This state of things would continue until terror had become general. Then the fury of the people would die out, the people and the administration of the law would fall asleep again, and the old state of things would return.

Such a form of government, the *democratic** form of government, in the real signification of the word, is the unsafest which is possible, since each citizen has constantly to fear not only the attacks of other citizens, but also the blind rage of a maddened mob, which will carry out injustice under the name of law.

* Democracy, as it was understood in Greece, namely, the direct rule of the people without a government.—TRANSLATOR.

Our problem, therefore, has not been solved; and the condition of men is as unsafe as ever. The true ground of this unsafety is, that the people can not be at the same time both *judge and a party* in the administration of the law.

This discovers to us the solution of our problem. In the administration of the law, judge and party must be divided, and the people of the commonwealth can not be both together.

The people can not be a party in this matter. For the people must remain the supreme power, and hence no judge, if the people were a party, could carry out his sentence against them, unless they should voluntarily submit, which is not to be supposed; for if they did, they would respect the law above every thing, and no law-dispute could possibly arise.

In short, there must be a law,* according to which it can be decided whether the power of the state has been properly applied or not; and in this law-dispute the same person can not be both judge and a party to the case. Now, as the people must be one or the other in the law-dispute, and as they can not be *party*, from the reason stated above, the people can not retain the supreme power in their own hands.

It is, above all, important to be convinced of the

---

* There must be, besides the power of government, which enforces the laws, another power, which makes it impossible for the power of government to violate the laws. This other power is, our American system of *checks and balances.*—TRANSLATOR.

strictness of this argument, since it furnishes the *a priori* deduction, which, to my knowledge, has never before been given, of the absolute necessity of *Representation* in a commonwealth. It shows that a representative government is not only useful and wise, but is absolutely required by the Conception of Rights, and that a Democracy, in the above-mentioned sense of the word, is not only an impolitic, but an absolutely unlawful form of government. Perhaps the statement, that the people can not be both judge and party to a case at the same time, will meet less objection than the other statement, that a check upon the administration of the supreme power is absolutely necessary. Nevertheless, it is the certain result of all we have said before. Each member of the state must be convinced of the impossibility that his rights will ever be violated. But this impossibility does not exist so long as the administrators of the supreme power are not held accountable.

The people of a commonwealth must, therefore, relinquish the administration of the supreme power to one or more persons, who remain responsible for the proper application of that power. A form of government which does not provide for this responsibility of the administration is a *despotism*.

Hence, it is a fundamental law of every rational and legal form of government, that the *executive power*, which embraces the executive and judicial, should be separated from *the power which controls and checks the administration of that executive and judicial power.*

I shall call the latter power the *Ephorate.* It must remain with the entire people, whilst the executive power must not remain with the entire people. A form of government, therefore, must be neither *despotic* nor *democratic.*

Much has been said concerning the division of powers, that is, of dividing the one common power of government into many. It has been said that the legislative power must be separated from the executive ; but this proposition seems to be somewhat indefinite.

For, after the people of a commonwealth have once agreed upon living together in a legal relation, all specific laws are only applications of the one fundamental law, to which they have subjected themselves. It is, therefore, all the same if the men who are intrusted with the executive power, also frame new specific laws ; for in doing so they only execute the one fundamental law, which they were elected to carry out. If their specific provisions are unjust, or unlawful, the *Ephorate* holds them responsible.*

Utterly useless and only seemingly possible is the separation of the judicial from the executive

* Here FICHTE does not perceive that such a separation is one of the very best means of checking the abuses on the part of the supreme power. The conception of an *Ephorate* is precisely realized by this separation of the form of government into several branches.—TRANSLATOR'S REMARK.

power, using the latter word in its more limited sense. For if the executive power has no veto upon the judicial power, then it is the unlimited power of the judiciary itself, separated into two persons ;* but of which two persons only one has a will, the other being merely a physical power directed by another will. But if the executive power has a veto, then it is itself the highest judicial power, and both powers are again one and the same. According to our doctrine, only the executive power and the Ephorate, or checking power, are to be separated.

The executive power of a commonwealth may be intrusted either to one person—as is done in a Monarchy—or to an organized body established in the constitution, as is done in a Republic. But since even in a monarchy one person does not really execute all the power, intrusting it rather to subordinates, the real distinction between a monarchy and a republic is this, that in a monarchy the final decision of all questions rests with one permanent

---

* It is very true that all separation of power is only a separation of one power amongst different persons, but this separation amongst different persons is one of the best safeguards against abuses of power. There is really but one executive power—and only the checking power is opposed to it ; and this one power is divided out amongst a number of persons, some of whom exercise the legislative, others the judicial, others the strictly executive functions. The whole machinery of government is established merely to carry out, to execute, the fundamental law ; and none of the wheels of this machinery are independent of each other ; yet is each of the wheels also independent enough to check the other.—TRANSLATOR'S REMARK.

president, (the monarch ;) whereas in a republic it rests with the majority of votes—the ballot-box. Hence, in a republic, the permanent monarch is a mythical and often changeable person, since it is composed of all those who decide by their votes the question at issue.

Again : The administrators of the executive power may be either elective or not ; and in the former case *all* or only some of them may be elective. They are elective in a proper *democracy*, that is to say, in a democracy which recognizes representation. If *all* the public officials are directly elected by the whole people, the democracy is a pure democracy ; if only some, it is a mixed democracy. The public officials may also fill vacancies themselves ; this is the case in a pure *aristocracy*. But if only some of the magistrates are thus replaced by the public officers, and if the others are again directly elected by the people, then the form of government is that of a democratic aristocracy. A permanent president (monarch) may also be elected to exercise the executive power during his lifetime.

In all these cases, either all citizens of the commonwealth, or only some of them, are eligible to office. Eligibility may, therefore, be limited or unlimited. It can be effectively limited only through birth ; for if every citizen is eligible to any office in the state, and the limitation is merely that he shall not fill, for instance, the higher offices until he has filled lower ones, then his eligibility is not absolutely but only relatively limited. If eligibility is absolutely limited, and hence grounded upon birth, the form of government is that of an *hereditary aristocracy;* and this leads us to the second supposition, that the administrators of the executive powers are not elective.

They are not elective in a form of government which recognizes born representatives, persons who are representatives either immediately through their birth, as hereditary princes in every hereditary monarchy, or who, at least, are, through their birth, the only eligible representatives, as the nobility in all monarchies, and the patricians in hereditary-aristocratic republics.

All these forms of government become legal through the law ; that is, through the original will of the people, expressed in the adoption of their constitution. They are all lawful, provided that a checking power is established effective enough to prevent any abuse of power.*

* This *provided* annuls all the foregoing, which, indeed, as based upon facts taken from experience, is a purely subjective judgment. It is, for instance, *a priori* clear that no checking power can be efficient if a monarch remains the *permanent* executive ; or if there is not a power to punish his unlawful actions, by depriving him of his executive office. It is equally clear that an hereditary aristocracy does not permit of an efficient checking system, and that hence it is an unlawful form of government; for there is no power sufficient to prevent their abuse of power ; or, if there is, then the aristocracy is not hereditary and exclusive possessor of certain rights.

It is certainly not the province of the Science of Rights to determine which is the better form of government, but it is equally truly its province to determine the conditions of a lawful government.

The question, Which is the better form of government for any particular state ? is not a question for

We have already shown that one of these conditions is universal applicability to the whole human race, and hence the form of a Confederate Republic. Another condition is, as FICHTE has clearly shown, an effective checking power. How this is to be established is certainly a problem for the art of politics ; and it is also clear that this art can constantly be improved upon. No one will deny that, however excellent, our system of checks and balances, both in our general form of governments and in our state governments, can be vastly improved. Our state governments particularly seem much in need of such improvements.

All we desire to assert in this note is, that the conditions of the effectiveness of such a system of checks can be much closer determined than FICHTE has done here. The reason why he found this subject so difficult to manage was probably because he could not see that the Ephorate, of the necessity of which institution he was absolutely convinced, would be realized in those very separations of powers and systems of checks which he attacked ; and this he could not see because he did not see this, their true character. *A priori* he was convinced that a checking power must be established ; but how to establish it was a question to which history alone could suggest answers, and neither the history of the ancient republics nor the recent experiments of France furnished the proper answer. American history was little known at FICHTE's time. Thus it puzzled him continually ; and hence, also, no chapter of his Science of Rights was looked upon with more wonder by the public than this one upon the *Ephorate.* Unable to suggest a solution, FICHTE, some ten years later, withdrew his proposed establishment of such an *Ephorate,* but took, at the same time, occasion to reassert his firm conviction in the correctness of the *idea.* He added that, after all, such an *Ephorate* did already exist in every civilized commonwealth, *in the force of public opinion,* which kept a continual check upon the executive power. We append that retraction at the end of this book, so that the reader may fully see how a philosopher may be absolutely certain of the correctness of a principle, and yet find it impossible to give it reality in the world as it is.—TRANSLATOR'S REMARK.

the Science of Rights to solve, but for the art of politics ; and the solution of that problem depends upon the investigation, under which form of government the checking power can be made to work in the most effective manner.

The persons who have been intrusted by the people with the administration of the executive power, must have accepted it, and made themselves responsible for its administration.

Of course, this acceptance can only be voluntarily ; and both parties must come to an understanding about it. For although the Conception of Rights requires that a public power, and expressly appointed administrators thereof, shall be established, it does not say to what particular persons that power is to be intrusted.

It is clear enough that, since the Conception of Rights requires such an establishment of a government, each person can be compelled to vote for or against the establishment of it ; and likewise, that, if he happen to be elected as one of that government, he must declare whether he will accept the office or not.

It is also clear that the vote on the constitution, as the instrument which establishes the form of government, must be a *unanimous* vote. For although there exists a right of compulsion, to compel every person to become member of a commonwealth, there is no such right to compel him to become member of *any particular* commonwealth. If

the vote is not unanimous, the majority will probably remain in the country, and constitute themselves a commonwealth under that constitution ;
whilst those in the minority, as they can not be
tolerated in the commonwealth unless they become
members of it, have no other choice than either to
make the vote unanimous by accepting the constitution, or to make the vote unanimous by leaving
the commonwealth.

Those who have once accepted an office under
the constitution, can not again resign it without the
consent of the people, since such resignation would
perhaps interrupt the rule of the law, or make it
impossible for a while, if no one could be found to
take their place.   On the other hand, the people can
not take the office away from them ; for their office
is now their vocation, their possession in the state,
and they have no other property.   The other citizens received their property, and these got their
offices as their property ; hence their legal relation
with the other citizens would be annulled, if the
offices were taken away from them one-sidedly.   Of
course, if both parties agree, no objection can be
raised.

Again : Since those who are to administer the
public power made themselves responsible for the
maintenance of justice and security, they must
necessarily insist on being provided with the means,
and the free use of them, requisite for that purpose.
They must have the privilege of determining what
each citizen shall furnish as his share of those

R

means, and of using them according to their best knowledge and conviction. (How far this power is, nevertheless, to be limited, we shall soon see.) They must, therefore, be intrusted with unlimited control of the public power.

This public government must, in each specific case, protect the rights of citizens and punish violations of these rights. It is held responsible for this, and hence must have the power and the right to watch the conduct of the citizens ; in other words it must have a *police power** and a *police legislation*.

It needs scarcely be added, that this public administration is also a judge from whom there is no appeal, since all citizens have agreed in their original compact to submit their law disputes to the common power, which has now, through the constitution, been established as an administrative power.

* Our Grand Juries are such an institution.—TRANSLATOR'S REMARK.

§ 2.

THE ESTABLISHMENT OF A CHECK UPON THE GOVERNMENT.

WE now proceed to the second problem in the establishment of a constitution: How can this supreme power of the commonwealth, which has been constituted its government, be prevented from ever executing what is not lawful; and likewise from ever neglecting to execute what the law requires?

We have already suggested in general how this is to be accomplished. Their private end, the end of their own security and welfare, must be the same as the common end, and must be attainable only through the common end. It must be made impossible that they should have any other object than to promote the general object.

The law is merely *formal;* hence there must be no *material* interests possible for their law decisions. The only interest possible for them must be to watch, that their decisions are conformable to the law.

They must, first of all, be placed in a position of complete independence from all private persons, so far as their private needs are concerned. They must have a sure and sufficient income, so that no private person can offer them any benefits, and that all inducements which may possibly be offered to them can have no value in their eyes.

They must also have as few friendships, personal connections, attachments, etc., as possible, in order to be indisposed to show partiality.

It was stated before as a principle, necessary to compel equal legislation for each person, that the law must judge cases in time-succession, and that no future case must be decided until all past cases have been decided. This principle falls away as soon as a regular judicial power has been established through the constitution, which is held responsible for the pure administration of the law ; for it may be more expedient to first decide cases which require little time ; and the great object is, after all, to lose as little time as possible ; but nevertheless, it is absolutely necessary that the judicial power should always be able to show that it has taken cognizance of all cases brought before it, and likewise that a certain time should be fixed within which cases—according to their nature—must be finally decided upon. If such a time is not fixed, it is impossible to ascertain whether each citizen has obtained his rights, and impossible to prove a neglect on the part of the judicial power, since it can always refer the complainants to the future.

But the following is a sure criterion whether the

law is administered as it should be: The administration of the law must never contradict itself. Each public act of the public government must become established rule for all the future. This will bind government to the law. The government officials now can not proceed unjustly, since that would involve continued injustice for all the future, which again would lead to their own unsafety. Or if they should ignore again the unjust rule once adopted, they would thereby confess their unjust procedure in the previous case.

To make such a criterion possible, all acts of the administration, with their connected circumstances and grounds of decision, must receive the greatest publicity, at least after their final settlement. It might often be necessary, for the sake of public security, to keep these proceedings secret whilst still pending; but after the final decision, secrecy is no longer necessary.

If the state officials administer their power in accordance with these principles, right, justice, and security are fully guaranteed to each citizen of the commonwealth. But how—since confidence and fidelity are qualities never to be presupposed in legal relations—can the officials be compelled to proceed according to these principles? This is the final problem for a rational state constitution.

The executive power has final jurisdiction in all cases; there is no appeal from it. Such appeal is neither permissible—since it is a condition of a legal status that no appeal shall be made from the executive power—nor is it possible, since the executive power wields supreme power. The presumptive law, which has been constituted the infallible law of the commonwealth, speaks through the person of the judges, elected as infallible, from whom there is no appeal. The decisions of that power must, therefore, be carried out in the sensuous world.

A clear proof that the constitutional law has been violated by the executive power, can be furnished only when it is shown, either that the law has not been executed within the time fixed in the constitution, or when it is shown that the state officials contradict themselves, or commit evident injustice in order to avoid the appearance of self-contradiction.

It has further been shown, that only the people can judge the administrators of the public power. But the difficulty is this : where and what is the people ? Is it any thing more than a mere conception, and if any thing more, how is it to be realized ?

Before the tribunal of the public power or state government, all the members of the state are only private persons and not a people ; each person is always subject to the government. Each will is considered by the government as only a private will, and the government considers itself the sole expression of the common will. The people, as a community, have no separate will ; and hence a people as a body to sit in judgment upon the government, can not at all be realized until the people have withdrawn their declaration that the will of the government is their own will.

But how can this be done? No private person has the right to get up and say: " Let the people of our state come together in a convention to sit in judgment upon the government!" For if the will of such a person does not agree with the will of the government which continues to represent the common will, then the will of that person is a private will rising in opposition to the government, and hence a rebellious will, punishable as such ; and his will certainly will never agree with that of the government. For either that government is conscious of its just administration, and in that case such a proposition for a convention would be utterly opposed to the common desire that no unnecessary disturbance of private business and of the administration of the law shall be tolerated, or it is conscious of its injustice ; in which case it is not to be presumed that it will give up the power which it still holds in its hands, and will itself call together its judge. Hence, the government officials always remain their own judges, because the realizing of a judicial power to judge them depends upon themselves ; and thus the form of government remains, after all, a despotism.

In short, since the people, as one body, can call itself together in convention only through itself, and since the people can not be one body until they have been thus called together, its calling together is impossible.*

How can this contradiction be solved? It is solved; *When the constitution is made to provide in advance that the people shall, in a certain case, be called together in convention.*

Such a constitutional law might provide, for instance, that the people should assemble together in convention at certain times, in order to consider the administration of the government officials. This arrangement is possible in small states, where the people do not live far apart, and can be called together without much loss of time, and where the administration of a government, moreover, can be easily surveyed. Yet even in such states this great law-ceremony would lose its dignity by too frequent a recurrence ; and what is worse, a foreknowledge of its occurrence would enable parties, to a great extent, to control such conventions, and thus make them rather the representatives of their own than of the common will. In larger states, however, such an arrangement would be altogether impossible. It may, therefore, be stated as a principle of such a provision : *That the people shall never be called together without absolute necessity; but as soon as it is necessary, they shall be called together at once, and shall have the power to judge.*

---

* As would be the case in a state under a constitution providing no mode for calling together a constitutional convention, and as was the case in the State of Missouri in 1861.—Translator.

There is no necessity for such an assembly, nor will the people desire it, unless law and justice have utterly ceased to be effective ; but when this necessity arises, the convention must be called.

In a properly organized state, law and justice in general are dependent upon the maintenance of the rights of each single individual ; and hence the whole law is overthrown if a single case of injustice occurs.

But who shall ascertain whether this case has occurred ? The people can not, for they are not assembled ; nor can the government, for that would be making it judge its own case. Nor can the party which complains of injustice, for it also is interested in the case. Hence, *there must be a special power established by the constitution to take cognizance of such cases.*

This power must be intrusted with continual supervision over the conduct of the government, and hence we may call it the *Ephorate.*

The executive power is responsible only to the people assembled in convention ; hence the Ephorate can not sit in judgment upon the government ; it must, however, be intrusted with the power to constantly watch the conduct of the government, and hence, also, to obtain information concerning it. The Ephorate must not have the power to stop the decisions of the executive officials, since from them there is no appeal ; nor must it have the right to decide law disputes, since the government is the only magistrate in the state. The Ephorate *has, therefore, no executive power at all.**

But the Ephorate has an *absolute prohibitory* power—power to prohibit, not the execution of this or that particular decision of the government, for then it would be a judge, and the executive power would not be supreme, but to utterly suspend the administration of the law and the government in all its branches. I will call this suspension of all law power the state interdict, (in analogy with the church interdict. The church has long since invented this infallible means to enforce the obedience of those who need her.)

It is, therefore, fundamental principle of a rational and proper government, that the *absolute positive* power should be complemented by an *absolute negative* power.

But since the Ephorate is to have no power at all in its hands, and since the executive government is the supreme power, it might be asked how the Ephorate can enforce its declared suspension of the government. But this enforcement will come of itself. For by the publicly announced suspension of all law, all the subsequent acts of government become illegal and null and void. Every body will, therefore, refuse to submit to the decisions of government if the decision is against him ;

---

* In this the power of the Ephorate, deduced from pure reason, is utterly distinct from the *Ephores* of the Spartans, from the state inquisition of Venice, etc. The tribunes of the people in the Roman republic had somewhat of the character required here.

and no one can rely on its decision if it is in his favor.

By the announced suspension of the government, the state officials are declared to be mere private persons, and all their orders to use executive power are declared null and void. From the moment of this announced suspension, every act of the government, whereby it exercises executive power, is resistance to the common will of the people, as expressed through the Ephorate, and hence is a rebellion, and is to be punished as such. But since by such a resistance a government would in advance subject itself to the highest punishment, whereas by quietly awaiting a trial before the people, it might, perhaps, successfully refute the charges of the Ephorate, a resistance of this kind is scarcely to be apprehended.

The announcement of the suspension of the government is at the same time a call for a convention of the people. The greatest misfortune which could possibly happen to them, has forced the people to come together in convention. The Ephorate is, of course, the accusing party, and has to prefer its charges.

It is, of course, not necessary, and would be in most cases impossible, to call all the people together ; it is sufficient if all of them take part in the convention. How this is to be accomplished, or how the result of the will of the people is to be clearly ascertained, is a question for the art of politics to solve. Still it will be necessary, from a reason we shall shortly develop, that at various places large gatherings of the people come together.

The resolves of this convention of the people become constitutional law.*

It will be, therefore, necessary, first of all, that the convention declare the suspension of the government, and hence its own existence, to be in accordance with the constitution, and that the decision of the convention, no matter which way it may turn, be declared to be supreme law of the land.

Again : So far as the decision itself is concerned, it will necessarily be just, that is, in accordance with the original common will of the people.   For if the convention should absolve the government from the charge preferred by the Ephorate, that the government has allowed a crime to remain unpunished, (the *fact*, as such, must not admit of a doubt ; this the Ephorate will have to take care of ;) then the convention would thereby resolve that the unpunished crime should be considered a lawful act, which every citizen of the state might commit.   Or if the government is charged with contradicting itself, or with an evident injustice, and the convention should absolve the government, then the convention would thereby make that contradictory or unjust principle a fundamental law of the state, ap-

---

* The state of things in Missouri, from 1861 to 1864, affords an exact analogy to the condition of things here described ; and our practical American solution of the difficulty was precisely in accordance with the principles here established.—TRANSLATOR'S REMARK.

plicable to each citizen. The convention will certainly be very careful to avoid a wrong decision.

The losing party, whether it be the government or the Ephorate, must be declared guilty of high treason. The Ephorate, because it has suspended the administration of the law without just cause; the government, because it has abused the power intrusted to it to suppress the law.

Few persons will hold it too hard that the government, if declared guilty, should be pronounced guilty of high treason; but some may consider this too severe a punishment for the Ephorate. It may be said that its members were positively convinced that the commonwealth was in danger, that they have acted conscientiously and have only erred. But the same may be said of the government, and the only answer to this is: Error in such matters is quite as dangerous as a bad intention; and the law should be quite as careful to prevent the former as to suppress the latter. The wisest of the people should be elected to the offices of the government, and none but old and experienced men should be elected as Ephores.

Moreover, it is quite probable that, previous to suspending the government, the Ephorate will consult with the government officials and induce them, if possible, voluntarily to remedy its fault or neglect. By doing this the Ephorate will, at the same time, obtain a thorough knowledge of the merits of the case.

The action of the convention has retroactive

power. The judgment pronounced under the rules, which the convention has disapproved, are annulled, and the parties who have suffered under these judgments are reinstated in their previous position without detriment, however, to their opponents, since these have acted only in accordance with the law, although the law has now shown itself to be an invalid law. The damages devolve upon the judges who have pronounced the unjust judgments.

The ground of this retroactive force is this : the party who lost under the unjust judgment was prohibited from appealing from it, since the presumption was, that the will of the judge who pronounced it was in accordance with the common will of the people. At present the contrary appears, and when the ground falls away, so also does the grounded. That judgment, therefore, is annulled.

The positive and negative powers—the government and the ephorate—must be heard before the convention of the people. They can not be parties in their own cause, and hence do not belong to the people. The truth is, all government officials. though before their election they belong to the people, cease to belong to it the moment they become officials. If they are born such officials, as is the case with hereditary princes, they have never belonged to the people. Born aristocrats and noblemen belong to the people, but not after they are elected into the government. Before election, they are not government officials, although they are exclusively eligible. The constitution must make provision that their votes, in view of their probable partiality for the executive power, shall not have an injurious influence upon the actions of the common will. How to make such provision is a problem for the art of politics.

As soon as the candidates for offices are elected, they cease to belong to the people, even though they have not yet accepted the election. Making themselves, as they do, responsible for the public safety and the administration of justice with their own person and freedom, it is necessary that they should have a *veto* in the legislation ; that is to say, they must have the privilege of stating : We will not govern under such laws. But the people then must also have the privilege of replying : If you will not govern under laws which appear good to us, we will elect others.

As soon as the government has been established, the people, as a unity, cease to exist ; the people are no longer a people, a Whole, but an aggregate of individuals subject to the government, which is now not a part of the people.

It appears, that the safety of the whole common- wealth depends upon the absolute freedom and per- sonal security of the Ephores. It is they who are to keep the supreme power of the government in proper check. It must be impossible, therefore, that they can ever become dependent upon the government so far as their personal welfare is con- cerned. They must, therefore, be particularly well paid. Moreover, they are exposed to the persecutions and threats of the government, and have no other defense than the people.

Their persons, must, therefore, be made secure by the law ; that is, they must be declared inviolable. The least violence or threat of violence against them is *high treason*, that is, is an immediate attack upon the commonwealth. The mere threat of violence against them on the part of the government is, indeed, in itself a declaration that all law is suspended ; for by such a threat the executive power clearly separates its will from the common will.

Again, *the power of the people must surpass by far the power of the government.* For if the power of the government were but in any ways equal to that of the people, the government might resolve to resist the people, and a war would be possible between the people and the government; but such a war must be rendered impossible by the constitution. If the executive power of the government were superior to that of the people, or could become superior·in a war, the government might at any time undertake to subjugate the people and to reduce them to perfect slavery.

It is, therefore, a condition of the lawfulness of every civil government, that under no circumstances must the power of the government be able to oppose the least resistance to the power of the people as a whole. Every end must be sacrificed to this highest of all ends, which is equivalent to that of maintaining the rule of law itself.

For this reason it is also one of the chief aims of a rational constitution to provide that when the people are called together in convention by the Ephorate, larger masses of people shall congregate in different places, ready to quench any possible resistance on the part of the government.

The following important question might still be asked: How shall the people decide? By a majority of votes or by unanimity?

We have shown that, in the original compact of the people amongst themselves, unanimity is necessary. Each individual must declare that he is desirous of entering with all the others into a commonwealth for the maintenance of the law.

In electing magistrates, the matter already assumes a different shape. True, the minority is not compelled to submit to the majority; but being the weaker party, the minority may be compelled to leave the country within the limits of which the majority conclude to realize their constitution. If the minority does not choose to do so—as is most likely—it will have to indorse the action of the majority.

We said : being the weaker party, the minority may be compelled to leave. The reason is, evidently, because they are not strong enough to resist. The proof seems to consider, therefore, already, that the majority is a very decided one, strong

S

enough to make all resistance hopeless and a war—always an unlawful condition—utterly impossible. Until the minority is so strong, it must simply submit to the majority.*

In considering the justice or injustice of the charges preferred by the Ephorate against the government, little or no difference of opinion can possibly arise. The *facts* of the case must be apparent to all. The only question remains, therefore: is the charged conduct of the government just or not, and shall it be law for us in all future time or not? Only two answers are possible. Yes or no.

If the citizens have but ordinary power of judgment, the question is very easy to decide; and, indeed, it is so intimately connected with the welfare of each citizen, that the answer to it must be, from the nature of the case, almost unanimous, and that an opinion adverse to that of the overwhelming ma-

---

* This is a very ticklish question. It is clear, that the original constitution of a state must be adopted by an absolute majority, or unanimity; and such was the case with the United States Constitution. That original constitution, in order to settle all disputes as to the kind of majorities needed, before such disputes can arise, must specify them; as our general constitution, indeed, does. For all the cases provided for by the constitution, a dispute is, therefore, *lawfully* impossible. If, however, an unforeseen question should come up, of vast importance for the whole people, for which the constitution contained no provision, it is difficult to see how any other than an absolute majority could decide it. It will not do to say that the minority must submit. The minority have their rights under the original agreement, to take away the least of which involves an utter overthrow of all law; no matter how large the majority by which it is done.—TRANSLATOR'S REMARK.

jority may be safely put down as that of either incompetent or partial persons. The more rational citizens, if the first is the case, will try to convince them ; and if they can not be convinced, they will make themselves very suspect of being partial. But if the minority can not at all agree with the vote of the majority, then they are certainly not obliged to make their safety dependent upon a law which they do not recognize as just ; but neither will they desire to live among men who have adopted such a law, and hence the only course open to them is to emigrate from the state. As this is not always pleasant, it is to be expected that no one will insist on it ; unless, indeed, he is convinced that the passage of the law will destroy all safety. He will, on the contrary, rather indorse the vote of the majority, and thus make it unanimous.

It will be seen, that my theory of Rights always assumes the legal validity, not of a majority vote, but of a unanimous vote ; although it is admitted that those who refuse to submit to a very decided majority, (which may be fixed at seven eighths, perhaps, or still higher,) do thereby cease to be citizens of the state, and thus make unanimity possible.

Under the described constitution, Law must necessarily and infallibly rule at all times ; unless, indeed, the Ephorate should unite with the executive power to suppress the people.* This final and

---

* The excellent arrangement of our checking power makes such a union next to impossible. Even in our mere general form of gov-

greatest obstacle to a just government must also be removed.

The Ephorate must not be dependent upon the executive power, nor be in a position to receive favors from the government. It must have no friendly or social relations with the government. The people will look to this, and the Ephorate will take care not to lose the confidence of the people by such conduct.

Moreover it is advisable, nay, almost necessary. to make the tenure of government offices for lifetime, because the officials lose their other positions in life ; but it is equally advisable to make the tenure of the Ephores only for a specific time, since they need not give up their ordinary vocations. When retiring from office, the Ephores must give an account of what has occurred during their term of office ; and if any injustice has occurred. which still continues, the new Ephores must suspend the government and call together the people to sit in judgment upon the retiring Ephores as well as upon the government. It is clear, that the guilty Ephores must be punished as guilty of high treason. To have honorably administered the duties of the Ephorate ought to entitle to life-long distinction.

The Ephorate must be elected by the people, not

ernment, a combination of President, Congress, and the Supreme Court is out of the question. How, then, could the governments of all the states combine to suppress the whole people ?—TRANSLATOR'S REMARK.

by the government ; nor can the Ephores fill vacancies amongst themselves, the new ones being the judges of the old. The mode of their election should be specified in the constitution. No one should be allowed to apply for the Ephorate. The people themselves should select them ; and in this manner the people will learn to pay more attention to their wise and great men.

If all these provisions are observed, it is not well possible that the Ephorate will ever combine with the government against the liberties of the people. Unless every one of the first men of the country who may be successively elected into the Ephorate has been bribed when entering upon the duties of that office ; and moreover, unless each of them is so sure of a corruptible successor that he can afford to stake his whole security upon it, such a collusion is not well possible. A state of things like this is, however, impossible ; or, if it is possible, a people corrupt enough to make it possible may be said to deserve no better fate. Nevertheless, as a strict science should take cognizance even of the greatest improbabilities, the following must be added :

Each private person who calls together the people at large *against the will* of the government, which government represents the will of the people until the people are assembled in convention— it will always be against that will, since the government can never be induced to call the people together—is a rebel, since his will is in opposition to the presumptive .common will.

But *the people, as a whole, never can be a rebel;* and the expression *rebellion,* applied to the people at large, is the greatest absurdity ever uttered. For the people are, in fact and in law, the highest power and the source of all power; responsible only to God. By the convening of the people, the government loses its power, both in fact and in law.

Two cases are possible. Firstly, the people may rise up unanimously of their own accord and sit in judgment upon both Ephorate and government; for instance, when acts of injustice are too horribly apparent. In this case, the uprising is lawful both in form and in substance; for until insecurity and maladministration of the law oppress *every* citizen, each one takes care only of himself, and tries to get along as best he may. No people have ever uprise nor ever will uprise as one man, until injustice has become too intolerable.

Or, secondly: one or more private persons may call upon the whole people to come together in convention. In this case, these persons are certainly presumptive rebels, and until the people has so assembled, they will undoubtedly be so treated, in accordance with the presumptive common will, by the government, if that government can get hold of them. But an unjust power is always weak, because it is illogical; and because it has common opinion—often even the opinions of those whom it uses as tools—against itself. The more unjust it is. the more impotent and weak ; and the more probability, therefore, that those persons who have called the people together will escape the clutches of government.

The people may obey this call or may disregard it. If they assemble in convention, the executive power vanishes into nothingness, and the people sit in judgment upon it and upon those who have called the people together. If the people indorse the charges of the latter, they thereby declare their will to have been the true common will ; and its substance being acknowledged as the true law, its want of legal form is now supplied by the indorsement of the people. If, on the contrary, the people pronounce their charges unfounded, then these persons become rebels, and are condemned as such by the people.

If the people disregard their call, this disregarding proves either that oppression and public insecurity have not yet become general enough, or that they do not exist ; or secondly, that the people have not yet awakened to a desire to maintain their freedom and to a knowledge of their rights ; that they are not yet fit to decide upon the great law dispute brought before them, and hence that they ought not to have been called together. The persons who issued the call are, therefore, punished—with perfect external justice, as rebels ; although, according to internal justice, or in their conscience, they may be martyrs of true justice. They are perhaps, innocent in intention ; but in deed they

are punished as guilty.   They ought to have had
a better knowledge of the people.   For if a people
unfit to maintain its freedom had come together, it
would have resulted in a general annihilation of all
law.

All these provisions concerning the election of
executive officers, and concerning the establishment of a checking power, are provisions concerning the administration of the law ; and all these
provisions together are called the *Constitution.*

A lawful and rational constitution is unchangeable, valid for all time ; and is necessarily established
as such in its preamble.

For each single individual in the commonwealth
must agree to it ; and hence it is guaranteed through
the original common will.   Each individual has become a member of the state only under the guarantee *of this particular constitution.*   He can not be
compelled to approve another one.   If, therefore,
such another one contradictory of the original constitution should, nevertheless, be carried through,
he would be compelled to leave the state if he
could not approve of it.   But since he can not be
required to do this under the original agreement, it
follows that it is absolutely unlawful to change the
constitution, even if only one person is opposed to
it.   To effect a change of this kind in the constitution, therefore, *absolute* unanimity is required.

The distinction between the absolute unanimity
requisite for this change of the constitution and the

above relative unanimity is this, that the latter permits the exclusion of several persons from the state, while the former does not. In the former, the right to remain a citizen of the state is absolute ; in the latter, it is conditioned by his joining the majority.

We have said : A constitution which is a lawful one, that is, which provides for a responsible executive power, and for a checking power, is unchangeable ; that is to say, within its general scope. Infinite modifications are, of course, possible ; and in so far even the best constitution is subject to amendment.

If the constitution, however, is not a lawful one then it may be changed into a lawful one ; and no one has the right to say : I do not wish to give up the previous constitution. For the toleration of the previous illegal constitution was excusable only on the ground of previous ignorance or insensibility to the Conception of Rights ; but as soon as that conception is clearly apprehended, and the people have become capable of realizing it, each one is bound to accept it ; for *right shall rule.*

It is different with the amendments to the civil legislation. These will make themselves. At first, the state consists of a certain fixed number of men, carrying on these or those professions, etc. ; and the civil law is made accordingly. But as the people increase and new branches of business are created— of course, none must be created without the consent of the state—the laws also must change and be made to conform to the changed people.

The whole described mechanism is requisite for the realization of a lawful relation between men ; but it is not at all necessary that all these springs and wheels are always externally and visibly working. On the contrary, the better a state is organized the less it will be perceived, because its internal weight and quiet power cancel in advance all necessity for its exercise. The state prevents itself from being necessary.

The first object of the state is to decide the disputes of its citizens concerning their property. The more simple, clear, and comprehensive the law is, and the more infallible its execution, the less will be the number of these disputes, because every one may know with tolerable certainty what belongs to him or not, and will not be likely, therefore, to make the—presumptively abortive—attempt to secure the property of another. If the few disputes which may at first arise through error, are decided correctly in the conviction of both parties, there will be no crime. For where else is the source of crime concealed but in greediness and passions excited thereby, or in poverty and want, which are impossible if the law carefully watches over the property of each ? And how can crimes arise if their sources are stopped ? A good civil law and a strict execution thereof utterly cancel the application of the criminal law. Moreover, who will dare to commit a crime if he knows surely that he will be detected and punished ? A half a century of such a state of things, and the conceptions of crimes will have

vanished from the consciousness of the happy people who are governed according to such laws.

If the executive power has less to do, the possibility of its being unjust is lessened in an equal degree. The rare manifestation of the power of government will become an act which will excite the
veneration of the people and of themselves ; all
eyes will be turned upon the government, and the
necessary reverence of the people will make the
government reverence itself, if it should not do so
otherwise.

The power of the Ephorate also will find no occasion for its application, because the executive
power will always be just, and neither interdict
nor conventions of the people will ever be required.

If, therefore, any one should possibly allow himself to be frightened by these conceptions, and should
imagine heaven knows what horrors when he reads
of conventions of the people to sit in judgment
upon governments, he has two good reasons to
quiet himself. Firstly, it is only the lawless mob
which commits outrages, and not a legally assembled people, consulting in an established form of proceeding. (The *form* is, by the by, one of the greatest benefits for mankind. By forcing man to pay
attention to certain things, his attention generally
is concentrated. That man has not the interest of
mankind at heart who wishes to take away from
them all forms.)

Secondly : All these contrivances are invented,

not in order to be used, but in order to make the occurrence of cases, which might require their use, impossible. Precisely, in the states wherein they are established, they are superfluous ; and where they are not established, they are sadly needed.

CONCLUDING REMARKS.

The science which considers a particular empirically determined state, and proceeds to develop how the Science of Rights may be properly realized in such a state, is called the Science of Politics. All the problems of such a science have no connection with our science, which is purely *a priori*, and must be carefully separated from it.

To this class of problems belong all questions which may be raised concerning the particular determination of the one and only lawful constitution. For our established conception of a constitution solves only the problem of pure reason : How can the Conception of Rights be realized in the sensuous world ? If that constitution is, therefore, to be further determined, this can be done only by empirical facts. We now proceed, in conclusion, to specify the possible questions which may arise in this connection, and shall show that their solution depends upon the accidental position of the states to which the constitution is to be applied.

Our first *a priori* established rule in considering the constitution was this : That the power of a commonwealth must be transferred, and can not remain in the hands of the people. The question here arises: Shall it be transferred to one or to many; or shall the state, in regard to the persons who constitute its government, be a monocracy or an aristocracy? For a pure democracy is not a legal form of government.

The reply is: Both forms of government are lawful; it is a question of *expediency* which to choose. The ground from which to decide this question I will state in a few words: Of many, who modify each other's opinions more wisdom is to be expected; but on the other hand, they are slower, more inclined to throw responsibility the one upon the other. Nor will the power of the Ephorate be likely to have the proper influence upon them, since they will feel themselves more secure in the great number of the guilty. A perpetual president may, perhaps, be more liable to err; but power in his hands is more effective, and he is more responsible to the Ephorate. Hence, in states which need chiefly a strong government, partly because the people have not yet been used to strict obedience to the law, or partly by reason of their loose relations to other nations, a monocracy probably has the preference; but in states which have already been for some time under such an orderly government and in which the law works by its mere internal power, the republican form of government has the preference. It is clear, that all subordinate officials must be appointed by the highest regent, whether one or many, and must be subject only to his or their commands.   For only the highest government (the regent) is responsible to the nation, and responsible only for the administration of law and justice.   But to be so responsible, the regent must have complete control over the selection of those persons through whom justice is administered.

Another question is, whether it is better that the people should directly elect their highest representatives, (as is the case in a proper and lawful democracy,) or through mediate representatives ; or whether, perhaps, it is better to introduce hereditary descent of office ?

In regard to the Ephorate, this question has already been decided.   They must be directly elected by the people.   In regard to the executive power of the government, the decision can only be supplied by empirical facts, particularly by the degree of culture which a people possesses, and which is attainable only through a previous wise and just legislation.   A people which is to elect its own rulers must be very far advanced in culture, for the election must be *unanimous* in order to be valid.   But since this unanimity need only be relative, the fear always remains that a part of the minority will have to submit to rulers whom they do not like, or be compelled to emigrate.   The constitution ought, however, to remove all occasions for disputes and party divisions among its citizens.   Now, until the people have attained this high degree of culture, it is better that they should, in their constitution, delegate their right of election (of franchise)—

which, of course, they can thus delegate away only by *absolute* unanimity—and thus introduce a fixed succession of rulers. In a republic, the rulers may be allowed to fill vacancies in their own body ; for if the Ephorate is strong enough, they will take good care to make the best selections. In a monocracy, only the people, it would seem, could elect their ruler ; but since the people are not allowed to elect, they can only constitute their ruler hereditary. This hereditary descent has, moreover, other advantages, which render advisable its introduction ; for instance, the monarch is utterly cut off from the people ; is born and dies without any private relation to the people.

Questions might arise concerning the conditions of the contract between the people and their rulers, their personal rights, privileges, incomes, and the sources of these incomes. But all these questions must be decided empirically. The sources of income, or the *principle of finances*, we shall speak of hereafter. Each one must contribute according to the ratio in which he needs protection, and the protective power must correspond to the protection needed. This furnishes us at once with a standard of taxation. The rate of taxation is changeable as the requirement of protection is changeable. The ruler or rulers can, of course, be held accountable for the administration of the finances, through the Ephorate ; for it is one of the rights of the citizens not to pay taxes for any but public purposes.

A question might be raised concerning the nature of the judiciary.   It has been proved, that the executive power must also be the highest judicial power, from which there is no appeal.   It is also clear that subordinate courts and judges will be appointed, from whom appeal can be taken.   So far as the *form* of the judicial investigation or the *trial* is concerned, it is clear that judicial proofs are furnished like any other proofs, and hence the procedure of courts is based chiefly upon logic and sound common sense.   The sufficiency or insufficiency of the proof is decided by the judge.   One important point is, however, to be remembered concerning the proof *by oath*.   There are two ways of considering the oath.   It may be viewed simply as a solemn assurance, the external formalities accompanying it having no other end in view than to remove recklessness and to induce witnesses to consider the importance of such an assurance ; in which case the presupposition is, that he who is capable of publicly asserting a falsehood will also swear a false oath.   Or an oath is regarded as something more than such a solemn assurance, in which case the presupposition is, that a person who will not hesitate to publicly assert a falsehood will hesitate to swear a false oath.   Under the first supposition, it may be asked : Why should the state or the opposite party in a trial be compelled to accept such a statement on oath as absolute fact, and why should the judge be compelled to base his decision upon it, when the whole government is based, not upon trust, but upon distrust ?

Under the second presupposition, there arises this same question, and, moreover, the following higher question : What is there supposed to be in an oath calculated to restrain a man, who will publicly assert a falsehood, from making a false assertion under oath ? Since he does not fear the guilt of falsehood, it follows that he believes the calling upon God as a witness in the oath to be some sort of a supernatural, incomprehensible, and magical means of incurring God's anger by swearing falsely. This is, without doubt, in the true nature of a superstition, and is utterly at variance with moral religion. The state, therefore, in prescribing oaths, calculates upon the continuance of immorality, and must do all in its power to promote immorality, since it has staked its own existence upon a view of the oath, which is immoral. But this is absurd. Hence, the oath can only be viewed as a solemn assurance, and should not be administered except in private cases, where one party is willing to accept the sworn statement of the other as decisive. *Volenti non fit injuria.* On a public occasion the oath should never be administered ; nor will there be any need of oaths, if the state is properly organized.

Finally, a question might be raised concerning the manner of convening the people for the election of the Ephorate, or concerning the voting in convention, when the people are called together by the Ephorate to sit in judgment upon the executive power. As for the election of the Ephores—whose number is a problem of expediency and to be de-

T

cided by the number of the population and the culture of the people—a higher degree of culture requiring fewer Ephores—it will be immediately apparent that it should be conducted by the old Ephores, but in a manner which will prevent them from controlling the election, since the new Ephores are to be their judges. When passing judgment upon the executive power, the voting will have to be under the superintendence of men especially appointed for the purpose, the Ephores being themselves an interested party in the case.*

* We append FICHTE's later declaration on the subject of the Ephorate, which is taken from his Science of Rights of the year 1812: "Many years ago I made a proposition to establish a very complicated checking power—the *Ephorate*. The principles of law which led me to do so are perfectly correct. It is a very true principle, that the government officials should be made responsible to each citizen, and it would be well if such a responsibility could be realized in the sensuous world. It is also clear, that no man ought to be a member of the government whose understanding of the law is considered insufficient by the Ephorate or by the people themselves. But so far as the practicability of such a checking power is concerned, I must now, after mature consideration, decide against it. For, who shall again check the Ephorate, that it may not commence a revolution for some reason or another, although the government has not violated the law? Again: Will not the government, having all power in its hands, try to suppress the Ephorate at the very start? The Roman patricians will bear witness; for they killed the tribunes of the people. The Ephores once killed, government would find arguments and false charges enough to justify its conduct. Moreover, it has certainly been proved, that the decision of the people is always *formaliter* law, because there is no higher judge. But how *materialiter?* Is not more confidence to be placed in a number of the wisest of the people than in a majority which has been gathered together, God only knows how?

"This consideration did not escape me at the time. I admitted all this, but added, that a people whose Ephores, being selected from the very best of the people, could be corrupt enough for such conduct, did not deserve a better government, and were not fit for a better one. This is, after all, the truth of the case. The realization of a checking power as a part of the constitution is not practicable, because mankind at large is too bad as yet; but until men grow better, they will have to get along with a government which needs no really established *Ephorate*.

"One circumstance, however, seems to have escaped all, who have expressed surprise at this idea of an Ephorate; namely, that this idea is, in point of fact, realized wherever a civilized people is to be found. As soon as thinking is developed among the people, a power which observes and checks the action of the government is also developed. This power has two purposes to fulfil: To warn the government; and secondly, if that is of no avail, to call the people together. The first purpose it generally accomplishes, unless free speech is forbidden, (which is a dangerous undertaking on the part of the government,) and government usually listens to those warnings and obeys them. For no government dares to remain behind the people. But if government does not listen to them, the people are called together. As a sure proof that this is practicable, I need only say that it has been done in this age and under our very eyes, and that it has resulted in the overthrow of the government. [Alluding to the French Revolution.—TRANSLATOR.] It has also, however, as far as can be judged at present, resulted disastrously for the people; not by accident, but in obedience to a necessary law. For so long as there are more good than bad people, it may be safely assumed that the propositions of the bad, and not those of the good and wise, will be adopted. Hence, the expedient of calling the people together through the Ephorate, or of revolutions, will be only a substitution of one evil for another and greater one, until a complete change has been effected in the human race. A greater evil: for the principles of government, which are always conformable to the character of the age, will not change, and the regent of a people which has revolutionized will try all the more to root his power firmer, in order to prevent the recurrence of a revolution. The only thing from which we can expect improvement is the progress of culture and morality, and a consequent steadily increasing influence of the Ephorate in this progress."

Book Third

CONCERNING MUNICIPAL LAW

§ 1.

CIVIL LAW.

THE first compact of persons entering with each other into a legal relation, and which we have called the property-compact, is the true original basis of that relation, and hence is equally the basis of what is usually called civil law. To exhaust our present investigation, therefore, all we need to do is to analyze that compact thoroughly.

The conception of original rights we have shown to be that of a continuous reciprocal causality between the person and the sensuous world, which causality is dependent solely upon the will of the person. In the property-compact each person has assigned to him a determined sphere of the sensuous world, as the exclusive sphere of his reciprocal causality ; but with these two conditions, to wit, that he will not disturb the freedom of all others in their sphere, and that he will protect them by his contribution against the attacks of any third party.

Firstly: A sphere is assigned to him for his freedom ; nothing more. This sphere contains certain objects, determined by the freedom assigned to him. *His right of property to these objects extends, there-*

fore, as far as the freedom assigned to him extends, and no further. He receives them only for a special use, and he has only the right to exclude every one else from this special use and from what might be injurious to this special use. The object of the property-compact is a determined activity. (This appears, indeed, already, from what we have said previously. For the fundamental ground of all property is, that I have subjected something to my end. But what end? This question each one has to answer when entering the property-compact, which compact must be throughout determined and determining. It is only this declared and recognized end and purpose in the objects which that compact guarantees; and the property of the object extends no further than to the attainment of this end.)

But these ends may be very different in the use of one and the same object, and hence also in the use of different objects. The question is, whether all possible ends of a citizen may not be subordinated to a single one?

The person, in acting, always presupposes his own future existence; the object of his present acting always lies in the future; and he is a cause in the sensuous world only in so far as he proceeds from the present to the future moment. Freedom and continued existence are essentially united, and he who guarantees the one necessarily guarantees the other. *Present activity includes the future.*

Nature has destined man, who alone concerns us here, for freedom, that is, activity. Nature attains all her ends, and hence must also have made arrangements to attain this one. What arrangements could she contrive to incite man to activity?

If we presuppose that each man has wishes in the future, then nature could attain that end by making the possibility of a future for him *dependent upon his present activity*. The wish for a future, on the other hand, would involve the necessity of present activity. The future would be conditioned by present activity ; in the present activity the future would necessarily be contained.

But since it is possible that there may be men who have no wishes in the future, and since, moreover, the desire for a future is grounded only in present activity, which present activity is itself again grounded in the desire of a future; and since the contrivance of nature would, therefore, be a faulty circle, it is necessary that she should unite both in a third present moment, and this is *Pain.* The present pain, threatening continued existence, involves both present activity and the wish for and the possibility of a continued existence. This pain is *hunger* and *thirst ;* and we thus discover that the need of nourishment is alone the original incentive, as its satisfaction is the final end of the state, and of all man's life and doing ; of course, only so long as man remains under the guidance of nature, and does not arise through freedom to a higher existence. This need of nourishment is, therefore, the highest synthesis, which unites all contradictions. The highest and universal end of all free activity is, therefore, that men may live. This end each one has, and the guarantee of freedom involves this guarantee. Unless he attains it, freedom and the continued existence of his person will be impossible.

We thus obtain a more special determination of the exclusive sphere of freedom, guaranteed to each in the property-compact. To be able to live is the absolute, inalienable property of all men. A certain sphere of objects is guaranteed to a person exclusively for a certain use ; but the ultimate end of that use is, that he shall be able to live. The spirit of the property-compact is the guarantee of this end, or of life. It is the fundamental principle of every rational form of government, that each person shall be able to live from the results of his labor.

Each individual has made this agreement with all others, and all have made it with each. Hence, all have promised to all that their labor shall be the means to attain this end, and in the state organization provision must be made to realize this purpose.

Again : all right of property is based upon the agreement of all with all : that each will acknowledge the possessions of the other, provided the other will acknowledge his. But as soon as any one can no longer live from the results of his labor, that which belongs to him is no longer his; the agreement with him is, therefore, completely annulled, and he is no longer legally bound to respect the property of any one else. Since this insecurity of property is to be avoided, all must in law and by agreement give him of their possessions sufficient to live from. From the moment that any one suffers distress, that part of the property of each citizen, which is necessary to remove that distress, no longer belongs to them, but in law and justice belongs to the suffering individual. The original compact should make provision for such a repartition of property among the sufferers, and this contribution to the distressed is as much condition of all civil rights as the contribution for common protection. Each one retains possession of his property only in so far, and on the condition that all other citizens can sustain their lives from their property; and if they can no longer sustain their lives therefrom, his becomes their property: of course, in such proportions as the state government may determine. The government is responsible for this as well as for all other branches of state administration; the poor citizen has an absolute claim to support.

The principle established was this: Each one must be able to live *from the results of his labor.* Labor is, therefore, the condition of being able to live, and when this condition has not been fulfilled the right also does not exist. Since all are responsible for the support of all who can not live from their labor, they necessarily also have the right to watch that each labors sufficiently ; and this right of supervision they transfer to the government. No one has a legal claim to the support of the state until he has shown that he has done within his sphere all that was possible for him to do in order to make his living ; and that, nevertheless, he was unable to do it. But since, even in the latter case, the state could not permit him to die, and would be, moreover, liable to the reproach that it had not compelled him to work, the state necessarily must be intrusted with the right of supervising the manner in which each citizen administers his property. Precisely as there must be no poor man in a rational state, so also must there be no idler. A legal exception to the latter result will appear hereafter.

The property-compact comprises, therefore, the following acts :

1. All state to all what they intend to live from. This holds good without exceptions. He who can not state this can not be a citizen of the commonwealth, since he can not be forced to respect the rights of property of the others.

2. All permit to each this occupation, exclusively, in a certain respect. Each one must expressly state his occupation ; and hence no one becomes a citizen in general, but becomes, at the same time, entitled to a certain occupation. There must be

no undeterminedness whatever in a state organization. Each, of course, has possession of objects only so far as the ends of his occupation require it.

3. The end of all this labor is, to be able to live. All guarantee to each that his labor will achieve this end, and guarantee this end with all their means. These means belong to the rights of each, which the state must protect. The agreement in this respect is as follows : Each promises to do all that is in his power to do, in order to make his living from what has been ceded to him as his property and rights ; and in consideration of this promise, all others, or the state, promise to cede more to him, if he should not be able to make his living therefrom, guaranteeing this promise by obliging themselves to furnish contributions. Hence, precisely as the original compact provides for the erection of a protective power of government, so must it also provide for a supporting power. In other words, the state government must not only protect the citizens, but must also support the poor.

The arrangement contrived by nature to compel us to free activity is as follows :

Our body is an organized product of nature, and the progress of organization goes on in the body uninterruptedly. Nature proceeds herein in two modes : Either the body takes in organic matter, and nature first organizes that matter in the body ; or the body receives matter already organized, and nature merely further organizes it in the body.

Moreover, nature may either bring herself the matter to be organized within the sphere of causality of the body, or may arrange the body so as to betake itself by free activity to the materials needed by it. The latter condition occurs in beings that are articulated for free movement; and, since nature would seem to rise to greater perfection in these latter bodies, it seems not unlikely that both conditions should go together; that is, that articulated bodies should be able to supply their organization only from organized matter. Without investigating here why and by virtue of what laws this is so, we content ourselves with stating the simple fact that it is so. The plants are formed from inorganic matter; at least, matter which appears inorganic to us; whilst animals feed from the organized products. What seems to be an exception to this rule is none. When animals swallow earth, stones, or sand, etc., it is not to derive nourishment therefrom, for these materials are not digested, but to expel injurious ingredients from the body.

It may also be possible, that articulated creatures again, on their part, supply their organization from other articulated creatures, or eat meat. It seems, indeed, as if these meat-eating creatures occupied, likewise, a higher stand-point of organization.*

---

* Quite the contrary doctrine to that of the vegetarians, yet undoubtedly more plausible. Such improper generalizations are, however, all faulty. Since all matter is organic, all creatures are meat-eating; and whether we eat only small animals, in vegetable food, or big ones, in animal food, is all the same.—TRANSLATOR'S REMARK.

Man is evidently made to supply his nourishment from both spheres of organized nature.

It is a condition of the continued existence of the state, that a sufficient amount of food should be on hand ; for otherwise men would be forced to emigrate.

All organization proceeds according to laws of nature, which man can learn and direct or apply, but which he has not the power to change. Man may place nature in the known conditions of the application of her laws, sure that she will not fail then to apply them ; and by doing so, man exercises the power of promoting and increasing organization. It seems likely that nature will need such assistance from man in places where men congregate through freedom, which freedom nature could not have taken into consideration in arranging herself. If this is a fact, then the promotion of organization is the fundamental basis of the state, since it is the exclusive condition on which men can live together.

Man will find it requisite, first of all, to promote the organization of plants, in order to feed himself and the animals. Plants are fixed to the ground so long as their organization lasts. It seems, therefore, probable that many men will devote themselves exclusively to the cultivation of plants ; and such a right must be admitted, since the existence of the state depends upon its exercise.

All organization progresses according to certain laws, and must not be interrupted in this its progress. In each cultivated part of the plant kingdom, therefore, every thing must remain precisely as the cultivator has designed it to be ; and hence the ground, which he needs for this cultivation, must be exclusively granted to him for that specific purpose.

PROPERTY IN LAND.

Land is the common support of mankind in the sensuous world, the condition of man's existence in space, and hence of man's whole sensuous existence. The earth in particular, considered as a mass, is not at all a possible object of property ; for it can not, as substance, be submitted to any possible exclusive end of a person ; and it is not lawful for any one, according to our above results, to exclude all others from the use of a thing without assigning himself a use for it. Even if some one should say : the earth is useful to build houses upon, he already ceases to speak of it as a substance, modifies it, and uses it as an accidence. Hence, the right of the agriculturist to a fixed piece of ground is solely the right, exclusively to raise products upon it and to exclude all others from doing the same, or from using it for any purpose which would conflict with that use.

The agriculturist, therefore, has not the right to prevent another use of his property, provided it does not conflict with his own. He has not the right, for instance, to prevent others from using his lands after harvest for pasturage, unless he has obtained also the right of cattle-raising; nor to prevent the state from mining on his lands, unless, indeed, his lands should thereby receive damages, in which case the state must reimburse him.

The lands of the commonwealth are chosen by the individuals, and guaranteed by the state to each. Their limits are designated by fences or other marks, so that they may always be known. To wantonly remove such marks is a crime, because it leads to endless law disputes.

Each agriculturist, who is nothing but agriculturist, must be able to live from the cultivation of his lands. If he can not do so, an additional piece of land must be given to him, since he is only agriculturist. Whether he has worked sufficiently in the cultivation of his lands, the state decides.

As citizen of the state, the agriculturist must contribute toward the needs of the state. So far as we can see now, he will have to make these contributions from the products of his field. Until he makes this contribution, he has no property, because he has not fulfilled the agreement which makes it his property. Whatsoever remains after this contribution is his own; the state has, so far as appears now, no claim on it, and must protect him in the possession of it against all attacks. Only the *products* of his lands are, therefore, the absolute property of the agriculturist. They belong to him, substance and all; whereas, of the lands, he owns only an accidence.

U

Whatsoever grows wild on cultivated lands must be assumed to have been subjected by the proprietor to his ends ; hence it rightfully belongs to him. Moreover, if a stranger should interfere with such wild products, he would interfere with the proprietor's right to dispose of his lands as may seem best to him.

Uncultivated lands are property of the whole commonwealth, for they were assigned to no one when the lands were distributed. Of course, the state distinguishes between the substance, the ground itself, and its accidences, that which grows upon it. These accidences will most properly be taken by the state for public purposes, (forests.) But if they shall be so taken by the state, then the state must expressly declare them to be state property ; and what is not so declared thereby becomes the property of the first one who chooses to appropriate it, (wild fruits, berries, etc.)

Whenever a citizen wishes to cultivate any of these uncultivated lands, they must be divided. Whoever obtains such lands as his property must cultivate them. The state will thus be indemnified for the loss of the accidences on these lands by receiving contributions (taxes) from their new cultivators.

MINERAL LANDS.

Minerals are the transition of nature from inorganic matter to organic products. The laws by which nature produces them are either not at all discoverable, or, at least, are not yet discovered. Metals can, therefore, not be arbitrarily reproduced by art and cultivation like fruits. They are found as nature made them.

It seems as if each one ought to have the right to say : I intend to hunt for minerals ; just as each has the right to say : I intend to cultivate fruits ; and hence as if the interior of the earth could be divided among the miners precisely as the upper crust is divided among the farmers. The metals found would thus belong to the miner, as the fruits cultivated belong to the farmer. Nevertheless, there is a difference ; partly because mining is risky, and can not be surely known to support the miners, and partly because the land once investigated by the miner can not be reinvestigated. Mining must, therefore, be assigned to a permanent corporation, which can afford to *wait* for success ; and no corporation is better adapted to do this than the state, which, moreover, has still another reason for obtaining possession of the metals, as we shall soon show. Hence, the interior of the earth remains the common property of the commonwealth, and the miners become the regularly employed laborers of the state, receiving their wages whether they find any metals or not.

The same principle applies to all similar products of nature ; precious stones, quarries, sand, etc. The state has the right to make these objects its own declared property, and to prohibit all others from ap-

propriating or using them.   If it does so, it must,
of course, guarantee to furnish these products in
sufficient quantities to all who may desire to use
them.   If the state does not choose so to do, it
may extend the privilege of working them for certain districts to such individuals as may apply for
the privilege ; or may tacitly agree to let any one
take possession of them who chooses to do so.   The
principle which rules is always that unless the state
expressly declares these objects to be its property,
they may be taken possession of by the first comer.

PROPERTY IN ANIMALS.

There are also animals upon the earth who may
be useful to men in their accidences, or whose substances may be useful to men ; their meat to eat,
their skin for various purposes, etc.   If any citizen
intends to subject only the accidences of such animal to his ends, he must first make the animal sub-
servient to him.   Moreover, since the animals are
fed and kept alive only by organized matter, and
since it is not to be expected that nature will take
care of them after they have once been made art-
products, he must replace nature in becoming their
nourisher.   This, again, is conditioned by the *exclusive possession* of the animal ; only *I* must feed
and attend the animal always, and only I, therefore,
must be allowed to enjoy the advantages it may
confer.

There is no reason why each one should not have

the same right to take possession of an animal Hence, exclusive property in animals can be obtained only through the original property-compact in a state.

There is, however, this difference between property in land and property in animals, that the land can always be designated by the place in space which it occupies, whereas the animal has free motion and can not be so specified. How then is it to be made known what particular animal belongs to a certain person and to no one else?

If it should, firstly, be the case that only certain kinds of animals are ever made exclusive property of persons, it would be, above all, necessary to specify to what kinds of animals the right of property can extend. This would enable every one to know at once whether an animal, coming within his reach, is the property of any body or not. For instance, if I have a right to hunt, I may shoot the deer, because it is a deer; but I may not shoot the horse, although I do not know who owns it. Why not? Simply because I know that horses have been declared property by the state, and that, hence, some one is surely the owner of the horse, although I do not know who. If some one should tame a deer, it doubtless becomes his property. But if the deer runs away and I shoot it, am I, therefore, responsible for it as for the horse? Clearly not, since the state has not declared that the right of property extends to deers. The right of the original owner of an animal remains, although the animal may run away from him, because in the original compact it has been agreed upon in what kinds of animals the right of property may rest. Such animals are called *tame animals.* The ground why precisely these kinds of animals have been declared property in a state and none others, lies in their fitness for serving the needs of men in their accidences, in the possibility of taming them, and in the necessity of taking care of them.

But let no one believe that this taming and feeding of the animals is the true legal ground of the right of property in them. That legal ground is to be found only in the property-compact. Hence, if any one should introduce a new kind of tamed animals, for instance, buffaloes or kangaroos, the state would first have to declare them animals to which the right of property should extend, since otherwise they would be properly treated like wild animals. If they were kept locked up in such a one's house or yard, they would, of course, thereby become part of his house property. It is also clear, from the foregoing, that the state has a perfect right to prohibit the keeping of certain animals, for instance, of lions, bears, monkeys, and unnecessary dogs.

But the next question is : To whom does this or that animal which in its kind has been declared property, belong? These animals may either remain under the immediate supervision of their proprietor, so that he can at any moment prove them to be his—unless, indeed, they be unlawfully in his possession—or they may be feeding in a common pasture with the animals of other proprietors. How, in the latter case, can ownership be proved ? Happily, animal instinct has supplied the neglect of the lawgiver. Tame animals accustom themselves to their stables, and the judge decides according to the instinct of the animal as to who is its owner. Yet, would it not be proper to have all tame animals marked in some way, the marks to be as inviolable as those which designate the several pieces of landed property, and thus to place them under the direct protection of the law? (In the armies the horses are, indeed, so marked.) Each bill of sale of an animal ought to be accompanied by a specification of the mark upon the animal, so as to guarantee perfect safety to the purchaser.

In reference to some animals, the right of property is determined by the space they occupy, to wit, when they are of a kind which can be confined to a certain locality, and must be so confined to serve their end. In such cases the owner is proprietor of the animals, because he is proprietor of the locality wherein they exist, (fish-lakes, birdhouses, etc.) When the fish is out of the lake, or the bird out of the cage, they have no owner.

The right of property is always granted with reerence to the end to be accomplished by it ; so, likewise, the right of property in animals. Now, most animals are useful, not only in their accidences, (as milk, eggs, and their labor,) but also in their substance ; we eat their meat, make use of their skins, etc. etc.

It may, perhaps, be deemed expedient to limit this right of property in the *substance* of the animals, and to specify this limit in the original property-compact. Such a limitation would not invalidate the right of property in the animals, so far as it has reference to their accidences, but it would restrict the right to do with the substance of the animals as might please the owner. The state, for instance, might provide that a certain number of cattle shall always be kept in the state, and that, therefore, only a limited number may be slaughtered. If such a law is passed in a state, another law must be passed, of course, providing that, at all times, a certain amount of food for cattle shall be raised and set aside, since otherwise the former legislation would cancel itself.

Animals propagate themselves, and their young ones are their accidences. The ownership of the old animals involves the ownership of their whole future breed, precisely as the ownership of a grain of wheat involves that of all the future wheat which may grow out of it. It may be lawful, however, to limit the number of cattle which shall be kept in a commonwealth.

The animals have free movement and feed from the products of the field. Hence, when an animal trespasses upon the fields of a farmer, there arises this dispute between the agriculturist and the cattle-raiser :

The former says : " I have the right to cultivate land in this state, and the products of the field are mine." The latter replies: " I have the right to raise cattle in the same state, and the state knows well enough that animals are determined by their nature to hunt food."

This dispute the state has to settle by establishing laws, based on the original property-compact, whereby either the one party alone is compelled to keep his cattle in a closed pasture, or, which is more fair, the other party is also compelled to fence in his fields. Whosoever neglects to do his duty in this respect, must not only repay damages, but also makes himself liable to an additional fine. If accidents happen in spite of all precautions, they are to be considered as misfortunes for which neither party is liable, and which the state has to repair.

Wild animals are animals the accidences whereof can not be subjected to the use of men. Their substance, however, may be useful, and since they can not be tamed, it becomes useful only through the death of such animals. In so far they belong to the whole state, or are undivided property. They become the property of individuals only by being caught or killed.

There is, however, one great distinction between these animals. Some of them are inclosed in an element which is not subject to men, at least in so far as these animals live *in* and *of* it, namely, the fishes in rivers and seas. Hence, they do no harm to men. It is the same with some other animals, which, though they live in and of the same element as men, the earth, yet do so little damage to it, that they are not materially injurious; namely, the birds. The harm which they do to the crops, etc., is amply repaid by their killing off injurious insects.

It is quite different with another class of wild animals, which are injurious to men and destroy man's labors. All kinds of game belong to this class. Now, since the state guarantees to each person his property, it must protect that of the agriculturist against the devastation of these animals. Everywhere wilderness must give way to culture, and the irregular modes of living, which can not be surely known to suffice for man's subsistence, must give way to regular pursuits.

Hence, the state must make fishing a lawful pursuit, which is best accomplished—with a view to make it an *orderly* business—by assigning specific districts of rivers and lakes to fishermen, who thus become the proprietors of these districts in the manner of agriculturists, of course only in regard to the *use* of these districts. They would not have the right, for instance, to prevent navigation within their districts, since that would not interfere with their pursuits in the same localities.

But all wild animals of the second class must be regarded by the state as absolutely injurious; not as a source of emolument, but as a class of enemies. The first object of hunting is not, therefore, to possess the game, but to protect the farmer; and the state must undertake this protection precisely as it undertakes to protect property against thieves and incendiaries, namely, by appointing men especially intrusted with this duty. Of course, the agriculturist retains the right to shoot any piece of game or wild animal which may stray within his fence, and does not need to wait for the official gamekeeper's arrival, precisely as each citizen retains the right to quench the flames, if his house should be put on fire, without waiting for the arrival of the official firemen.

Now, since the chase affords considerable profits, it is not to be assumed that the people ought to pay taxes for sustaining it; rather, it ought to pay itself. For this reason it will be most advantageous to grant to a certain class of persons, game-keepers, the right of chase in specified districts—as in the case of the fishermen—which right thus becomes their property. Let it be well understood, that the right of property is not vested in the animals, as such, but only in the killing of this class of animals within the specified district. Nevertheless, since it is the chief object of the chase to protect the agriculturist, the game-keeper can receive this right only on the express condition that the game is truly kept harmless by him, and that he holds himself responsible for all the damages farmers may receive by reason of such game.

No one but the gamekeeper can possibly have the intention to take care of or protect the game, and this end is granted to him only in so far as the game is not injurious to the purposes of culture; or in so far as the game remains in the forest. Whoever kills them there, trespasses upon the property of the gamekeeper ; whereas, he who kills them upon his fields is perfectly justified. For the life of the game is not guaranteed by the state ; indeed, the game has no end for the state ; on the contrary, their death is the end which the state has in view. The killed game belongs to the gamekeeper of the district ; the damage they have inflicted whilst at large must be paid by him, whether the animals be worth much or nothing at all.

The first end of the chase is to protect culture ; all other ends are accidental. Hence, it is properly made the duty of the gamekeeper to exterminate, likewise, wild animals, from which he himself derives no benefit, and which may not be immediately injurious to himself ; as, for instance, eagles, hawks, sparrows, nay, even caterpillars and other injurious insects. Other animals, which are immediately injurious to himself, because they destroy his game, such as foxes, wolves, etc., he will exterminate of his own accord.

If the chase were a burden without profit, government would have to undertake it. But since it is combined with considerable advantages, which generally increase in value the less attention the gamekeeper pays to his proper business—and herein lies the root of the chief difficulty—and since, therefore, complaints will often be preferred against the gamekeepers, it is expedient to keep them under the close supervision of the government. The right of keeping game, being combined with emoluments, can not remain, therefore, in the hands of the government. Government would always be an interested party as the possessor of the game, and the agriculturist would have no impartial judge.

PROPERTY IN PRODUCTS OF INDUSTRY AND ART.

All rights of property, heretofore considered, are vested in products of nature, as such, whether nature has heen assisted in producing them, as is the case in agriculture and cattle-raising, or whether her products are merely hunted up, as is the case in mining, hunting, fishing, and cutting down of timber. We will call all the citizens, who have rights of this kind, *Producers*.

Now, it is very probable that these raw products of nature need a particular preparation through art to render them useful for the purposes of men, and in our present wholly empirical investigation we will assume, without further *a priori* deduction, that such is the case. It is, therefore, to be expected that another class of citizens will devote themselves wholly to this art-preparation of the raw material. I shall call this class of citizens *Artists*, in the widest significance of the word.

The distinction is sharply defined, and the designation in itself perfectly correct. For the former class of citizens leave nature to herself, do not prescribe to nature, but merely place her under the conditions of the application of her power. Those of that class who merely hunt up products do not even so much. As soon as nature has achieved her work, the labor of the producers is finished ; the product is ripe, or the raw product has been found.

But the second class of persons who now enter on the scene, do not calculate at all upon the assistance of nature, since the organizing power of the product has already been deadened by its ripeness, or else must be deadened by them to become useful for their purposes.

They compose these parts according to their own conception altogether ; the moving power lies in *them*, not in nature. Every thing composed in this manner is called a product of art. Each thread of the spinner is a work of art. It is true, the word *Artist* has been applied to particular classes of these laborers ; but this use of language need not interfere with ours, which is based on a correct *a priori* division, and which we do not desire at all to make universal.

A number of persons must have the exclusive right to thus artistically prepare certain objects in a certain manner. If they have no exclusive right, they have no property ; for in that case they have recognized the labor-vocations of all others, whereas their own has not been recognized by these others in return. Their property-compact, in that case, is one-sided, merely obligatory, not granting rights, and hence is null and void.

A class of citizens exclusively entitled to prepare

certain objects in a certain manner is called a profession. To leave all professions open at all times to all citizens, renders a property-compact impossible.

The artist must be able to live from his work. Two classes of artists are to be distinguished; such as merely furnish their labor and do not own the materials of it, and such as own the material. To enable them to make their living, the state must guarantee to the former class labor, and to the second class sale of their wares.

The substance of the agreement which all others make with the artists is as follows : You promise us to furnish this sort of work in sufficient quantity and of excellent quality ; we, on the other hand, agree to purchase it only from you. If the professions do not furnish excellent work, they lose the exclusive right granted to them in the compact. Hence, the examination of candidates for a profession is a matter of common interest. The government, or each profession in the name of the government, must calculate how many persons can live from each profession, and how many are necessary in each to satisfy the needs of the public.

If all can not make their living, government has made a miscalculation, and must bear the consequences. Those who can not sustain themselves from the profession must be assigned to other branches of business.

But the artist can not live from his works. He must have the products of the other class. It is, therefore, necessary that there should be in the state at all times products enough to supply both the needs of the producers themselves and of the artists. These products the producers supply to the artists, and receive in return the works of the artists; and *vice versa*. Thus an exchange takes place, which government should regulate in the following manner: Each piece of work must be exchanged for as many products as the artist needed *during the time of making that work;* and *vice versa*. Each product of the producers must be exchanged for works of the artist in the same ratio. Ir short, there must be a complete equilibrium between raw products and manufactured wares.

There must not be any more artists in a country than can be supplied by its products. An unfruitful soil does not admit of luxury. The people must retrench their needs. Of course, this principle is limited by the results of external commerce, which we do not consider here, since we speak of each state as a whole in itself. But since such external commerce renders states dependent, each state should try to arrange itself so as to be able to do without it.

Every person must have his requirements supplied as soon as possible. To facilitate this exchange, therefore, it is well that a class of men should devote themselves entirely to it—merchants. The right to be a merchant is conferred exclusively upon a certain number of citizens, which number the government must determine by calculation, as their property in the state. Of course, they also must be able to live from its results.

All contracts of exchange, whether concluded between the producers and artists directly or by means of the merchants, are guaranteed by the government, and government must look to see that they are fulfilled, since without them a legal relation between persons is impossible. But since the state can not guarantee that whereof it has no cognizance, it must establish by law what contracts are to be valid and what contracts not. A contract concluded *in violation* of the laws of the state has no validity ; if concluded *without* legal form, it has no *legal* validity, and becomes a matter of private honor and morality. The validity of all contracts is derived, immediately or mediately by means of positive law, from the supreme principle of law, according to the rule : that, without which a legal relation between persons would be impossible, is absolutely valid in law.

In this exchange of products for manufactured wares and labor, the advantage is, of course, decidedly in favor of the producer. He can get along, at least to a great extent, without the works of the artist ; but the artist can not live without the products of the producer. But it has been agreed in the property-compact that the artist shall be able to live from the results of his labor, that is, that he shall always be able to obtain the proper amounts of products for his works, according to the standard already established. The pro-

x

ducer is, therefore, bound by the property-compact to sell. But these products are, as we have seen, his absolute property, and hence he ought to be at liberty to sell them at as high a price as possible. It now appears that this liberty can not be extended to him. It will, therefore, be necessary to fix a *highest price* for all articles of food and for the most necessary articles for manufacture. If the producer is not willing to sell at this price, and if the state has not the power to force him to sell, the state may, at least, induce him to sell. This it can best accomplish by storing away all the articles which it receives from the producers as their contribution toward the support of the government, and selling them at the highest price at which the producer declines to sell. The artist is never in a position to oppress the producer to any extent; for he is always in need of articles of food (I speak here, of course, of a state organization such as has been described, and not of the existing state, in which the farmer has to pay his taxes in money, and may, therefore, be compelled to sell by those who hold the money.)

A distinction must be established, however, between those manufactured wares which are indispensable to the producer and those which are not so. The former class comprises all tools of agriculture, clothes, houses, etc. Of these articles, likewise, the highest price must be established, so that if the artists should refuse to work or sell their wares at that price, the state may do it. Hence,

government will also have to store away such tools,
clothes, etc. ; and will also have to engage masons
and carpenters, who may build houses on its account if necessary. The needs of luxury are not
guaranteed by the state, and hence need not be
kept on hand. The state ought to take care, likewise, that those articles which are dispensable—
particularly those which can only be imported from
other countries, and the import whereof may, therefore, become interrupted—shall not become indispensable. This can best be attained by levying
high taxes on such articles. The object of these
taxes must not be to make the income from the tax
large, but to stop it altogether ; and the tax should
be increased·until the importation stops. This, however, must be done at the very commencement, and
not after the state has encouraged the enjoyment
of such articles by its neglect, and has thus tacitly
guaranteed their enjoyment.

MONEY.

It seems that we have involved ourselves in a
contradiction.

THESIS.—The state guarantees to each citizen,
who contributes toward the protection of the state
and to the support of the poor, the absolute and
unlimited property of the remainder of his possession. Each must have the right to waste, destroy,
or throw away what belongs to him, provided he
thereby inflicts no injury upon other citizens.

ANTITHESIS.—The state continually takes possession of all the remainder—of the products of
the producers, and of the wares and labor of the
artist—in order thereby to make possible the necessary exchange, without which each can not be sure
that he can sustain himself from the results of his
labor.

To solve this contradiction we must discover its
ground.

The state takes possession of the remainder, not
in respect to its *form*, as remainder and as property,
but in respect to its *substance*, as something which
is necessary to sustain life.

In order to solve the contradiction thoroughly,
form and *substance* must, therefore, be separated.
The state must have the power of taking the *substance* without touching the *form*.

Without exhibiting here unnecessary profundity,
I shall solve the problem at once. We must discover a mere form of property, a mere sign of it,
which is a sign of whatever is useful in the state,
without having in itself the least use ; for if it were
useful in itself, the state would possess the right to
claim it, like the other products, for public purposes. Such a mere *form of property* is called *money*. The use of money must be introduced in a
state necessarily ; and this solves our problem. The
producer has not the right to keep his products ;
he must sell them. Nevertheless, they are his absolute property, guaranteed to him by the state.
True, he is not to give them away for nothing, but

in exchange for wares. But he needs no wares at present, at least not those which are offered to him. Hence, he receives *money*. The same applies to the artist.

The state is obliged to furnish to the producer wares for his products, and to the artist products for his wares. They have received money for their respective property, not wishing to exchange for wares or products at present. Hence, as soon as they desire to make this exchange, they must be able to effect it by means of that money, which they hold as the sign of the value of those articles. In other words : by the issuing of money the state guarantees that it will furnish to the holder of money at any time, for his money, those articles whereof the state has guaranteed the enjoyment to every one ; for each piece of money in the hands of a private person is a sign of an indebtedness on the part of the state.

The amount of money current in a state represents all that is purchasable on the surface of the state. If the quantity of purchasable articles increases while the quantity of money remains the same, the value of the money increases in the same ratio ; if the quantity of money increases while the quantity of purchasable articles remains the same, the value of money decreases in the same ratio. Hence, if a state is considered as isolated, it is all the same whether there is much or little money in it ; the increase or decrease is merely seeming, since in either case the existing quantity of money always represents the total of all purchasable articles in the state, and since, therefore, any part of it can always purchase a corresponding part of that total.

The conception of money involves, as we have seen, that its material must have no utility for men ; its value must depend altogether upon agreement and common opinion. Each must merely know that every other one will recognize it as the equivalent of a particular part of all purchasable articles in a state. *Gold* is, therefore, excellent money ; for its true value, its utility, is as nothing in comparison with its imaginary value as a sign. *Silver* is not so good for money, for it is intrinsically very useful in itself. These two substances have become money for all the world, both by reason of their rarity, and because states can not arbitrarily increase them.

Paper or *leather money* is the best money for an isolated state, if counterfeiting can be prevented, because its intrinsic value is as nothing compared with its artificial value as money. The objection, that a state may easily over-issue it, is of no force, since it is all the same whether the amount of the circulation is large or small ; its value rising and falling, as we have shown, in proportion to its amount.

But since all civilized states of the present age carry on foreign commerce, and since foreigners are not generally inclined to receive a currency which can be contracted or expanded *ad libitum*, these paper issues must be at a considerable discount against gold and silver. The discount will be the greater the more such a state imports from abroad, and the less it has to export in return.

Coining money is the privilege of the state alone; for the state alone can guarantee its value to all citizens. Hence, mines are a necessary property of government.

Citizens pay their taxes with their products or manufactures; if they choose, however, they may also pay in money, since that is the state's authorized representative of all things. But the citizens must have the privilege of paying in those articles; and the amount of taxes must also be calculated by products and manufactures, for the reason that the value of money is constantly fluctuating.

Whatsoever remains to the citizens after they have paid their taxes, is their property; but since the state has the power to compel the exchange of such articles for others, each citizen receives money for that remainder. This money *is absolutely pure property, over which the state has no longer any control.*

Each piece of money which I possess is, at the same time, a sign that I have fulfilled all my civil obligations. The state has no supervision over it. Taxation on *money* is absurd.

Whatsoever citizens have bought with money for their private use—not for trade, which is under the supervision of the state—all furniture, clothing, jewelry, etc., etc., is, for the same reason, absolute property.

THE HOUSE.

The state is obliged to protect all absolute property, as specified above, and to guarantee to each citizen its secure possession. But all these things, and particularly money, can not in any way be designated as belonging to such and no other persons. In the case of land, corner-stones or wooden posts designate property, which can, therefore, be described on the record-books of the governments as belonging to such or such an individual ; but all dollar-pieces look alike, and must look alike, since they are intended to change owners ; how then can property in them be specified ?

Again, the state can not take notice at all of how much money each citizen possesses ; and even if it were possible for the state to do so, the citizen need not suffer it. But how can the state protect that whereof it does not know, and which, in its nature, is wholly undeterminable ? If the state is bound to afford this protection to the undetermined, that undeterminable property must be inseparably connected with something else which is determined and which is expressly posited as the *symbol of all absolute property*, thereby being removed altogether from the supervision of the state. This determined something must be visible, known and determinable through the person of the owner.

This determined something, with which the undeterminable property is to be connected, may be of two natures, as will appear immediately. The state has guaranteed to each citizen who has paid his contributions the full *use* of all his manufactured, built, or bought possessions. By this guaranteed use the state has characterized or determined property. It is, therefore, to be presupposed, until the contrary is proved, that that which a person immediately uses is his ; for in a well-administered state it is not to be assumed that a person should be making use of any thing against the will of the law. Immediate use, however, connects articles with the body. Hence, whatsoever a person carries in his hands or on or upon his body, belongs to such a person. Money, which I carry in my hands or in my clothes, is *mine*, as the clothes are mine to which the money is attached. (The Lazzaroni always carry all their absolute property on their body.)

Not only that which I use immediately, however, but also that which I intend for future use, is my absolute property. Now it is not to be assumed, nor can it be required, that I shall always carry it all on my body. Hence, there must be a surrogate of the body, whereby that which is connected with this surrogate may be designated as my property absolutely by reason of thus being connected with it. Such a surrogate we call the *house*, using the word in its widest significance as designating equally the room which a person has rented, the trunk of the servant, etc. My house is immediately under the protection and guarantee of the state, and through its means all that it contains. The state guarantees me against all violent entrance into my house. But the state knows not and has no right to know what is in the house. Hence, the single objects in it, *as such*, are under my own protection and under my own absolute control. In like manner all my actions in the house are under my own absolute control, provided their effect does not extend beyond the house. The supervision of the state extends to the lock upon the door, and there begins mine own. The lock is the boundary line between the power of the government and my own private power. It is the intention of locks to make possible self-protection. In my own house my person is sacred and inviolable even to the government. In civil cases government has no right to attack me in my house, but must wait till I am upon public ground. In our investigation of *Criminal Law*, we shall see how this sacred *house-right* may be lost.

The house designates and determines my absolute property. Something is my absolute property, because it has got into the house—of course with the knowledge and consent of the government. The fact of my having a house and something in it is the best proof, in a state such as we are describing, that I have completed my obligations toward the state, for the state first appropriates what I owe to it.

If I am absolute master and protector in my house, using the word as described above, then every thing that enters my house stands under my authority and my protection.

No one has the right to enter my house against my will. Even the state can not compel me to extend this permission, since even the state can not enter against my will. In the house we are no longer under the supervision and guarantee of the government, but under our own supervision and protection, and hence we enter each other's houses, so far as our personal security is concerned, on trust and faith in each other. Whatsoever occurs in the house is a private affair, and may be forgiven by the injured party ; but whatsoever occurs publicly is a public crime, and can not be so forgiven. In the house a tacit agreement of mutual personal security is presupposed. Whosoever violates this agreement becomes *infamous*, that is, untrustworthy for all future time.

(Thus, indeed, has a deep-rooted moral sentiment decided long ago among all nations. Everywhere it is considered infamous, if a landlord insults his guest, or a guest his landlord in his own house. Everywhere secret theft has been held to be infamous to a degree which never was attached to open and bold robbery. Perhaps the latter is quite as dangerous as the former ; and hence this general opinion is not inspired by egotism. But robbery is bold, and opposes, confessedly, force to another force, which is not deceived ; whereas theft is cowardly, using the confidence of the other with a view to violating it.)

Whatever is in the house—cash, furniture, victuals, etc., (except the goods of the merchant)—is beyond the supervision of the state, and hence the right of property to such articles is not immediately guaranteed by the government. If I lend my money to the other on his word, and he denies the loan, I have no redress from the state, since our contract was not concluded under the guarantee of the state, and since I can not, therefore, legally prove the debt. But if I take his note—the state having announced such a note to be a legal proof of the debt—then the state owes me protection and redress against him. Contracts concluded upon mere trust and faith admit of no legal redress ; their violation is punished solely by loss of character.

GOOD NAME.

The honor or character of a citizen is constituted by the opinion of his fellow-citizens, that he is faithful and trustworthy in all cases which are beyond the reach of the state ; for where the state extends its power of compulsion, trust and faith are not taken at all into consideration.

The government has neither the right nor the power to command that the citizens shall trust each other ; for the state is the very result of distrust ; nay, it is even the *object* of distrust, as shown in the constitution.

But neither has the government the right to prohibit trust and confidence. True, it has a perfect right to decree that none of its own affairs shall be transacted on the basis of trust and confidence, and to annul the legal results of all enactments thus made. For instance : the state has a perfect right to pass a law, that land or houses shall not be sold otherwise than in the prescribed legal form ; for the government must always know the legal owner thereof. But since the state has no supervision over the whole region of absolute property, nay, has not the right to take any notice of it whatever, it follows that each citizen must be permitted to do with his absolute property whatever he pleases to do with it. He may throw it away or destroy it, and hence he may also loan it upon trust. Money, or any articles of personal, absolute property, may, therefore, be loaned without the authority of the law.

Nevertheless, the state must protect the absolute property of each citizen. How, then, can it protect him against infamous characters ? Simply *by warning all citizens against all men known to be infamous.*

The property-compact involves both the right and duty to do this ; for the state must protect against all dangers, and infamy is a great danger. Hence, the state ought to make that danger impossible as much as it may. This it can do by inflicting upon the acts hereinbefore specified the punishment of infamy.

No one has the right to demand that other citizens should trust him, or that the state should compel them to trust him. Confidence is required and given voluntarily. But each one has the right to demand that he shall not be proclaimed infamous without legal conviction. The confidence of his fellow-citizens is worth a great deal to him, and perhaps he may require it hereafter. Hence, no one has a right to deprive him of this possibility by falsely charging him with infamy.

The right to a good name is, therefore, simply the right not to be falsely proclaimed infamous. It is a mere negative right. The state has guaranteed it by agreeing not to interfere with public opinion, and the natural order of things in this respect.

THE RIGHT OF PERSONAL SECURITY.

The freedom and absolute inviolability of the body of each citizen is not expressly guaranteed in the municipal compact, but is rather constantly presupposed together with the personality of each citizen. The very possibility of the compact, and of all its contents, is grounded upon it. No one may beat, push, or hold a citizen without infringing upon the use of his freedom, and diminishing his activity and well-being. Blows or wounds inflict pain ; and each one has the right to be as well as nature permits him to be ; and another free being has not the right to infringe upon it. An attack upon the body of a citizen is an attack upon *all* the rights which a citizen has in a state, and is, therefore, indeed, a crime in the state.

Hence, whenever I am on *public* dominion, that is, outside of my house, I am always under the protection and guarantee of the state. Each attack on my-person in such places is a public crime, which the state is obliged to investigate and punish, and which the parties interested must not be allowed to settle among themselves. But whilst I am in my house, I am not under the protection nor under the jurisdiction of the state, although the house itself stands under that jurisdiction. Hence, a forcible entrance, whether by day or by night, is a public crime, and must be punished as such. But persons who enter quietly, *without having broken open the lock*—and for this reason the custom of knocking at a door has been introduced, and should always be upheld ; the " Come in !" giving the necessary legal authority to enter—have entered with my consent, and stay with me as a matter of mutual faith and trust in each other. I have not presupposed that they will attack me or my property, or else I should not have admitted them.

But supposing that, nevertheless, they should attack me, my body or my property, or both, if I defend my property with my body, is the state in such a case bound to protect me or not ?

The state does not know what happens in my house, has not the right publicly to know it, nor to act as if it knew it. If the state is to take cognizance of it, it must be because I myself have legally made it known to the state, that is, by having preferred complaint.

The rule, where there is no plaintiff there is no

judge, applies only to the cases which happen within *private* dominion ; but on no account to occurrences upon public dominion. Bar-rooms, coffee-houses, in short, all places which one may enter who proposes to spend money, are under public jurisdiction ; and all violations of law happening in such places must be investigated and punished by the state, whether complaint has been preferred or not.

But is the state really obliged to take cognizance of my complaint concerning occurrences in my own house, and if so, why ? The reason is this : the state is obliged to protect me and all my property in my house ; not immediately, however, but only mediately. The immediate protection of the state would violate my right because its condition, the taking cognizance of it by the state, would violate my right. If I resign this right by voluntarily giving the state notice of the facts, I submit immediately to the state what previously was only mediately under the state's jurisdiction. Of course, this must be specified in the penal law, so that every citizen may act accordingly.

But by this arrangement we get into a great difficulty. For if a citizen is killed in his own house, he can not prefer complaint. Perhaps he also has no relatives, who may do it for him ; or his relatives may have been implicated in his murder. Since the state has no jurisdiction over the house, it would seem that there is no legal protection against such murder ; nay, more, that the law expressly invites thieves and robbers to add murder to their crimes, so that no complaint can be preferred against them.

This can not be the case. There must be some rational solution of this difficulty. Let us look for it.

If the murdered man were alive, he might prefer complaint or might pardon. He has been unjustly killed ; he ought still to live, and the state does not know of him yet except as living, since he has been killed beyond the jurisdiction of the state. The state has still the right to ask him what he has resolved to do concerning that occurrence, and hence his will is to be assumed, with perfect external right, as still continuing to exist for the state. The murdered man has not determined this will of his ; but it is determined, declared, and guaranteed by the general will of all the citizens of the state, *regarded as separate individuals ;* not by the common will of the state as a body, for the state judges, decides, and grants, but does not demand and sue in the present case. (We shall speak of this general will of the *individuals* of a state again, when we come to speak of Wills ; for this general will is manifested always when it is the interest of all the individuals of a state that a deceased citizen should have had a will, and that his will should be still valid ; because they all wish that, in a like case, the same should be assumed of them.) How, then, is the will of the murdered man determined by the general will of all citizens ? They all say, his will would have been to prefer complaint. Hence, there should be a representative of the general will in regard to this last will of the deceased—a sort of public prosecutor ; for the state can not prefer the complaint, since the state does not and can not know of the murder ; and each private citizen has the right to see that this public prosecutor does his duty. Each one has the right to notify him of such occurrences, and to prefer complaint against him if he neglects to prefer complaint against the murderer.

Each private citizen must not only have the right, but must be obliged to give public notice of what he knows of such occurrences, and must become liable to punishment if he neglects to do so. Nay, even the government takes, to some extent, notice of the occurrence, since it must take notice of the death and the manner of death of all citizens—for to die is a public act. All doctors must be under the supervision of the government. Hence, it is rather in the interest of the offender to spare the life of the attacked party ; for so long as that party lives, he may forgive ; but when he dies, his cause devolves upon the people and the public prosecutor ; and the people can not pardon, for the sake of their own security.

THE RIGHT OF SELF-DEFENSE.*

No one has the right to defend with his own body *property which is marked by the state*, and thus to jeopardize his own life and the life of his opponent; for so far as such property is concerned, title can always be proved, even if it should be taken possession of by the other party, and the true owner can be reinstated and have his aggressor punished by the state.

But property which is not thus marked, the title to which can only be proved by its actual possession, either upon one's body or in one's house, each person has the right to defend even at the risk of the life of the assailant. The question, What is money worth compared to life? can not be properly asked in such cases. For that question rests upon moral, not legal, considerations. Each person has the absolute right to prevent any one from taking things away from him by force, and to prevent it at all hazards. A violent attack upon my property, if I protect it by my own person, thus becomes an attack upon my body, and I have the same right of self-defense. The ground of this right is, that the assistance of the state is not immediately on hand, and that the defense—since the property to be defended *can not be replaced*—must be immediate.

We have thus obtained, at the same time, the

---

* The limitations of this right, as here exposed, deserve particular notice in our republic, where no right is more shamefully abused.—TRANSLATOR.

limit of the right of self-defense.   I have this right only in so far as the state can not defend me ; hence, it must not be my fault that the state can not do so, and I am legally bound to do my best to make it possible for the state to do so.   I am bound to call upon the state for help, and this is done by *calling for help*.   It is absolutely necessary to do this, and it is the exclusive condition of the right of self-defense.   The code of laws should specify it, and citizens should be taught it from their earliest youth, so that they may accustom themselves to it.   For how, if I murder some one, and say : He assailed me, and I could save my life only by taking his ? The murdered man can not expose my lie.   But if I call for help, I can prove that I was the attacked party ; or, at least, if the contrary can not be proved against me, the presumption remains in favor of my innocence.

(The laws of the twelve tables justified the killing of a thief who defended himself, and very correctly, if he had stolen unmarked property ; for no one can be required to let things be taken from him to which he can not afterward prove his right of property.   He was justified in reclaiming the articles by force.   If the thief defended himself, the attack upon the property became an attack upon the person of the injured party, and hence he was justified in defending himself at the risk of killing the thief. But the law required him, as a condition of that right of defense, to cry out for help ; and again very correctly, for only by thus crying out for help did he place himself in a position to get the public to witness his innocence, or to obtain assistance which might secure the thief and obviate the necessity of killing him.)

Such an attack upon unmarked property may occur either upon public territory or in my house. In the first case, the application of the above principles is clear enough. In the latter case, no private person, not even government, has the right to enter my house. It is only by crying out for help that I justify government and every private person to enter my house. My crying out for help is a complaint preferred, and hence a voluntary abandoning of my house-right.

Each person who hears another one cry for help is lawfully bound by the state-compact to hasten to his assistance. *For all individuals have promised to all individuals to protect them ; and the cry for help is the announcement that a danger exists, which the representative of the protecting power, the government, can not immediately remove.* Hence, the cry for help confers upon each individual again not only the right but also the obligation to render immediate protection. If it can be proved that a citizen heard the cry for help and did not hurry to assistance, he is liable to punishment ; for he has violated the original municipal compact, and the law should provide punishment for such cases. Such assistance in need is not only *moral and religious duty,* but is the *absolute duty of citizenship.*

Those who hasten to render help have no further

duty than to part the combatants, but on no accoun
have they a right to decide their dispute.   For the
grounded extends no further than the ground.   The
immediate right of protection is grounded upon the
present danger ; and that danger has been removed
by the interference of the others.   The judicial decision and investigation on the part of the state
can now be safely awaited for.   It is, for instance,
an unlawful barbarism which should be severely
punished, when mobs punish criminals after they
have been caught.   As soon as the immediate danger has been removed, by the capture of such criminals, government again becomes sole protector and
judge.

There is still another case of self-defense, based
upon a pretended *right of necessity*, the theory
whereof we shall also consider in this connection.
This right is said to come into play when two free
beings are brought by mere natural casualty—and
on no account by any action of their own—into a
position wherein the one person can save himself
only by the death of the other, wherein both must
die unless one of them is sacrificed.   This category
of supposed cases includes that wonderful problem
of the law colleges, which assumes a board, to
which two shipwrecked persons cling, the board
being only large enough for one ; and which problem has recently been changed for the more ac-
commodating illustration of a boat of the same qualities as the board.   But having clearly determined
this whole class of cases, we may well refrain from
examples.

Much pains have been taken to solve this law-problem, and various solutions have been proposed, simply because the legal principle involved has not been clearly thought.

The problem of the Science of Rights is, How may many free beings, as such, exist together? In thus inquiring after the manner of such a coexistence, the possibility of such coexistence is evidently pre-supposed; and hence, when this possibility does not exist, the inquiry after the manner of its existence is clearly inadmissible. Such is the case in the assumed instance. Hence, there exists no positive right to sacrifice another individual to the preservation of my existence; but neither is it against the conception of rights, that is, it is not in conflict with any positive right of the other to sacrifice his life to the preservation of my own. In short, the question of right and not right does not enter here at all. Nature has canceled her permission *for both* of us to live; and the decision is a matter which physical strength or free will may settle. It may be, however, that this free will, which is not determined by the conception of rights in the present instance, stands under a higher legislation—the *moral law*. Such, indeed, is the case. Morality tells each of the two: Do nothing at all, but leave the matter to God, who can certainly save you, if it is his will, and to whom you must surrender your life if it is his will. This consideration, however, does not properly belong to a Science of Rights.

When the right of self-defense has been exercised, whether upon provocation or by accident, the person who has exercised it is obliged to surrender himself to the government for justification, and to prove that he went beyond the pale of the laws of the state only because a case had arisen in which those laws could not be applied. The person who does not voluntarily thus give notice of the fact, renders himself liable to suspicion.

The last will of the person killed is, presumptively, that the deed shall be investigated. It is, therefore, the duty of the public prosecutor to prefer the complaint. The defendant is not obliged to furnish the positive proof that he did act in self-defense ; for in the fewest cases, however just the provocation, could such a proof be procured. Provided it can not be proved against him that he acted without sufficient cause, judicial proceedings against him must be suspended. A complete exoneration can not be pronounced unless he can furnish positive proof. Concerning this mere suspension of judicial proceedings, we shall have more to say hereafter, when speaking of Criminal Law.

The property and honor of citizens is thus clearly defined and secured as perfectly as their life ; nor does it appear likely that greater security is obtainable.

ACQUISITION AND DERELICTION OF PROPERTY.

We speak here of acquisition of property only in the strictest meaning of the word, as signifying really the acquisition of a new kind of property, and not as signifying a mere exchange or trade of similar property.

All property is of a double nature ; it is either absolute, and hence not under the jurisdiction of the state, as money and valuables, etc., or relative, and immediately under the jurisdiction of the state, as real estate, houses, licenses, etc.

When both kinds of property are exchanged, that is, when a sale takes place, each party acquires a new kind of property, and hence the supposed acquisition takes place. It is clear enough that the deed of sale must be concluded under the supervision of the state, that is, according to the forms of law, and must be guaranteed by the state. For the state has all this property under its jurisdiction, protects it and assigns it to the proper person ; the state must, therefore, know the owner. No one is the legal owner of such a piece of property, except through the recognition of the state. The only question can, therefore, be, whether the state is obliged to give its consent to all such sales or contracts between private persons ; or whether the state may interfere, and to what extent.

The legal end of the state in all the property conveyed to citizens is, that this property shall be properly used for the necessities of the state. Hence, the purchaser must agree to use it, and must be in a position to be able to use it ; for instance, if he purchases lands, he must be able to farm ; if a profession, he must understand it.

Whether houses may be purchased for the purpose of pulling them down depends upon the special provisions of the law, which always shapes itself according to circumstances.

Again : since the seller retires from the jurisdiction of the state, so far as the money he receives in consideration is concerned, which is absolute property, and since, nevertheless, the state guarantees him a living, the sale must be of such a character that the sustenance of the seller is perfectly secured, and may never devolve upon the state. This can be done either when the seller retains a claim upon his property in the shape of a mortgage, etc., or when he loans out the purchase-money under the supervision of the state. He is not absolute proprietor of his money so long as it is his only sustenance, he being responsible to the state for his ability to make his living.

A second mode of acquiring and ceding property is, where the party who deeds it away receives no equivalent for it—*bequests and last wills.*

Property thus bequeathed may be either absolute or relative. Absolute property may, of course, be given away without form of law, the state having no jurisdiction over it. Relative property, however, can be bequeathed only in the form prescribed by law. The same condition applies here which applies to sales : the bequeather must retain sufficient to sustain his life. A bequest conveys full title, and can not be repealed.

A *will* conveys property after the death of the

grantor. The important question is here : How can the will of a dead person be obligatory upon the living ? The conception of rights applies only to persons who stand, or may stand in reciprocal influence with each other in the sensuous world. Dead persons have, therefore, at first view, no rights, and their property reverts to the state, which is the first claimant, since no individual can take possession without the state's permission. But it is very possible that a man may cherish in his life wishes for others after his death ; and the firm belief that those wishes will be carried out after such death as well, is frequently a real present advantage—for instance : better attendance, care, and love of those who are the presumptive heirs, are an actual benefit of life. In short, the conviction that wills are valid is an enjoyment of life, to which it may well be possible to acquire a right. This is the only proper point of view from which to consider this matter. The question is not one concerning the rights of the dead—the dead have no rights—but of the living.

Whenever the necessity of such a conviction arises among men, provisions will be made for it in the property-compact ; that is, all will guarantee that conviction to all.

But it should be constantly kept in mind that this agreement is arbitrary ; that is to say, a legal relation among men is possible without such an arrangement. It is not necessary that a law dispute should arise about the possessions of the dead, since the state is ready to claim them. I call this agreement regarding the validity of wills arbitrary, therefore, merely because it is not necessary for the realization of the conception of rights.

The conviction that wills will be considered valid after death can be realized only by establishing a law that all wills, without exception, shall be thus considered. Each one, then, guarantees for his own sake to all others the validity of their will, and in doing so guarantees his own will. The right of the dying is thus made to connect with the rights of all surviving citizens. It is not *the dying person's own* will which the state respects, but the will of all surviving individuals.

It is the business of the public administrator, as the representative of the will of all individuals of a state, to watch over the wills, and see that they are properly executed. He must not be a member of the government, since the government is an interested party in the matter, but simply a representative of the people, as individuals, precisely like the public prosecutor.

Hence, likewise, every private person must have the right to prefer complaint against him.

Wills should be executed in presence of this administrator and of witnesses who represent the public.

Since the legal validity of wills is arbitrarily established, it follows that the law may also provide *how far* the right shall extend to inherit at all. It is the duty of the legislator, with due regard to the peculiar circumstances and conditions of his state, to establish such provisions. There is only *one a priori* limitation to this right of willing away property, namely, that the heirs of the deceased must be provided for sufficiently, that is, that they may not become a burden to the state.

§ 2.

PENAL LAW.

THESIS.—Whosoever violates thé municipal compact in any manner, whether from neglect or intentionally, loses, strictly speaking, all his rights as a citizen and as a man, and becomes an outlaw.

PROOF.—A person has rights only on condition that he proves himself fit for a community of free beings, that is, that he makes the fundamental principle of law his constant rule of action ; and is also able to actually determine his free acts by the representation of that principle. He who willingly violates the law has not made that principle his rule of action ; and he who violates it through carelessness is not able to determine his acts by that principle. In either case, therefore, the condition of a person's having rights does not exist, and hence with the condition the conditioned also vanishes. In either case the person has no rights, and is an outlaw.

ANTITHESIS.—The only object of the erection of

a state government is to secure to each the full possession of his rights ; and the state has only to discover and apply the means which will secure this object.   Hence, if that object can be attained without the absolute outlawing of transgressors, the state is not necessarily obliged to affix this punishment to violations of the law.   It may do so or not as it pleases.   If, moreover, it should appear that the interest of the state requires the preservation of its citizens, and that each citizen is likewise interested in not having each little offense of the laws punished by outlawing the transgressor, a compact of the following character would become necessary : All citizens promise to all citizens that they shall not be outlawed and expelled from the state by reason of their offenses, provided such be compatible with public security.   Let us call this compact the compact of *expiation.*

Such a compact is equally useful for all (for the whole state) and for each single person.   For the whole state has thus the prospect of retaining citizens whose usefulness far exceeds the injury they may do, and obliges itself merely to accept the expiation.   The single individual, on the other hand, has thus the *perfect right* to ask that his expiation shall be received in place of the greater punishment which he has deserved.   It is a very useful and important right, this right of citizens to expiate offenses.

This compact becoming a law, the government is bound to act according to it.

Of course, the right of expiation extends no further than is compatible with public security. If it is made to extend further, it is irrational; and a state in which it extends beyond this limit, is not a legal state at all ; that is, does not sufficiently guarantee public security, and has no claim to toleration.

Punishment is not an absolute end. In fact, the proposition that punishment is an end for itself, as is, for instance, involved in the expression, " He who has killed must die," is positively meaningless. Punishment is merely a means for the end of the state "to maintain public security ;" and the only intention in providing punishment is to prevent by threats transgressions of the law. The end of all penal laws is, that they may *not* be applied. The threatened punishment is intended to suppress all evil purposes and to promote a good disposition, so that the punishment may never be applied. Hence, in order to attain this end, each citizen must know that the threat of the law will invariably become reality if he should commit any offense.

It is, therefore, to some extent true, that punishment serves as an example, namely, to convince all of the infallible execution of the law. But the original intention of punishment was solely to deter the criminal from the crime. Now, since this end could not be attained, he having committed a crime, his punishment has another aim in view, namely, to deter other citizens from committing the same offense. The execution of the penal law is, therefore. a public act. Each citizen who has heard of an offense, must also learn that it has been punished.   It would be an evident injustice toward all those who might, in future, be tempted to violate the same law, if the actual punishment of previous violations of that law had been concealed from them ; for such concealment would lead them to hope for escape from punishment.

The material principle of positive punishments in a state has already been suggested.   Each individual must stake precisely that portion of his rights and privileges (his property, in the widest significance of the word) which he is tempted to violate in the others, whether wilfully or through neglect. In other words, the punishment must be equal to the crime : *pœna talionis.*   Each one must know, that the injury he may intend to do to the other will be done to himself.

The essence of this principle is, as we have also seen, that a sufficient counterpoise must be established for the evil intention or the neglect.

Whenever this principle becomes applicable, the compact of expiation can become valid ; and hence the legal extent of the validity of that compact depends upon the answer to the question : How far is such a counterpoise possible ?

This counterpoise becomes possible or impossible, first, either from the nature of the case, or, second, from the peculiar position of the subject for whom the punishment is intended.

PUNISHMENT BY FINES.

I. *a.* Such a sufficient counterpoise, or a punishment which may be perfectly equal to the crime committed, is practicable from the nature of the case where a wrong has been committed through carelessness, and where the will of the criminal was a *materialiter evil* will, having selfish ends in view, and longing for the possession of another man's property. There is, however, this distinction : In the case of carelessness, a fine equal to the amount of damage done is equal to the injury committed ; but in the case of a crime, the criminal must not only restore what is taken, but must, moreover, pay an equal amount from his own property, in order to have the punishment made equal to the offense. For if you take away from him merely that which he has taken, he will always be tempted to commit the same crime, having nothing to lose and every thing to gain. By establishing the theory of a sufficient counterpoise, however, and hence by making him pay precisely the same amount which he has stolen, there is no inducement for him to steal. In case of discovery, he will lose precisely the amount he would gain if not discovered. Hence, the only incentive to rob would be the consideration that the chances of discovery were in his favor. But such a probability is not likely to happen in a well-regulated state.

b. The principle of a counterpoise is not applicable from the nature of the case when the will of the transgressor is *formaliter* evil ; that is, when the

z

violation of the law is done, not for the sake of getting possession of another person's goods, but merely for the sake of injuring the other. For such a *formaliter* evil will is not deterred by the punishment of an equal loss ; nay, an envious, malicious person may gladly submit to such loss, provided his enemy is also injured. Unless we find some other means of protecting citizens against such a *formaliter* evil will, the only punishment adequate to it must be outlawing, or exclusion from the state. Let us consider this subject.

Firstly, it is to be remarked that we have here a case where the sentiments and intentions which inspired the crime must be taken notice of. Nevertheless, it should not be held that this is a case wherein the *morality* of the act is considered. No man can and no man should be the judge of another's morality. The only object of civil punishment, and the only measure of its degree is the possibility of public security. Violations of the law, prompted by malicious intentions, are to be punished more severely than violations inspired by selfish motives ; not because they are *more immoral**—morality, indeed, has no degrees ; and there is only one morality—but because the fear of a milder punishment, a punishment simply of equal loss, would not afford adequate security.

Hence, the question arises : How can it be known

---

* Moreover, who would assert that the man whose malicious act evinces, at leas., ourage and energy, is more dead to morality than the man who is prompted only by egotism ?

and proved for external law what motives inspired the crime ; and what punishment shall be applied to crimes prompted by malicious motives ?

He who can prove that he stood in need of what he has appropriated from the other, and for what purposes he needed it, etc., is to be considered as having appropriated it for the sake of selfish gain. He who can not prove this, who, perhaps, did not even take or intend to take the property of the other, but merely destroyed it, has made himself liable to another doubt : Did he injure it intentionally and maliciously, or inadvertently ?

We have two criterions for malicious motives ; one external and one internal criterion. We have an external criterion when previous free acts of the same person can be proved, which can be interpreted only as means for the final end to effect a malicious injury.

On the other hand, the person who pretends that he has injured the other's property unintentionally, must be able to *furnish positive proof* that those other acts which are connected with the injury *had quite a different* end in view. Unless he can furnish this proof, he is to be held as convicted of a malicious act.

And yet remarkable connections of circumstances are possible which will give to an accidental crime all the appearance of premeditated maliciousness, without any true ground. Hence, regard must also be paid to the *internal* criterion of maliciousness, namely, whether the two persons have previously been enemies, and whether the accused has exhibited signs of malicious intent in his previous life.

But how if all this circumstantial evidence neither proves the suspicion nor removes it completely, as is very possible? A great number of jurists recommend in such cases a mild sentence; but such mildness exhibited toward a guilty person is a great injury to the commonwealth. By thinking the case clearly, the solution of this problem will show itself. The investigation is not yet closed, and can not be closed by the proofs furnished as yet; hence, the accused is not pronounced either guilty or not guilty. He has, however, been convicted, at least, of carelessness, and this punishment he has to suffer for the present. As far as his malicious intent is concerned, the state says nothing, but allows him to show, by his future life, proofs for or against it. Moreover, additional circumstances may be discovered in the future concerning the motives of the crime, and those additional circumstances, together with his behavior, will determine within a specified time whether he ought to be convicted or completely cleared. This suspension of judicial proceedings we have already had occasion to recommend in cases wherein the right of self-defense is exercised, and is, indeed, to be recommended in all cases of unproved suspicion. In a well-regulated state, no one should be punished innocently; but neither should any offense pass unpunished.

As a matter of course, the state will have to provide by law more severe punishment for offenses committed with malicious intent than for those committed for selfish motives of gain. For each one must know beforehand by what law he will be punished; otherwise, the punishment would involve an injustice; and the intent of the law, to deter men from committing offenses, can be achieved only by publishing the law. It is also clear, that the state must expressly provide by law what shall be held to constitute criminal neglect, and hence must specify the care which each citizen is required to observe in particular cases. Whosoever observes the care thus required by law, is to be released; and if any damage happens in spite of such care, it is to be considered as a misfortune, which must be borne by the sufferer; or it must be paid for by the state, if it was occasioned by a want of proper law or of proper police regulations.

The plea of anger or of drunkenness—as having placed the criminal for the moment beyond the control of his reason—relieves him from the charge of premeditated and malicious intent; but a rational legislation will rather provide more severe than milder punishment for such cases, particularly if such a state of mind is habitual with the accused; for a single unlawful act may well constitute an exception from an otherwise blameless life. But a person who pleads, " I habitually get so angry or so drunk as not to be any longer master of my senses!" confesses thereby that he changes himself into a beast on a fixed principle, and that he is, therefore, not fit to live among rational beings. He

must either be content to lose his freedom until his
recovery is sure, or else be excluded from the state
forever. Our laws treat far too leniently pleas of
drunkenness. True, if a nation or a class of men
in a nation can not renounce this vice, the laws can
not prevent them from shutting themselves up in
their houses with any one who chooses to keep
them company, and there to drown their reason,
provided they remain so shut up until they again
become rational; but the state may well lock up
every person found intoxicated on public territory.

II. *a.* The counterpoise becomes impossible of
application from the peculiar position of the subject
for whom the punishment is intended, when that
subject has nothing to lose but his body. Let no
one complain of injustice in this respect, because
the wealthier man, who has no need to rob, and in
robbing only risks his property, is allowed to expiate his offense ; whereas, the poor man, who needed
what he took for his absolute requirements, can not
expiate it, and hence must be completely outlawed,
simply because he has nothing. For such an objection would falsely assume that the state is the moral judge of men, and must make the punishment
equal to the moral depravity. But the state has no
such moral end in view. The state merely wishes
to secure property. Now the threat, " What you
steal from another citizen I shall take from your
possession," has little terror for a person who owns

nothing. Hence, the state must use another threat for such persons. Whether this threat must necessarily be exclusion from the state, or whether another punishment can be contrived for the poor, we shall see hereafter.

b. It is impossible to contrive a punishment as a counterpoise against the will, to arise in immediate hostility to the law and its power. The utmost that can be done and must be done, is that the law be made to maintain its authority ; and hence the law can not, as an equal punishment for the attempt to overthrow it, provide double severity for all its subjects. This would be to punish all citizens for the crime of one individual. The punishment of an equal loss is, therefore, not allowable here ; and there is no manner of expiating the original punishment for all crimes—to outlaw the criminal.

Two modes of committing this crime against the state are possible ; it may be committed mediately against the state in the person of its citizens, namely, by violating in them the compact to which the state, as such, is one party ; or it may be committed directly against the state, in which case the offense is rebellion or high treason.

1. We shall first explain the former. The original municipal compact contains two distinct compacts. Firstly, a compact of each citizen, as an individual, with all others, as individuals, concerning their property. This property-compact the *individuals* conclude, (not the state, as such, that is, not as the or-

ganized whole of all individuals, for the state only guarantees this compact.) In other words, the government is not a party to the original property-compact, but is merely a created organization to guarantee it.

But the original municipal compact contains, secondly, this very agreement of all citizens, as individuals, with themselves, as an organized whole, or as a state, in which agreement the state promises each citizen, when he has fulfilled all the duties of a citizen, to protect his *absolute property, his body, and his life.* The state has, of itself, renounced all claim to the absolute property ; it has no right upon it, only duties concerning it. The state is, therefore, *party* of the citizen, to whom it has guaranteed protection of this property against all violation. Hence, if some individual should break this compact of the state by robbery or by violent assaults upon a citizen's life or body, he would become guilty of an immediate attack upon the state ; for he would have broken the compact of the state, and have done his best to make the state faithless, and thus to destroy the compact existing between the state and the citizen. For the state having guaranteed the protection of that property, life, or body, the criminal directly offends against the state, and for this attack upon the state he should be declared outlawed according to the above.

2. To attack the state immediately is to be guilty either of *rebellion* or high *treason.* REBELLION is to attempt to raise, or actually to raise, a power in

hostility to the power of the state, and to resist therewith that power of the state. TREASON is to use a power which has been conferred by the state, to destroy or annihilate the ends of the state; or not to execute the ends of the state; hence, to take advantage of the confidence of the nation to render nugatory its purposes. Not to exercise the power of government is often as injurious to public security as to abuse it; and hence should be equally punished. It is all the same to the citizens whether government officials abuse their power for positive aggressions of their own, or whether, by neglecting to exercise it, they permit the aggressions of others. In either case, the citizens are oppressed. After an individual has signified his willingness to accept an office, the nation properly calculates that the duties of that office will be executed, and hence takes no other precautions to have them executed. If he had no intention to execute the duties of his office, he should have refused to accept it.

Only private persons can be rebels; only government officials can become guilty of high treason.

PUNISHMENT BY CONFINEMENT.

All these classes of offenses condition outlawing or complete exclusion from the state, because the only mode of expiation whereof we know as yet, that of fines equal to the loss inflicted, is not admissible in these cases. The question remains, however, whether there is not another mode of expiation which may be applicable to these offenses?

a. Let us first consider the case of the poor man who appropriates something from selfish motives, and who has not wherewith to expiate the loss. Why should the harsh punishment of exclusion from the state be applied in his case? There is, indeed, a way of settling the difficulty, whereby he also can participate in the benefits of the law of expiation. He has a property in the strength of his body, and hence he can expiate the fine by *labor.* This labor must, of course, be assigned to him immediately; for every offense, strictly speaking, annuls the citizenship of the offender. Only after the punishment of the offense has been expiated does the offender become a citizen again. It is also necessary that this labor must be carried on under the supervision of the state. Hence, the offender loses his freedom until he has expiated his offense. This is the punishment of the workhouse, as distinguished from that of the penitentiary and house of correction, whereof we shall speak hereafter. This punishment both satisfies the principle of an equal loss, and establishes a threat, which will be likely to deter all persons from committing crimes in any well-regulated state where the criminal is sure of detection.

We now proceed to consider the other cases.

b. A *formaliter* evil will, or an immediate attack upon the state, presupposes such sentiments, that the criminal who is guilty of either crime can not be tolerated in society; he must be outlawed, or expelled from the state. But since it is not necessary that the criminal should continue to harbor such sentiments, it may be possible to establish a second mode of expiation in the form of the following agreement: All citizens promise to all citizens that they will extend to them an opportunity of again becoming fit to live in the society of rational beings, should they ever have been convicted of unfitness therefor, and that after such reform they shall be again received as members of the commonwealth. Such an agreement is arbitrary and beneficial; but it benefits all; and hence, the criminal is invested by it with a *right* to an opportunity to reform.

The punishment which is established by such an agreement is an expiation of utter exclusion from the state; hence, it is a benefit extended by the law to the criminals. Each person has the privilege to reject his rights, and hence the criminal may reject this benefit granted him by the law; but by rejecting it he clearly proves himself an incorrigible scoundrel, and must be expelled without further delay. Let no one imagine, that by giving a criminal this privilege of accepting or rejecting the punishment of expulsion, the criminal obtains a means to escape punishment altogether. If a state is arranged rationally, and its neighboring states are also arranged rationally, there is no punishment so terrible as expulsion from the state ; and it is not to be expected that any one will choose it in preference over the established expiation, or that the prospect of having the privilege to choose it, if discovered, will quiet him when about to commit a crime.

(This same privilege of accepting the expiation established by law, or of submitting to the exclusion from the state, must, of course, be allowed also where the punishment is one of fines ; although it is not to be supposed that any one would ever prefer to be expelled from the state, and thus to lose all his property, rather than pay the fine.)

By means of this compact, a *reform* is to be made possible in the criminal. Not a *moral* reform, not a reform of inner sentiments ; for no man is a judge of another's morals ; but merely a *political* reform, a reform of obedience to the law and of rules of action. Moral sentiment is a love of duty for the sake of duty ; but political sentiment is love of one's self for the sake of one's self and care for the protection of one's own body and one's own property. This all-transcending love of one's self becomes the very means in the hands of the penal legislator by which to force each citizen not to violate the rights of the other ; for in the Penal Law it is established that every evil act you do unto another you do unto yourself. It is this care for one's own security which originally impelled man to build up a state, and he who has no such care has no reason to remain citizen of a state. It is this care alone by means of which each citizen gives to the state a sufficient guarantee, and is controlled by the state. The law has no hold upon a man who has not this self-love. There are two ways of escaping from it. Firstly, by pure morality, when each one forgets his empirical self in the ultimate end of all reason; in which case the Penal Law does not determine his acts, since duty itself causes him to obey the laws; and, secondly, by barbarism, when a man does not care for his own welfare; in which case he becomes unfit to live with other free beings, since the Penal Law can not apply to him. Political reform is a return to a care for one's own security and welfare.

He who has inflicted injury for the sake of the injury, has exhibited not only internal malice, which the state does not judge, but also barbarous manners and an unusual carelessness for his own welfare. If those barbarous manners are replaced by milder traits, and if the criminal learns to care for his own security, he may again be tolerated in society. Long confinement and its many evils are very apt to teach him this. The same holds good in regard to those who have attacked the body or property of other citizens. They are wild and untamed natures, and in the latter case, moreover, lusting after another's possessions. Let them first learn to live and take care of their own. It is only the reckless squanderer of money who is a thief or robber. Rebels may often be good-natured, but erring visionaries. Let them have their conceptions corrected, and learn to esteem the benefits of a civil government, particularly of that in their own state, and they may grow to be excellent citizens. It is only the traitor who has acted both faithless and infamous ; hence, he can never again be trusted with a public office. Used to power and to command, he will, however, not find it easy to stay content with modest retirement and a small private business. The only question is, whether he can not be tamed down ? It may be a difficult matter, but who would assert the absolute impossibility of it ? (Dionysius became schoolmaster in Corinth.) The chief rule is, that we should not despair of their reform, nor make them despair of themselves ; and secondly, that they should always be made to retain some degree of satisfaction with their condition, and some hope of a future better fate. To some extent this is accomplished by allowing them the privilege of choosing between expulsion and expiation. They will trust themselves when they perceive that the state trusts them.

The institutions of correction for these offenders must be practically arranged. They must be removed from society, and the state must be made heavily responsible for any injury which may be inflicted upon society by persons who have been sentenced to these institutions. Hence, the freedom of such persons must be completely taken away from them. But he who is to reform his manners must be free ; and he must be free, moreover, in order to render possible a judgment as to his reform. Hence, it is a chief maxim, that these men must be free within necessary restrictions, and must live socially together.

Nothing for them without labor. It would be the greatest mistake if these institutions were so arranged that the prisoners received their food whether they worked or not, or if laziness were punished by the most degrading treatment—blows— instead of by its natural sequence—lack of food. Again: All the production of their labor, after deduction of their board, must remain their own. In the same manner, their property in the state must be kept for them under the supervision of the government. The object of their confinement is, to awaken in them love of order, of labor, and of property. But how could this love arise, if order and labor were to them of no advantage, and if they could not acquire property? They must be under the supervision of the state, and yet they must also be free; in other words, so long as they act properly they must seem to be perfectly free; but when they act wrongly, punishment must follow immediately.

It will be well to use remote countries, uninhabited islands and deserts for such institutions. To urge the expense would be criminal. For what are the revenues of the state for, unless for such purposes? The expense, moreover, will not be very great, if such colonies are properly arranged, and if each person is employed in the occupation with which he is familiar.

The object and condition of allowing criminals

to expiate their offences is their reform. Unless, therefore, they really do reform, the conditioned, that is, the patience of the state, ceases. It would be very practicable if each criminal could be required to prescribe a fixed term for his own reform, which term he might, perhaps, be allowed to extend a little if it should be considered advisable. But a certain general term must be peremptorily fixed for all. We have already said, that the object intended is not moral, but political reform ; and acts alone can decide whether it has taken place or not. Hence, if the discipline of government is relaxed as each prisoner gives evidence of improvement, it will not be difficult to determine soon whether a reform is taking place. It will be necessary to appoint sensible and conscientious men for these offices, who will make themselves responsible for the future good conduct of all persons whom they pronounce reformed.

The reformed criminals return into the commonwealth and are reinstated in their previous condition. They have been completely reconciled with society by their punishment and subsequent reform. Nor will there be entertained any more distrust— but rather confidence—in these reformed criminals, when men have once resolved to consider such institutions as really means of reform, and not merely as means of punishment ; and when only those are allowed to return into society who have reformed, but not, as is done at present, all who have been de-tained for a fixed term, and who have only been made worse by irrational treatment.

All prisoners who have not reformed within the prescribed term, are excluded from the state as incorrigible.

These institutions are to be not only places of conversion, but also of punishment; and hence they must be of a nature to deter citizens from committing crimes. Loss of freedom, exclusion from society, and strict discipline—all this is terrible enough for men accustomed to freedom; but there is no reason why the fate of the prisoner should not be generally considered to be still more severe than it really is, or why distinctions should not be made in their treatment which terrify others without being in themselves an evil; as, for instance, a peculiar dress, or a chain which does not pain much. The prisoner gets used to it, and on the outsider it makes the proper impression.

MURDER.

The only crime which does not allow of an attempt to reform the criminal, and which must, therefore, be punished immediately by absolute exclusion from the state, is *intentional and premeditated murder.* (Not a murder which is merely the accidental result of another violence.) The ground is this: Of him who has committed murder, it is to be apprehended that he may murder again; and since the state has no right to compel any one to expose his life, no one can be compelled to undertake the supervision over the murderer, who must be allowed some degree of freedom, if he is to reform ; nor can the other criminals be compelled to tolerate a murderer in their midst. True, if any one is willing voluntarily to risk his life in behalf of the murderer, he may do so. Hence, societies might be permitted to establish institutions for the purpose of attempting the reform of such criminals ; but such societies must guarantee to the state the safe-keeping of the murderer.

THE PUNISHMENT OF OUTLAWING.

But what shall be done with those who are absolutely excluded from the state, either without preliminary attempts to reform them, or because they did not reform within the prescribed term, or because they refused to expiate ? This is by far the most important investigation in the theory of punishments. We hope by its means to put an end to a number of confused notions ; and we shall not merely, as is usual, assert, but *prove*.

1. The declaration that a citizen is an outlaw is the highest punishment which the state can inflict upon any rational being. For the state exists for the individual as state only through the compact. The utmost the state can do, therefore, is to declare this compact annulled. Both the state and the individual do not now exist for each other any more. The compact, the legal relation between them, and

indeed all relation between them, has been utterly canceled. The state has now no right upon the individual by virtue of the compact ; and since there is no other positive, determined, and determinable right than through the compact, the state has no right whatever upon the individual thus outlawed.

2. But what, then, are the results of this declaration ? The perfectly arbitrary treatment of the outlawed. Not as if you *had a right* to treat him thus ; but there *is neither a right against it.* The outlawed person is, therefore, declared to be a thing—an animal. For, in regard to animals and their relation to us, the question is never one of right, but of physical force. I can not say, I have a *right* to kill this animal ; but neither can I say, I have not a right to kill it. It is so with the outlaw. No reason can be shown — from positive law — why the first citizen who meets him should not kill or torture him ; but neither can any reason be shown why he should do so.

3. Supposing some citizens should thus treat the outlaw, what would follow ? No proceeding against them on the part of the state, for the outlaw has no rights ; but certainly the contempt of all men, or infamy. He who tortures an animal for mere pleasure, without having any positive advantage in view, is justly held in abhorrence as an inhuman barbarian ; how much more he who would torture or kill, for mere pleasure, a being which at the worst has, at least, a human countenance ! It will not be done, therefore ; not because that outlaw has

any rights, but from motives of self-respect and of the esteem of other men. (The moral view of the act we do not take into consideration here ; but merely its civil aspects.)

4. How, then, is the state situated in regard to this outlaw ? We have already shown, that by the breaking of the compact the state ceases to exist as a state for the outlaw. Hence, if the state should kill him, it does not kill him *as state*, but as the *stronger physical force*, as a mere natural force. But the state has the same reasons for not killing or torturing him which we discovered to influence the private individual, namely, respect for itself, for its citizens, and for other states.

Nevertheless, there is a possible ground why the state should kill the outlaw, to wit : Because it is the only manner in which the state can protect itself against him. Since there is no reason why it should not kill him, this consideration is, therefore, decisive in such a case. The outlaw is considered simply as a wild beast, which must be shot ; or as an overflowing river, which must be stopped ; in short, as a force of nature, which the state must render harmless by an opposing force of nature. The death of the outlaw is not a means of punishment, but merely of security ; and this consideration gives us the whole theory of capital punishment.

THE PUNISHMENT OF DEATH.

The death of the outlaw is not decreed by the state as a judge. The state, as judge, has merely pronounced the sentence of exclusion from the state, and this is the only public act of the state If, after such sentence, the state, nevertheless, kills him, it does not kill him through the judicial power, but through the police power. The condemned has been placed beyond the pale of the judiciary; he belongs to the police. The killing is not done by virtue of a positive right, but from sheer necessity. Such matters, however, are not honorable, and hence, like all that is dishonorable and yet necessary, must be done secretly and shamefully. Let the criminal be throttled or beheaded in prison. His civil death has been pronounced publicly by the sentence of expulsion, and that sentence has killed him in the memory of all citizens. The citizens do not care what is done with the physical man after that sentence.

(What a disgrace to reason that so much pomp should accompany executions; or that the dead bodies of the criminals should be hung up for public show, tied to the wheel, etc., just as the Indians hang up the scalps of their enemies around the walls of their wigwams!)

The death of the criminal is something accidental, and hence can not be officially announced; but the exclusion from the state must be officially announced.

To increase the death-penalty by torture is barbarous. It changes the state into a wild, malicious, revengeful enemy, who loves to torture his enemy and to make him *feel* death.

It is often necessary to strengthen the proofs of reason by facts of experience. Here is one well known : In the Roman Republic, those who were condemned to death were allowed the choice of exile. It was only when danger was to be appre‹ hended of them, as in the case of Catilina's conspirators, that the Romans permitted their death. But they killed them secretly, in prison ; not publicly. The consul Cicero was sent into exile, and very justly, in so far, not because of that execution itself, but because the trial of those conspirators had been decided in the senate, and not before the people, as the law required.

One other circumstance is to be considered in the execution of criminals, which we can not well pass by here, although it is not of a legal nature. For the moral law explicitly prohibits in each case the intentional killing of another. Each man must be regarded as a means to promote the object of reason ; and no one can renounce the belief that the other, however corrupt he may now be, may reform his moral character, without renouncing his own end, as necessarily established for him through reason. The strict proof of this assertion is to be furnished in a Science of Morality. Hence, a private person has never a right to kill, but rather than kill should endanger his own life. It is different in the case of the state, which, as police power, is not a moral, but simply a legal body. Government officials may be often morally obliged to expose their own lives to danger rather than kill the

life of another ; but they have not the right to expose the life of others, still less the life of the state—
that is, the life, security, and legal relation of all—by
allowing a dangerous outlaw to remain alive.

Hence, the execution of incorrigible rascals always remains an evil, though a necessary one, and
it is the problem of the state to render it unnecessary. But what is to be done with them, if they
must not be killed ? Imprisonment for life is a
burden for the state ; and how, indeed, could the
state require its citizens to pay taxes for something
which will realize none of the ends of the state,
since there is no hope for reform ? The only remaining punishment is banishment for life ; not
deportation, for deportation is, as we have shown, a
means of conversion, and is carried on under the
superintendence of the state. If there is any fear
that the criminal may return, let him be branded*
in a manner as little painful as possible, for the state
must not appear as a torturer. The branding, also,
is not punishment, but a means of public safety, and
devolves upon the police.

What shall be done with the criminals who have
thus been branded and expelled from the state?
This is a question put, not by the *citizens*, but by
men. Let the branded criminal go into the wilderness and live among animals. This has accidentally happened to many who were not criminals ; and

---

* The custom in Nebraska, Kansas, and all border states of civil-
ization.—TRANSLATOR'S REMARK.

the criminals, branded under laws as we have described, are incorrigible.

Against the theory of punishments as established
here by us, there is usually opposed another theory,
which establishes an absolute right of punishment,
and looks upon judicial punishment not as a means,
but as an end in itself. Since this latter theory
claims to rest upon an unprovable assertion, and
hence manages very cleverly to escape furnishing
proof, it is easy for its advocates to sneer at all
those who think differently, to charge them with
sentimentality, *affected* humanity, etc., and to call
them sophists and legal quibblers ; quite in violation
of the much-praised and justly-to-be-demanded
equality (*of reasons*) and freedom (of opinions, *sup-
ported by reasons*) on the field of philosophy. The
only prominent side of this system, by which it ex-
poses itself to attacks, seems to me to be this : It
has often been remarked, that no person condemned
to death for murder has ever been known to complain that he was being punished too severely or
unjustly ; and if any one should so complain, all
sensible men would laugh in his face. Now, apart
from the laughing in his face, this is so very true
that a murderer could not say he were suffering too
much or unjustly, even though he should have been
sentenced to the gallows by a government which
was entirely ignorant of his crime of murder, and
which was hanging him altogether unjustly. There
is nothing more true than that we are forced to confess : In a moral world, governed by an all-knowing

judge, and according to moral laws, no one who is treated according to the same law which he himself established suffers unjustly ; and this confession, which forces itself upon all men, is based upon a categorical imperative. Hence, the question is not at all whether *the murderer* suffers unjustly, when he also loses his life in a violent manner ; but the question is : Whence does any other mortal derive the right to personify this moral rule of the world, and to punish the criminal according to his deserts ? A system which asserts the supreme ruler of a state to have this right is undoubtedly compelled to say that the title to it is beyond demonstration, and hence to call it a right given by God. Such a system is, therefore, bound to consider the monarch as the visible representative of God in this world, and to consider all government as a theocracy. In the Jewish theocracy, the doctrine was, therefore, eye for eye, tooth for tooth, and very properly.

PILLORY, DAMAGES, ETC.

He who maliciously defames another citizen, naturally defames himself, for he renders himself unfit for the confidence of others. But since the state owes retribution to the one who has been innocently slandered, it must make public the defamation of the slanderer.

Pillories are a means to call the attention of the public to this defamation, and to symbolize infamy. They must be as little painful as possible, and are a punishment in themselves ; hence they must not be connected with other punishments, unless, indeed, when a crime has been committed which involves the infamy of the criminal, as, for instance, burglary. For the common criminal does not become infamous when there are hopes of his reform ; and if there are none, if he is an outlaw, it would be no punishment to put him on a pillory.

The one who has been injured must receive damages in all cases. He holds the state directly responsible for his damages, since the state guaranteed him protection against all injuries ; and the state holds the criminal responsible. It is clear that the injured party must not be made to pay the costs of the proceedings. What does he pay his taxes for ? The state must hold the criminal responsible. When the criminal is outlawed, all his property is, of course, confiscated by the state.

There are two distinct kinds of punishment, as we have seen, such as are based upon a compact, and such as are based upon the absolute nullity of the compact. It is clear that the citizen is obliged to submit to the first class without compulsion, since they are in a certain other respect also his rights, and that he may very properly be compelled to submit to them voluntarily, since there are worse punishments possible, and since the remainder of his property is still to the state a guarantee of his submission to the law. He must, therefore, voluntarily appear at the investigation of his crime, and can be punished if he does not appear. Hence, there is no reason why his body should be taken possession of by law.*

But the guilty person can give no proper guarantee when his crime involves punishments of the second class ; that is to say, when it involves either exclusion from society or deportation to institutions of reform. The reason is, that in the first case he has lost all his rights categorically, and in the second case problematically, that is, unless he reforms. Hence, the state must take possession of the bodies of such offenders. The right of compulsion which the state has commences with the relative property of citizens ; if that is not sufficient, the state takes hold of their absolute property ; and if the guilty person refuses to pay, the state enters his house by force ; and, in the extreme case, the state takes possession of their persons.

* In other words : for all such crimes each citizen has an absolute right of *bail*.—TRANSLATOR'S REMARK.

§ 3

POLICE LAW.

WHAT is the Police? This we can best answer by a deduction of the conception of the police power of the state. The state, as such, has entered into a common compact with its citizens by which each party assumes certain duties and receives certain rights. We have shown the means of connection between the state and the citizens in all cases in which the citizen can and undoubtedly will prefer complaint. But we have also shown up a number of matters regarding which no complaint will be preferred, because the state is officially *obliged* to watch over them. Hence, there must be a peculiar means of connection for these cases between the citizens and the government; and this means of connection is the police power of the government. By its means the reciprocal influence between government and citizens first becomes possible. Hence, it is one of the necessary requirements of a state.

The state has a twofold relation to its subjects: it has duties to perform, namely, to protect their rights; and it has rights, namely, to require their obedience to the laws and the fulfillment of their

duties as citizens. In either case the police power
is the mediator between state and citizens. As the
judicial power is related to positive law in its application to the citizen, so the police power is related
to positive law in its application to the government.
The police furnishes the case of the application of
the law.

It is, as we have said, the duty of the state to
protect the rights of its citizens, and the police
power is the executive power of this protection.
Some persons might object that citizens are very
apt to remind the state themselves when the protection stipulated in the constitution is required.
But very often a damage received can not be made
good ; and it is far more the object of the state to
prevent attacks upon the rights of its citizens, than
to punish attacks after they have been committed.
Hence, the arrangements necessary for protecting
and securing the rights of citizens are the first
branch of the police power.

Each citizen must be able to travel throughout
the whole state free and safe from all accidents,
whether he does so by virtue of his right to cultivate the ground, or to purchase products, or to
carry on trade, or to enjoy his capital. The greater
the number of men is who are gathered at one
place, the more effective must be the arrangements
for protecting them. Hence, armed police-squads
are necessary in the streets, and on the roads where
roads are unsafe. These subordinate officials have
no judicial power, but simply the power to tempo-

rarily arrest suspicious persons. They are to be held heavily responsible for all crimes committed within their precinct.

This protection of the safety of life and property involves also a superintendence of roads. Each citizen has the right to demand good roads or streets, for the state has guaranteed to him the speediest and most comfortable mode of carrying on business, or most agreeably enjoying his justly acquired gains. Hence, signs must be put up at all unsafe places. Persons who are injured at places which have no such signs are entitled to redress from the state, for the state has guaranteed to them *security in all acts not prohibited by law.* Persons who are injured where such signs have been put up have no redress ; but neither must they become liable to a fine, for each person is master of his own body.

This protective power of the police involves, likewise, superintendence of doctors and apothecaries. The examination of physicians is best left to the medical colleges, who in this examination are, therefore, considered as government officials. Quackery, etc., must be prohibited, that is, *for those who carry it on ;* but not for those who make use of it ; for each person is master of his own life.

The police must also afford protection against robbery, against fire, and against the overflowing of rivers, etc., etc. All this is the absolute duty of the state, and is not merely to be regarded as a benefit conferred.

But besides this direct protection by means of

the police, the state has also the right, for the same purpose of protecting the rights of its citizens, to pass certain laws tending to facilitate the police superintendence, the discovery of guilty persons, and the general security of citizens. These laws are called *Police Laws*, to distinguish them from the real *Civil Laws*. For, whereas the latter laws prohibit merely the *actual violation* of the fundamental compact, the police laws are made to prevent the *possibility* of such violation. Thus, the civil laws prohibit acts which directly interfere with the rights of others, as, for instance, theft, robbery, assault, etc., and hence these laws are not likely to be considered unjust by any one. The police laws, however, prohibit acts which may appear perfectly indifferent, and which in themselves harm no one, but which are calculated to facilitate the wronging of others, and to render difficult the protection of the rights of citizens by the state. Hence, these laws, the violation whereof is not injurious in itself, are often considered unfair by people who do not comprehend their peculiar nature, and the right of a state to pass them has often been doubted. But the right and the duty of the state to pass such laws appear clearly from the police power of the state. Let me illustrate the matter by an example : If a citizen carries arms, he thereby does not directly violate the rights of any other citizen ; for what can it matter to the other citizen what I choose to carry about my person ? But my carrying arms facilitates the injuring of other citizens ; and hence the state has, in my opinion, a perfect right to prohibit the carrying of arms. Nay, it would have the right to prohibit the harboring of arms in my house, if the state could only be sure that I would never require to use them in self-defence. (In the Roman Republic it was prohibited to appear armed in the city ; and the general who awaited the honor of his triumph was required to remain outside of the city until the day of his solemn entrance, or, if he chose to enter before, the law required him to lay aside his arms and renounce the expected honor.) At any rate, the state has the undoubted right to prohibit the possession of certain weapons, such as airguns, which seem especially made for assassination, and are not necessary for self-defence.

Another instance : It would be a very proper police law to prohibit citizens from walking the streets at night without a light. The object of this law is that each citizen may be easily recognized by the policeman. True, by walking without a light, the rights of no citizen are injured ; but in the darkness it is much easier to injure a citizen, and this possibility is to be removed by the police law.

He who violates a police law must suffer all the disagreeable consequences which may result to him, and is, moreover, liable to a fine.

The chief principle of a well-regulated police is this : *That each citizen shall be at all times and places, when it may be necessary, recognized as this or that particular person.* No one must remain unknown to the police. This can be attained with certainty only in the following manner : Each one must always carry a pass with him, signed by his immediate government official, in which his person is accurately described. There must be no exception to this rule. In the case of important persons, who can afford to pay for it, it may be well to use their portrait (photograph) in the place of word-descriptions, which are always more or less insufficient. No person should be received at any place who can not thus make known by his pass his last place of residence and his name. But in order not to interfere with the innocent enjoyment which may arise from temporary *incognito*, policemen should be strictly prohibited from ever demanding the exhibition of such passes from mere curiosity. It is only to be required when necessary to identify the person.

The state does not know what passes in the house, but it does take cognizance of what happens in the streets, which, after all, we must pass in order to get into the house. Hence, the citizens can not assemble in a house without the knowledge of the police ; and the police have thus not only the power, but also the right to prevent such assemblages—since the streets are under their superintendence—if they excite suspicion. If enough men gather together to possibly endanger public safety, which is always the case when the number is large enough to resist effectually the armed power of the government at such a place, the police has the right to ask of them their intentions, and to watch that these intentions alone are carried out. The house-right ceases in such cases ; or, if the owner of a house does not wish to give up that right, he can assemble the masses in a public house, where house-right does not exist. Gatherings of the people in the streets, market-places, etc., belong to the same class, and may likewise be prevented by the police, or at least watched. The state may properly arrange this matter by providing that, when a certain number of people gather together, they must notify the police of their intention, so that the police may act understandingly.

In regard to the security of absolute property, two more questions are to be answered : firstly, how is the counterfeiting of drafts to be prevented ? and secondly, how the counterfeiting of gold and silver ? I am the more inclined to reply to these questions, since I can thus illustrate how that which is deemed impossible is easy enough for a well-regulated police.

Firstly, concerning forged drafts. I refer here only to those which are transferable by indorsements. In large cities, such drafts often change owners many times in a day. Perhaps the persons through whose hands the draft passes know each other not at all or only slightly. Now, it is very true that merchants do not usually take a draft unless they know the maker or makers, and his or their signature to the draft. But signatures can be forged ; and the simple fact is, that forged drafts are passed, and that hence it must be possible to cheat by means of them. The forgery is finally discovered. But how is it now possible to find out the man who is guilty of the forgery, and to get hold of him? There is no difficulty about the matter under such police laws as we have described.

The names of those through whose hands the draft has passed are written on its back. Under present circumstances, however, people can easily adopt false names, and it is impossible, therefore, to trace them. According to our proposition, each person who indorses the draft must show by his pass that he is this particular person, and where he resides. The one who receives the draft makes a note of this by writing on the back of the draft over the name, "Pass from ——," naming the government official who has issued the pass. These few additional words are all that is necessary to make known the true name and residence of the indorser.

But how can the indorser be found again, if the draft, after the lapse of some time, should turn out to have been forged by him? Under our police laws, no one can leave one place without announcing his next place of residence, which must be marked on the pass and recorded in the books. No other place receives him except the one mentioned in his pass, and when he leaves that place again the same rule holds good.

But how if he is a foreigner or travels abroad? All police-states, particularly those who are also commercial, must come to an agreement about this matter, so that the forger may be arrested in any country. The pass of a state which has not entered into this agreement must not be recognized, and hence people who present passes from such a state can not have their drafts cashed. Such an understanding would force all commercial states to adopt this agreement.

But how if some one should also forge such a pass ? The forging of passes ought to be made impossible ; to accomplish which there are doubtless ample means. For instance, by a paper or parchment prepared exclusively for this purpose, as was used for the French *assignats*, the secret of making which must be known only to the government. But can not this paper be forged, as was done in that same case of the French *assignats ?* It was done in that case, because a great interest, as well of pecuniary gain as of political animosity, was to be satisfied ; and because the forged paper could be used hundred-fold. But when only *one* pass is to be forged, will any one go to all that trouble ? Not likely, unless a forged draft of a very large amount is to be passed. But the dangers which would accompany such an undertaking would in all probability deter from the costs and trouble of it.

As regards the second point, the counterfeiting of money, there is this to be considered : The state guarantees the value of the money, and whoever accepts a piece of money accepts it on the faith of the state, the seal whereof is stamped upon it.

Hence, the state must guarantee to each citizen the genuineness of the money, and whoever is cheated, *without any fault of his own*, by counterfeited money, should be justly indemnified by the state, and have his false money exchanged for genuine money.

But when is a citizen cheated *without any fault of his own?* Under what conditions is it to be believed that he could not distinguish the false money from the genuine? It is a part of the education of each citizen to learn to know money, and it should be held as a rule that counterfeit money can not be readily recognized as such when *many* citizens are cheated by it.

It is, therefore, in the immediate interest of the state, and a part of its police laws, to discover counterfeiters and to prevent the counterfeiting of money. How is this to be done? It can not be accomplished by means of passes; for no one can say from whom he has received certain pieces of money, unless he has received them in very large quantities. Hence, it must be accomplished by keeping a strict watch over the materials which may be used in counterfeiting coin, and which chemistry can designate, and by providing that such materials shall not be issued except to such as *present their pass* and give notice of the use they intend to make of them. This is all the easier for the state, since the state is exclusive possessor of all mines, as has been shown above.

Besides these *duties*, the government has the *right* to see that the laws—civil laws as well as police laws—are properly executed. The state has to indemnify for each offense which is committed within its limits, and to bring the offender to justice. It is clear, however, that no particular or additional arrangements are necessary for this guardianship over the laws; for, in each case of such violation of the laws, there is some one who must be protected, and hence all the arrangements made for protection cover these cases.

The exclusive condition of the efficiency of legislation, and hence of the whole state organization, is this, that each citizen shall know beforehand that, if he commits a crime, he will be surely discovered and punished in the manner prescribed by law. For, if the criminal can entertain hopes of escaping detection, what is to deter him from committing a crime? In such a case, we merely continue to live, no matter how wise the laws we have, in our previous condition of nature, wherein each depends upon the good intention of the other; and it is injustice to punish the detected criminal according to the strict letter of the law, since we allowed him to hope that he would escape unpunished, like all the other criminals whom he knows to have escaped unpunished. How could a law deter him which he could not but consider null and void? The sarcasm which the common people love to levy against our laws and government—namely, that they do not punish men for having committed crimes, but for having been foolish enough to allow themselves to be detected—is just and appropriate. It is an indispensable requirement addressed to the police, as the servant of the government, that each guilty person, without exception, should be brought to trial.

I have heard many objections raised to the possibility of satisfying this requirement. If such objections were grounded, I should not hesitate to draw the conclusion : In that case government and law are equally impossible among men ; all so-called states are nothing else and never will be any thing else but the oppression of the weak by the powerful under the pretense of law ; and the science of law is nothing but the science of how the stronger may be unjust without injury to themselves, as Montesquieu ironically describes it. But is there really any valid reason for this assertion of the impossibility of satisfying that requirement ? Whence does that assertion arise ? It arises from this, that the conception of a state as here established, that is, as an organic whole, is not firmly entertained, but is constantly darkened by the image of our modern states. In our modern states, as they are constitu ted now, it would, of course, be impossible to bring to trial the author of every offense ; or if it could be done, that is to say, if some one state should make use of some of the police regulations suggested by us, it would involve an injustice which no people would be content to suffer. For a state wherein disorder and injustice rule, the government can maintain itself only by also allowing the people a good deal of disorder, provided that disorder does not injure the government itself.

The source of all evils in our present states, as they are constituted, is *disorder*, and the impossibility to produce order.   The fact that it is so very difficult to discover a criminal arises solely from the fact that there are so many persons in a state who have no fixed position, and about whom the state does not concern itself.   In a state such as we have described, each citizen has his fixed position ; and the police know pretty well where each citizen is, and what he does at every hour of the day. Each one must work, and each one who does work has enough to live.   Loafers (*chevaliers d'industrie*) are not tolerated in any part of the state.   By means of his pass, each citizen can be identified at a moment.   Crime is something very unusual in such a state ; and is preceded by a certain unusual emotion, which the police, quickly observing, proceed to watch.   I, for my part, can not see how, in such a state, an offense and the offender can remain undiscovered.

It is also to be considered, that, with such a police establishment, detectives or spies are not needed. Secrecy is always petty, low, and immoral.   Each one should have the face to do before the whole world whatever he dares to do at all.   Moreover, to *whom* could the state intrust such a dishonorable occupation ?   Shall the state itself encourage infamy and immorality ?   If the state authorizes secrecy in the conduct of some men, who will guarantee that these men may not make use of that secrecy for their own purposes and for the commission of crimes by themselves ?

Again : Why should a government secretly place a watch over its citizens ? In order that they may not believe themselves watched. But why should they not believe themselves watched ? That they may discover their thoughts respecting the government and its plans, and may thus become their own betrayers ; or may betray whatever they know of other secret and illegal acts. The former is necessary only where government and citizens live in perpetual war with each other ; where the citizens are unjustly oppressed, and seek to regain their freedom again by employing all the means and tricks of war : the latter is necessary only where the police are not watchful enough.

The Paris chief of police, who proposed to clothe his detectives in uniform, became the laughing-stock of a corrupt people, and saved his life thereby. But in my opinion he evinced healthy common sense. In a state organization such as we have described, the police official can be uniformed. They are quite as much the venerable witnesses of innocence as the accusers of crime. Why should honesty hate the eye of watchfulness ?

FIRST APPENDIX

TO THE

SCIENCE OF RIGHTS.

———◆———

FUNDAMENTAL PRINCIPLES

OF THE

RIGHTS OF FAMILY.

DEDUCTION OF MARRIAGE.

I.

PRECISELY as we were compelled to deduce the necessity of the coexistence of rational beings, and their relation to a sensuous world, in order to obtain an object for the application of the conception of rights, so shall we now be compelled to obtain a knowledge of the nature of marriage by its deduction, in order to be enabled to apply the conception of rights to it understandingly. It is not to be understood as if the conception of rights gave rise to marriage ; for marriage is not merely a legal association like the state, but rather a natural and moral association. Hence, the following deduction is not legal, but is necessary in a Science of Rights, as giving an insight into the legal propositions which follow it.

Nature has based her end of propagating the human race upon the existence of a natural impulse in two different sexes, which impulse seems to exist only for its own sake, and to crave only its own satisfaction. That impulse is itself end of our nature, although it is only means for nature in gene-

ral. While men have no other object than to satisfy this impulse, the natural consequences of this
satisfaction result in the end which nature had in
view, without any additional coöperation of man.

The ground why nature must separate two different sexes, through the union whereof alone the
propagation of the race is possible, I shall suggest
here only in outlines, since it is an investigation
not properly belonging here. The formation of a
being of its own kind is the last degree of creative
power in organic nature ; and that power necessarily works whenever the conditions of its causality are given. If these conditions, therefore, were
always given, nature would be an everlasting transition into other forms, but never a permanency of
the same form ; would be an everlasting Becoming,
but never a Being ; nay, even transition and becoming would be impossible, since there would be
nothing to change and to become ; all of which is,
indeed, an unthinkable and contradictory conception.

If a nature was to be possible, it was necessary
that the species should have another organic existence besides that of the species, and yet that it
should remain species, so as to be able to propagate
itself. This was possible only by separating the
organic power, which forms the species, into two
absolutely connecting halves, as it were, which only
in their union would form an itself propagating
whole. In this separation that organic power forms
only the individual. The individuals are and form

the species only, (for to be and to form is the same in organic nature,) in so far as they are united and can be united. The individual is permanent only as a tendency to form the species. Only thus did rest and permanency of power enter nature, and with that permanency *form*, and made it nature ; and hence this law of a division into two separate sexes necessarily pervades all nature.

II.

The particular determinedness of this institution of nature is this, that in the satisfying of the impulse, or in the promotion of the end of nature, so far as the real act of generation is concerned, the one sex keeps purely active, and the other purely passive.

The ground of this determinedness also can be discovered. The system of all the conditions for the generation of a body of the same species had to be completely united somewhere, and, when put in motion, to develop itself after its own laws. The sex which contains these complete conditions is called throughout all nature the *female* sex. Only the first moving principle could be separated from it. The sex in which this principle generates itself, apart from the substance to be vitalized by it, is called throughout all nature the *male* sex.

III.

The character of reason is absolute self-activity; pure passivity for the sake of passivity contradicts reason, and utterly cancels it. Hence, it is not against reason that the one sex should propose to itself the satisfaction of its sexual impulse as an end in itself, since it can be satisfied through activity; but it is absolutely against reason that the other sex should propose to itself the satisfaction of its sexual impulse as an end, because in that case it would make a pure passivity its end. Hence, the female sex is either not rational even in its tendencies, which contradicts our presupposition that all men should be rational, or this tendency can not be developed in that sex in consequence of its peculiar nature, which is a self-contradiction, since it assumes a tendency in nature which nature does not accept; or, finally, that sex can never propose to itself the satisfaction of its sexual impulse as its end. Such an end and rationality utterly cancel each other in that sex.

Nevertheless, the sexual impulse of this female sex, as well as its manifestation and satisfaction, are part of the plan of nature. Hence it is necessary that the sexual impulse should manifest itself in woman under another form; and, in order to be conformable to reason, it must appear as an impulse to activity; and as a characteristic impulse of nature, it must appear as an activity exclusively appertaining to the female sex.

Since our whole subsequent theory rests upon this proposition, I shall endeavor to place it in its proper light, and to disarm possible misunderstanding of its meaning

Firstly : we speak here of *nature* and of an *impulse of nature ;* that is, of something which a woman will find in herself as something given, original, and not to be explained by any previous act of her own, nor originated by any application of her freedom whatever ; something which woman will thus find in herself as soon as its two conditions, reason and activity of the sexual impulse, exist. But we do not at all deny the possibility that woman may not sink below this condition of nature, or may not through freedom elevate herself above it, which elevation, however, is itself not much better than the sinking below it. A woman sinks below nature when she degrades herself to irrationality ; in which condition the sexual impulse may manifest itself in consciousness in its true form, and may become a well-considered object of activity. A woman elevates herself above her nature when the satisfaction of the sexual impulse is not an end for her, neither in its coarse form nor in that form which it receives in a well-formed female soul ; hence, when it is considered by her as means for another end, which she has with free consciousness proposed to herself. Unless this other end is to be an utterly wicked and degrading end—as, for instance, if she should have done it for the purpose of becoming a married woman, and in view of a pros-

c c

pect of a secure income, thus making of her person the means to obtain an enjoyment—we must assume it to be the same end which nature has in view, that is, to have children, and which some such women, indeed, claim to have been their motive. But since she could attain this object with every possible man, and since thus there is no ground to be discovered in her principle why she should have chosen precisely this man and none other for that purpose, we must assume, as, after all, the least degrading motive, that she chose this man because he was the first one she could get, which surely does not evince great personal self-respect. But even apart from this grave circumstance, and admitting for the moment that such an end would justify the resolve to cohabit with a man, the serious question would still remain: Whether the end will be produced by such means, or whether children are really begotten by the resolve to beget them?

We hope this plainness will be pardoned in our endeavor to show up certain dangerous sophistries in all their nakedness, by means of which sophistries many seek to palliate the repudiation of their true destination, and to perpetuate it forever.

Let me characterize this whole relation in an image: The female sex stands one step lower in the arrangement of nature than the male sex; the female sex is the object of a power of the male sex, and no other arrangement was possible if both sexes were to be connected. But at the same time both sexes, as moral beings, ought to be equal. To make this possible, a new faculty, utterly wanting in the male sex, had to be given to the female sex. This faculty is the form in which the sexual impulse appears to woman, whereas to man it appears in its true form.

Man may confess to himself that impulse, and may seek its satisfaction without thereby losing his self-respect or the respect of others. I speak, of course, of the sexual impulse in its original condition; for a man who should propose to himself the satisfaction of that impulse for its own sake with a loving wife, would show himself to be a coarse character, whereof we shall discover the ground hereafter. But a woman can not confess that impulse to herself. Man may court, but not woman. A woman who were to do so would exhibit the highest self-contempt. For a refusal received by a man signifies merely, "I will not submit myself to thee!" and this may be borne. But a refusal received by a woman would signify, "I will not accept the submission thou hast offered me!" and this is insupportable. It is nonsense to apply legal arguments in this case. If some women claim that they ought to have the same right to court as men, we would answer: "No one disputes you that right; why, then, do you not make use of it?" The truth is, such arguments are as absurd as it would be to question whether man has the same right to fly as the birds have. Of course he has; so let him fly!

This one distinction constitutes, indeed, the whole

difference of the sexes. It is this natural constitution of woman which gives rise to female modesty,
which modesty is by no means developed to the
same extent in the male sex. Vulgar men some-
times boast of their deeds of voluptuousness; but
even in the times of the worst demoralization into
which the female sex has repeatedly sunk, and then
by far exceeded the demoralization of the men,
women have never been known to do so; and even
the prostitute will rather confess that she carries on
her horrible trade from lust of gain than from voluptuousness.

IV.

Woman can not confess to herself that she gives
herself up—and since, in a rational being, every
thing is only in so far as it arises in consciousness—
woman can not give herself up to the sexual impulse merely to satisfy her own impulse. But
since she can give herself up only in obedience to
an impulse, this impulse must assume in woman the
character of an impulse to satisfy the man. Woman
becomes, in this act, the means for the end of another, because she can not be her own end without
renouncing her ultimate end—the dignity of reason! This dignity she maintains, although she becomes means, because she voluntarily makes herself means in virtue of a noble natural impulse—
love!

Love, therefore, is the form in which the sexual

impulse appears to woman. But love is, to sacrifice one's self for the sake of another not in consequence of a reasoning, but in consequence of a feeling. Mere sexual impulse should never be called love ; to do so is a vulgar abuse of language, calculated to cause all that is noble in human nature to be forgotten. In fact, my opinion is that nothing should be called love but what we have just now described. Man *originally* does not feel love, but sexual impulse ; and love in man is not an original, but a *communicated, derived* impulse, namely, an impulse developed through connection with a loving woman ; and has, moreover, quite a different form in man to what it has in woman. Love, the noblest of all natural impulses, is inborn only in woman ; and only through woman does it, like many other social impulses, become the common property of mankind. The sexual impulse received this moral form of love in woman, because in its original form it would have canceled all morality in woman. Love is the closest point of union of nature and reason ; it is the only link wherein nature connects with reason, and hence it is the most excellent of all that is natural. The Moral Law requires that man should forget himself in the other ; but love even sacrifices itself to the other.

Let me state it concisely : In an uncorrupted woman the sexual impulse does not manifest itself at all, but only love ; and this love is the natural impulse of a woman to satisfy a man. It is certainly an impulse which urgently requires to be satisfied, but its being thus satisfied is not the satisfaction of the woman. On the contrary, it is the satisfaction of the man, and for woman it is only the satisfaction of her heart. Her only requirement is to love and to be loved. Only thus does the impulse which the woman feels to sacrifice receive that character of freedom and activity which it must have in order to be rational. Perhaps there does not exist a man who does not feel the absurdity to turn this around and to assume in man a similar impulse to satisfy a need of woman; a need, in fact, which he can neither presuppose in woman nor consider himself as its tool without feeling himself disgraced to the innermost depths of his soul.

Hence, also, woman in the sexual union is not in every sense means for the object of the man. She is means for her own end, to satisfy her heart; and she is means for the end of the man only in so far as physical satisfaction is concerned.

The attempt to hold up this mode of regarding woman as deceptive, and to say, for instance, "After all, it is only the sexual impulse which impels woman, under the deceitful cloak of love," is a dogmatic error. For woman sees no further, and her nature goes no further, than love ; hence woman *is* only love. It does not matter to woman whether man—who does not possess that female innocence, nor is intended to possess it, and who may become conscious of all that is within him—proceeds to analyze that impulse or not ; it suffices to woman that the sexual impulse is to a woman only love.

If women were men, it would certainly be otherwise.

V.

Woman, in making herself the means to satisfy
man, gives up her personality; and she receives
this and her whole dignity back again only by thus
making herself means to satisfy man from love for
a particular one.

If this sentiment ever should cease; if woman
ever should cease to regard in the man whom she
satisfied the most lovable of all his sex, this
thought alone would make her contemptible in her
own eyes. If it were possible that he should ever
not be in her eyes the most lovable of all his sex,
then the presumption would be, that in giving herself up to him she gave herself up only from a concealed natural impulse to give herself up to the
first one who might come—a thought which would,
doubtless, dishonor her in her own eyes. As surely, therefore, as she thus gives herself up with
full preservation of her dignity, she does it under
the presupposition that her present feelings can
never change, but that they are as eternal as she is
herself. The woman who gives herself up once,
gives herself up forever.

VI.

The woman who thus surrenders her personality,
and yet retains her full dignity in so doing, neces-

sarily gives up to her lover all that she has. For, if she retained the least for her own self, she would thereby confess that it had a higher value for her than her own person ; and this undoubtedly would be a lowering of that person. Her own dignity requires that she should give herself up entirely as she is, and lives to her choice and should utterly lose herself in him. The least consequence is, that she should renounce to him all her property and all her rights. Henceforth she has life and activity only under his eyes and in his business. She has ceased to lead the life of an individual ; her life has become a part of the life of her lover. (This is aptly characterized by her assuming his name.)

VII

The position of the man, meanwhile, is this : Since he may confess all to himself, and hence finds in himself the whole fullness of humanity, he is able to overlook his whole relation to woman, as woman herself can never overlook it. He, therefore, sees how an originally free being voluntarily submits itself to him with unlimited confidence, and that she makes not only her whole external fate, but also her internal peace of soul and moral character —at least her own faith in it—dependent upon him, since the faith of woman in herself and in her own innocence and virtue depends upon this, that she may never cease to esteem and love her husband above all others of his sex.

As the moral impulse of woman manifests itself as love, so in man that impulse manifests itself as *generosity.* His first wish is to be master ; but if another being surrenders itself to him in perfect confidence, he lays aside all his power. For to be strong against the vanquished is fit only for the weak-hearted who can not oppose force to resistance.

In consequence of this natural generosity, man, in his relation to his wife, is compelled, first of all, to be worthy of esteem, since her whole peace of mind depends upon his being held in esteem by her. Nothing so irrevocably kills the love of the wife as the meanness or infamy of her husband. Indeed, the female sex will pardon in our sex every thing but cowardice and weakness of character. The ground of this is by no means a selfish calculation upon our protection ; but solely the impossibility to submit to such men, as woman's destiny nevertheless requires her to submit.

The peace of the wife depends upon her being utterly submitted to her husband, and having no other will than his own. Now, since he knows this to be so, his character of manly generosity, which he can not deny without denying his own nature and dignity, requires that he should make it as light as possible for her to do so. This he can not do by allowing his wife to rule him ; for the pride of her love consists in being and seeming to be submitted and not knowing otherwise. Men who submit themselves to the rule of their wives thereby make themselves contemptible in the eyes of their wives, and destroy all their matrimonial happiness. He can do it only by attentively discovering her wishes, and causing to be done, as if it were through his own will, what he knows she would most gladly have done. It is not to be taken that he thus gratifies her notions and whims merely in order to have them gratified, but that he has the far higher purpose of thereby making it easier for her to love her husband always above every thing, and of thus retaining her innocence in her own eyes. It can not fail but that the wife—whose heart can not be satisfied by an obedience which calls for no sacrifice on her part—will seek to discover, on her part, the concealed higher wishes of her husband, in order to satisfy them at some sacrifices. For the greater the sacrifice, the more perfect is the satisfaction of her heart. Hence arises connubial *tenderness ;* that is, tenderness of sentiments, and of the whole relation. Each party wishes to give up its personality, so that the other one may rule alone. Each finds content only in the satisfaction of the other ; the exchange of hearts and wills becomes perfect. It is only in connection with a loving woman that the heart of the man opens to love, to the love which confidingly surrenders and loses itself in the beloved object ; it is only in the tie which connects the wife with the husband that she learns generosity and conscious self-sacrifice ; and thus the tie unites them closer every day of their wedded life.

COROLLARIA.

1. In the union of both sexes, and hence in the realization of man as a *whole*, or as a completed pro· duct of nature, but also *only* in this union, is there to be found an *external* impulse to virtue. Man is compelled by his natural impulse of generosity to be noble and venerable, because the fate of a free being which surrendered itself to him in full confidence depends upon his being so. Woman is compelled to observe all her duties by her inborn modesty. She can not act contrary to reason in any manner, because it would lead her to suspect herself of having acted so in the chief manner, and that she had chosen her husband, not from love—the most insupportable thought to woman—but merely as a means to satisfy her sexual impulse. The man in whom there still lingers generosity, and the woman in whom there still dwells modesty, are open to the utmost degree of culture ; but both are on the sure path to all vices when the one becomes mean and the other shameless, as indeed experience invariably shows it to be the case.

We have, therefore, also solved here the problem : How the human race can be led to virtue through nature. This can be done only by restoring the natural relation between both sexes. Moral education of mankind is possible only from this point.

2. Such a union as we have described is called a *marriage*. Marriage is a *complete union* of two

persons of both sexes, based upon the sexual impulse, and having its end in itself.

It has its *ground* in the sexual impulse in either sex, that is, for the external observation of the philosopher ; but it is not necessary that either of the persons who desire to conclude marriage should be conscious of it. A woman can never confess this to be the case. She can only confess the motive to be love. Nor is the continuance of marriage in any way conditioned by the satisfaction of this impulse ; for that end may vanish utterly, and the marriage relation may, nevertheless, continue in its whole intensity.

Philosophers have hitherto considered it necessary to assign some end to marriage, and have specified that end variously. But marriage has no other end than itself ; it is its own end. The marriage relation is the true mode of existence of grown persons of both sexes, required even by nature. In this relation all man's faculties develop ; but out of it many, and among them the most remarkable faculties of man, remain uncultivated. Precisely as the whole existence of man has no relation to any sensuous end, so neither has its necessary mode, marriage.

Marriage is a union between *two* persons—*one* man and *one* woman. A woman who has given herself up to one, can not give herself up to a second, for her whole dignity requires that she should belong only to this one. Again, a man who has to observe the slightest wish of one woman can not conform to the contradictory wishes of many. Polygamy presupposes that women are not rational beings like men, but merely willess and lawless means to gratify man. Such is, indeed, the doctrine of the religious legislation which tolerates polygamy. This religion has—probably without being clearly conscious of the grounds—drawn one-sided conclusions from the destination of woman to remain passive. Polyandry is utterly against nature, and hence very rare. If it were not a condition of utter brutishness, and if it could presuppose any thing, it would have to presuppose that there is no reason and no dignity of reason.

The union of matrimony is in its nature inseparable and eternal, and is necessarily concluded as being eternal. A woman can not presuppose that she will ever cease to love her husband above all of his sex without abandoning her personal dignity ; nor can the husband presuppose that he will ever cease to love his wife above all of her sex without abandoning his manly generosity. Both give themselves to each other forever, because they give themselves to each other wholly.

3. Marriage is, therefore, no invented custom, nor an arbitrary institution, but a relation necessarily and perfectly determined through nature and reason in their union. Perfectly determined, I say, that is, only a marriage such as we have described, and absolutely no other union of both sexes for the satisfaction of the sexual impulse is permitted by nature and reason.

It is not the business of the Science of Rights, but of the far higher laws of nature and reason to establish and determine marriage. To look upon marriage as merely a legal relation leads to improper and immoral conceptions. The reason why, nevertheless, it has been done, may be found, perhaps, in the consideration that marriage, like all that is determined by the conception of rights, is a living together of free beings. But it would be bad if this cohabitation had no higher ground, and no other regulative principle, than a law of compulsion. Marriage must exist before we can speak of any matrimonial rights, precisely as man must exist before we can speak of rights at all. The Science of Rights neither asks how matrimony originated nor where men came from. After marriage has been deduced, as has just now been done, the question first arises as to how far the conception of rights is applicable to it, what law disputes may enter it, and how these disputes ought to be decided ; or, since we teach here an applied Science of Rights, what rights and duties the state has in regard to the relation of both sexes in general, and particularly in regard to the marriage relation. We now enter upon this investigation.

LAW OF MARRIAGE.

I.

THE conception of personality involves the conception of all the rights of man, and hence it is the first and highest duty of the state to protect the personality of its citizens. A woman loses her personality and her whole dignity when she is compelled to submit herself to the sexual lust of a man without love. It is, therefore, the absolute duty of the state to protect its female citizens against this compulsion, a duty which is not at all based upon any particular arbitrary agreement, but upon the simple nature of the case, and the immediate principles of municipal law—a duty as holy and inviolable as the duty to protect the life of citizens, for it is the internal, moral life of the female citizens which is thus to be protected.

II.

Such a compulsion may be effected upon a woman by immediate physical force, in which case it is called *rape.* Of course, rape is a crime ; for it is a most brutal attack upon the personality of a woman, and hence upon all her rights.

The state has the right and duty to protect its female citizens against this compulsion, and does so partly through the watchfulness of the police, partly by providing for its punishment. This crime evinces, first of all, brutality in the criminal, making him incapable of living among human society. Violence of passion is no excuse, but, on the contrary, increases the crime. For a man who has not control over himself is a wild beast, and society, not being able to tame him, must not tolerate him in its midst. It evinces, moreover, an unlimited contempt for, and neglect of, all human rights. Some laws punish rape by death, and a legislation which recognizes the punishment of death certainly acts logically in prescribing it as a proper punishment for this crime. According to my system, I should send such men to the colonies for correction ; for, although their crime is equal to murder so far as the contempt of human rights is concerned, still it is not impossible for men to live together with such criminals.

Restitution is, of course, impossible. For how can we restore to the unfortunate woman the consciousness that she may give up, at some future time, her whole untouched personality to the man she loves ? Nevertheless, restitution must be made so far as it is possible, and since the criminal can give to the offended woman nothing but money, and since she can receive from him nothing but money, I should vote that he be compelled to deliver all his property to the woman he has violated.

Unmarried women are, as we shall see hereafter, under the control of their parents ; married women under that of their husbands. Hence, the parents or husbands will be the plaintiffs in such cases. In the former instance, if the parents should refuse to prosecute, the woman might do so herself, but not if the husband should so refuse ; for women are submitted to their parents only conditionally, but to their husbands unconditionally.

III.

Or such a compulsion may be effected upon the female citizen *indirectly* through the moral influence of her parents or relations, in compelling her to consent to a marriage for which she has no inclination, either by means of harsh treatment or of persuasion. Harsh treatment is, of course, a legal offense ; but is persuasion also one ? In this case—although in no other possible case—persuasion is an indictable offense. For whereas in all other cases you can properly ask, Why did you allow yourself to be persuaded ? this question is not admissible here. The ignorant, innocent daughter has no knowledge of love, knows not at all the nature of the connection she is inveigled into ; she is, therefore, cheated, and used as a means for the ends of her parents or relatives.

DD

This kind of compulsion is the most dangerous, and far more insulting than violence, if not in form at least in its results. For, in the case of rape, woman, after all, regains her freedom afterward ; but in the case of a compulsion of this kind, woman is usually cheated for her whole lifetime out of the noblest and sweetest sentiment, that of love, and out of her true female dignity and whole character, and lowered completely and forever to a tool.

It can not, therefore, be at all a matter of doubt whether the state has the right and duty to protect its young female citizens against this kind of compulsion, by severe laws and strict vigilance. The only question is, Who is to prefer the complaint, since the unmarried daughter stands under the authority of her parents, who are her legal guardians, and who will not be likely to prefer complaint against themselves ? The solution of this difficulty we shall find when we come to see that the daughter escapes that parental authority the moment she marries. Hence, the law can very properly provide that a daughter shall become independent the moment her parents propose marriage to her, and shall, therefore, be full master of her own rights in such case.

The final decision of the state in such a case would be this : Parents who have abused their power for the purpose of enslaving their children during their whole lives, must be deprived of that power, and the children, together with their inheritance, must be placed under the protection of the state. But since it might, nevertheless, happen, that young and inexperienced daughters, not accustomed to disobey parental authority, would rather submit than prefer public complaint, the state ought to retain the right to officially interfere on its own account in such cases, even when no complaint has been preferred.

IV.

It is quite different with the male sex. Firstly: No man can be compelled, in the true sense of the word, to marry, for it is against the nature of the thing. If he is persuaded, it does not signify much, for real love in man does not precede, but follows marriage. But if he knows his own advantage, he will not permit that any woman should be compelled to marry him, since this would be a violation of his human rights, depriving him, as it would, of all prospects of a happy marriage, which he has a right to demand. "Love will come afterward," say many parents. It is certainly to be expected in the case of the man, provided he marries a worthy woman ; but in the case of the woman it is very uncertain ; and it is terrible to sacrifice and degrade a whole human life upon the risk of this bare possibility.

The result of our argument is, that marriage must be an absolutely free act ; and the state, as the protector of the rights of each individual, and particularly of the female sex, has the right and the duty to watch over this freedom of all matrimonial alliances.

V.

This jurisdiction of the state over the freedom of all marriages involves, that the state must recognize and confirm all marriages of its citizens.

Every marriage must have legal validity, that is, it must not infringe upon the rights of the woman, who must give herself up with her free will, and from love. A citizen must be obliged to prove this to the state, unless he wishes to render himself suspicious of having used violence. This proof he can not well furnish otherwise than by causing the woman to declare the marriage to be her own free will before the law. This is done in the marriage ceremony. The " Yes !" of the woman declares in reality only that she has not been forced to the act. For all the other obligations which are entered into in the marriage ceremony are of themselves necessary results of *marriage.* The significance of the husband's " Yes !" we shall investigate later. That he is not compelled in the act appears clearly from his leading the woman to the altar. It is very proper and reasonable that marriages, being based upon and having their existence only in morality, should be celebrated by clergymen ; but in so far as the ceremony has legal validity, the clergyman is an official of the state.

It is beyond comprehension why the state, or the

clergy, should have the right to prohibit marriages between persons of a certain degree of relationship. If nature has provided a prejudice against such mixtures, the laws are superfluous ; but if there is no such natural disgust, then we should not produce it by our laws. It is plausible why some nations should believe such marriages to be an offense to their divinity, but that does not justify the state in prohibiting such marriages. Those who believe such to be the case will not conclude such marriages ; and those who do not believe it, or wish to risk it, will be punished by their own act if the belief of the nation is a true one. It is better to let the gods revenge their own insults.

But, independently of all religious grounds, might there not be political reasons for considering certain marriages as not allowable ? It seems to me that the best that has been said on this subject is to be found in Montesquieu. (*De l'Esprit des Loix,* liv. 26, chap. 14.) It has always been the natural destination of the fathers to watch over the innocence of their children, and to keep them as pure in body and soul as possible. Incessantly occupied with this care, the doing of any thing which might seduce these was furthest removed from them. The same reason implanted a disgust against mutual intercourse in son and daughter ; and is also the source why marriages between cousins are prohibited. For in the first times of our race all children remained at home, and the children of two brothers considered each other as of the same father and mother.

This preservation of chastity in families was under the care of the fathers of the family, but on no account an affair of civil legislation—as an actual violation of the rights of another family—or of police legislation—as merely facilitating such a violation. Hence, those who did not keep such care could merely be taught and educated by the more cultivated people to do so, but could not be compelled by force of law to keep this care over the chastity of their families. Again : the grounded vanishes when the ground vanishes, which in our instance is the living together of many relatives. So far as marriage between parents and children, and between brothers and sisters is concerned, this ground can never vanish in its generality. So far as the marriage of cousins, or of uncles and nieces, etc., is concerned, this ground rarely occurs in the present condition of mankind.

Cohabitation is the real actualization of marriage ; for only through it does the woman submit her whole personality to the husband, and shows him her love, from which the whole described relation between married people emanates. Where this cohabitation has occurred, marriage is always to be presupposed; where it has not occurred, any other union than a union of marriage has taken place. Hence, a mere engagement to be married, whether public or private, does not constitute a marriage ; and the breaking off thereof is not to be considered as a divorce. It may entitle to damages. The innocent party must be reinstated in her previous condition so far as possible. Even the performance of the marriage ceremony, if—as is conformable to propriety—it precedes marriage, does not constitute marriage, but merely legally recognizes in advance the marriage to be culminated.

VI.

Man and wife are intimately united. Their union is a union of hearts and of wills. Hence, it is not to be assumed at all that a law dispute can arise between them. The state, therefore, passes no laws regulating the relation of husband and wife, their whole relation being of a natural and moral, but not of a legal character. Both are one soul, and are presupposed to be as little likely to quarrel with each other or to prefer suit against each other, as one and the same individual is supposed likely to quarrel with himself.

As soon as a dispute arises, the divorce has already been accomplished, and it is only legalized by the judicial decree of divorce.

VII.

The conception of marriage involves the most unlimited subjection of the woman to the will of the husband ; not from legal, but from moral reasons. She must subject herself for the sake of her

own honor. The woman does not belong to herself, but to the man. The state, by recognizing
marriage, that is, by recognizing a relation based
upon something far higher than itself, abandons all
claims to consider the woman as a legal person.
The husband supplies her place ; her marriage
utterly annuls her, so far as the state is concerned,
by virtue of her own necessary will, which the state
has guaranteed. The husband becomes her guarantee in the eye of the law ; or becomes her legal
guardian. He lives in all her public life, and she
retains for herself only a house life.

The guarantee of the man is a natural consequence of the relation. Its limits we shall discover
hereafter. Nevertheless, it might be advisable to
have him so declare himself specially as the guarantee of this woman. The " Yes !" of the man in
the marriage ceremony may be regarded as such a
pledge, and obtains significance indeed, only when
so regarded.

VIII.

The conception of marriage involves, that the
woman who surrenders her personality shall at the
same time surrender the possession of all her property and her exclusive rights in the state. The
state, in recognizing the marriage, recognizes and
guarantees the possessions of the wife to the husband ; that is, *not as against the claims of the wife,*
for a law dispute with her is impossible, under our

presupposition, but against the claims and attacks of *all other citizens.* The husband becomes, in so far as the state is concerned, the sole proprietor of his previous possessions, and of those which his wife held at the time of her marriage.

These possessions of the wife have either been held by her before marriage, in her own name, and are, therefore, known to be hers by the state, in which case they are simply transferred to the husband ; or they are conferred upon her at the time of marriage by the parents, in which case the state is notified by the public transfer at the time. The absolute property, money, and valuables, the state, as we have shown before, takes no cognizance of ; nevertheless, for the sake of a possible future divorce, which necessitates repartition, as we shall see, it is necessary that this absolute property brought by the wife to the husband should also be known to the state, or at least that arrangements should be made whereby it can be proved in future cases of emergency. A sealed document or contract, deposited in a court of record, is sufficient.

The conception of marriage also involves common residence, common labor ; in short, living together. To the state both husband and wife appear as only one person ; what the one does is as valid as if the other had also done it. All public legal acts are performed only by the husband.

IX.

It needs no law of the state to regulate the relations between married persons, or the relations between them and other citizens. My views on laws concerning adultery, in so far as those laws are intended, or appear intended, to secure a property, the property of a man to his wife and of a wife to her husband, I shall express hereafter. Precisely as the state regards husband and wife as only one legal person, externally represented by the husband, and their property as one property, so each citizen also must regard them and their property. In law disputes citizens must deal with the husband ; none have a right to immediately appeal to the wife. The only consequence of this requirement is, that husband and wife are obliged to make their marriage publicly known, which, indeed, is necessary also for moral purposes, to prevent the annoyance illegal, or supposedly illegal, connections might give rise to ; and which is, therefore, most properly made the duty of the clergy.

X.

Originally, that is, so far as his mere natural inclination is concerned, man, it is true, seeks to satisfy his sexual impulse. But when he learns, either before or after marriage, through reflection or through the teachings of others, particularly through actual intercourse with esteemable persons of the female sex, (above all, from his mother,) that woman loves, and ought to give up her personality only from love, his mere natural impulse will become ennobled. He will no longer desire merely to enjoy, but also to be loved. Knowing that woman makes herself contemptible by surrendering herself without love, and that lust in woman is degrading, he no longer will wish to use her as mere means for sensual gratification. He would necessarily have to despise himself were he compelled to look upon himself as the mere tool for the satisfaction of an ignoble impulse. These principles govern all judgments respecting the effect of the wife's adultery upon the husband.

Either such a wife, who gives herself up to another man, does so from pure and whole love. In that case, since love does not admit of partition, she has ceased to love her husband, and the whole relation to him is broken of itself. Moreover, she has degraded herself, although she pleads love, for her first connection with her husband must now appear to her, if she is susceptible to moral feelings, as an ignoble and animal connection from the reasons assigned before. If she allows the sham of her relation to her husband to continue, she degrades herself still further to the utmost extent ; for, whether she does so from sensuous lust, or from some external purpose, she certainly uses her personality as a means for a low purpose, and thus makes also a means of the husband.

Or such a wife has surrendered herself to the

stranger from sensuous lust ; in which case it is to be assumed that she also does not love her husband, but merely uses him to gratify her passion, which is beneath his dignity.

In either case, therefore, adultery destroys the whole matrimonial connection ; and the husband can not continue to keep the wife without losing his self-esteem.

(This, indeed, has shown itself in the universal sentiment of all nations, even of the least civilized. A man who tolerates the dissipations of his wife is held in contempt, and a peculiar expression of ignominy has been invented for him. The reason is, that such a man acts dishonorably, and shows himself to be mean and ignominious.)

Man's jealousy has the character of a contempt of the faithless woman. If it has any other character, as, for instance, that of envy and jealousy, man renders himself contemptible.

X.

Adultery on the part of the husband evinces either a low mode of thinking, when the woman with whom he commits it surrenders herself, not from love, but from other motives ; or, when the woman gives herself up from love, it evinces the grossest injustice toward this woman ; for by accepting her he obliges himself to fulfill all the duties of marriage, to be unlimitedly generous and careful of her peace of mind, while he knows that he can not be so.

Now, although it is low in a man to merely gratify his passion, still to do so does not absolutely kill his character, as it does that of the woman. Nevertheless, his wife, seeing him commit adultery for such a low purpose, might thereby be properly led to suppose that he considers her in a like manner, and that all his pretended generous tenderness is merely sexual impulse—a supposition which would materially lower her in her own estimation. Even apart from this, it would certainly be painful for a loving woman to know that the same sacrifice she has made of herself to her husband has been made by another woman. (Hence the jealousy of woman has always a mixture of envy and of hatred against her rival.) It would thus become very probable that the wife's heart would be alienated from her husband; at least, it is sure that her relation would be embittered by such conduct on the part of her husband, and hence it is not conformable to the generosity which the husband owes to his wife.

Whereas, therefore, the wife's adultery necessarily destroys the whole relation between husband and wife, the husband's adultery does not do so necessarily, but, nevertheless, may possibly destroy it. His guilt is as great as that of the faithless wife, perhaps even greater, for he evinces lack of generosity, that is, meanness. The wife may pardon; and a noble, worthy wife certainly will pardon.

But it is painful for the husband to be pardoned, and still more painful for the wife that she should have something to pardon. The husband loses the courage and power to be the head of the family; and the wife feels pained that she can not esteem him to whom she has given herself. Their relation becomes reversed. The woman becomes the generous, and the husband the submissive party. This is, indeed, shown in common experiences. A wife who knows and tolerates the dissipations of her husband is not despised, but, on the contrary, is held all the more in esteem the gentler and wiser she bears it. The presupposition is, therefore, that she ought not to seek legal redress. Whence does this opinion rise, which is so deeply rooted in men's souls? From our legislation, or from our own sex? It seems not, since it exists also among the women, who complain about that legislation. It has its ground in the fundamental difference between both sexes, as pointed out by us.

XI.

In order to get a thorough view concerning the civil consequences of adultery, we must, above all things, investigate the relation of the state, and of legislation, toward the satisfaction of the sexual impulse outside of the marriage relation.

It is the duty of the state to protect the *honor* of the female sex; that is, to see that women are not compelled to give themselves up to a man whom they do not love ; for this honor is a part, nay, the noblest part, of their personality. But each woman has also the right to sacrifice her personality, that is to say, there is no *external* legal ground against her doing so. Precisely as each person has an unlimited external — not internal, or moral — right to take away his own life, the state having no right to make laws against suicide, so also has woman unlimited external right over her own honor. She is externally free to lower herself to a brute, as the man is also externally free to think meanly and low.

If, therefore, a woman chooses to give herself up from mere voluptuousness or from other motives, and if a man can be found who is willing to dis pense with love, the state has no right to pre- vent it.

Strictly speaking, therefore—we shall see here- after how this may be limited—the state can pass no laws against prostitution and adultery, nor affix any punishment to these offenses.

(Such, indeed, was the original rule in all Chris- tian states. Offenses of this kind were punished, not as violations of a civil law, but of a moral law, and hence were punished by the moral penal power, the church. Their chief punishment was always a church penance. We do not wish to discuss the propriety of this conduct here, since we do not speak of the church, but of the state. The Papal revenues from prostitutes, for instance, are a great consequence in inconsequence : for it is from the church that sanction must be obtained for this mode of life, if it is to be at all permitted ; and the money which is paid is the penance paid in advance for sins to be committed thereafter.)

XII.

A relation, the end whereof is mere gratification of the sexual impulse, and which is based upon egotism, may be public and permanent, in which case it is called concubinage. Its publicity results from the living together of both parties in a sufficiently public manner, at least, to be known to a watchful police.

The state, as we have seen, can not prohibit concubinage. But as the protector of women, the state must be satisfied that the woman has voluntarily entered the infamous compact. This can be achieved only by the declaration of such a woman, which declaration, however, on account of its infamous character, must not be a solemn ceremony before the teachers of morality, as the marriage declaration, but before such officers of the police as may be intrusted with affairs of this low character.

The state must also know that this connection, although it has the external appearance of a marriage, is none. It has not the legal consequences of a marriage ; the husband does not become the legal representative of the woman. The tie can be dissolved whenever either party pleases, without any formality. The state has not guaranteed it; nor does the state guarantee the conditions of the arrangement; and hence, the woman obtains no legally valid claim upon the man. For such claims can be obtained only in a relation recognized and guaranteed by the state. True, the state can not prevent such a relation as this of concubinage, but neither can the state confirm it, since it is immoral. If, therefore, the man refuses to conform to the obligations given to the woman, he certainly caps the climax to his meanness, and, it is to be hoped, makes himself universally contemptible; but the woman can not substantiate her claim before the law. The courts will refuse to entertain her complaint.

XIII.

A relation for the mere gratification of the sexual impulse may also be transitory and not public. Two cases are possible.

Firstly, the woman may submit to the will of the man without receiving any payment, or promise of payment—neither money, presents, services, or any other kind of payment whatever, and without expressly declaring that she does so from other motives than love. In this case, it is to be assumed that she has done so from love; for it is clear that she has not done it from motives of gain; and this is all the more to be presupposed, because it is against the nature of woman to do it from voluptuousness, unless, indeed, it can be proved that she is known to have intercourse with every body. She having thus surrendered herself from love, the relation between both persons is a true marriage relation, although no specific promise to marry has been given. The only thing wanting is the public recognition of this marriage, that is, the marriage ceremony. This the state, as the protector of woman's honor, owes to the woman. She herself is presupposed not to have sacrificed that honor, and hence, the state can not sacrifice it either. The man may be compelled to wed her. He is not compelled to marry her, for he has already married her, but merely to publicly declare this marriage. If he evinces an insurmountable aversion, or if there are other reasons which form obstacles to a continuance of marriage, (for example, perfect inequality of condition,) he may be divorced immediately after marriage, such divorce to be treated according to the general laws of divorce, which we shall speak of directly.

Secondly, the woman who has thus surrendered herself to the will of a man may have had previously or afterward intercourse with other men, or she may have done so for money. In the latter case, it must be evident that she has placed that price upon her personality, and has given herself up only for the sake of such price. The fact that she has received presents on other occasions from her lover is no proof against her virtue. But if that proof can be furnished, she is dishonored, and has no claim upon the law for protection; for the law can not protect an honor which does not exist, and which she has surrendered herself.

Prostitutes, who make prostitution their sole business, can not be tolerated in a state, but must be sent out of its limits, (although their freedom to do with their body what they please remains unimpaired,) for the following very simple reason : The state must know on what each person subsists, and must extend to each person the right (license) to carry on a certain business. A person without business (means of support) is no citizen. Now, if a woman should assign prostitution as her means of support, she would properly be considered insane by the state. *Propriam turpitudinem confitenti non creditur* is a just rule of law. It is, therefore, the same as if she had assigned no business ; *and this is the reason* why she can be expelled from the state unless she chooses to reform.

In a properly arranged state such a case can not well occur. Each person is rationally taken care of. If persons carry on another business than their legitimate occupation, the state ignores it, because it is not a public matter, and hence not subject to the law. The state knows nothing of such irregularities. The state does not guarantee to men the enjoyment of their dishonorable lusts, as it guarantees to all its citizens quiet and comfortable highways. Hence, it is not within the province of the police to be supervisors over the health of the prostitutes ; and I confess that I consider such a supervision unworthy of a state. Whoever chooses to be dissipated must bear the natural consequences of such dissipation. Nor does the state guarantee any contracts which may be made concerning these matters. A prostitute can not prefer complaint in such things.

XIV.

Let us apply these principles to adultery. The state can no more prohibit it or punish it by law than any other illegitimate satisfaction of the sexual impulse. For, let me ask, whose rights are violated by this offense? The rights of the husband whose wife, or of the wife whose husband, commits adultery? Is conjugal fidelity then an object of penal legislation? Or has it not, in fact, its ground in a connection of hearts? But such a connection of hearts is free, and can not be compelled by penal laws; and if *it* ceases, the compulsion of *external fidelity*—which compulsion alone is physically possible—is both illegal and impossible.

XV.

If the relation which ought to exist between married people, and which constitutes the essence of marriage, consisting of unlimited love on the part of the woman and unlimited generosity on the part of the husband—if this relation is destroyed, then the marriage is already canceled. *Married*

people divorce themselves as they have married them-
selves, out of their own free will. If the ground of
this, their relation, is canceled, their marriage does
not continue, no matter whether they remain together or not; henceforth their cohabitation is in
truth only concubinage ; their connection is no
longer end in itself, but has an external end, usually
some temporary advantage. Now, the law can require no one to do that which is dishonorable, as
concubinage is ; hence, it can not require persons
whose hearts have been separated, to live together
any longer.

From this it would appear that the state has
nothing to do in cases of divorce beyond making
the divorce public, as it made the first marriage
public. The legal results of the marriage which
the state guaranteed having ceased, of course the
divorce, which causes them to cease, must be
equally made known to the state, and through it
to its citizens.

XVI.

Nevertheless, most of our states assume to have
legal jurisdiction over divorces. Are they utterly
in the wrong? and if not, what is the ground of
their right?

The following : It may happen that the parties
to be divorced call upon the state for aid, in which
case the state has to judge whether it will extend
it to them or not. The result would be, that the

state gives no other decisions in divorce cases than
decisions as to the assistance it must furnish to the
parties interested.

XVII.

Both parties may have agreed about their separation and the partition of their property; in which
case there is no dispute, and all to be done is, that
they should declare their separation to the state.
They have settled the whole matter among themselves; the object of their agreement is an object
of their natural freedom; and the state, strictly
speaking, has not even the right to ask for the reasons of their separation.

Result: The consent of both parties separates
the marriage legally, without any further investigation.

XVIII.

One of the parties may not agree to the separation. In this case the notification to the state is
not merely a declaration of the fact of such divorce,
but also an appeal for its protection, and hence the
state may now take legal cognizance of the divorce.

What can the party demanding the separation require of the state? If it is the husband who ap-
peals for a divorce, the meaning of his request is: I
want the state to drive my wife out of my house.
If, on the contrary, the wife sues for a divorce, her

appeal signifies : That, since the husband, as representative of the family, owns the house and can not,
therefore, be driven out of it ; and since she, moreover, is willing to go, and possibly is also at liberty
to go, the state should force her husband to provide
for her otherwise.

According to what law is the state to settle this
matter ?

XIX.

Let us assume the case of a husband suing for
civil divorce on account of the adultery of his wife.
According to the above, it is against the honor of
the man to keep up his relation with her ; indeed this
relation is no longer a marriage, but a concubinage.
But the state can not force a person to do any thing
against his honor and moral feelings. It is, therefore, the duty of the state in this case to rid the
husband of his wife. What reasons, indeed, could
the wife have to desire the continuance of this relation ? Love is not to be presumed in her ; hence
she must have other ends in view. But the husband can not allow himself to be made the tool of
her ends. Even the church is not interested in
persuading the husband to retain the adulteress and
to pardon her, for the church can not advise him to
do that which is dishonorable and immoral.

Or let us assume that the husband sues for divorce
on the plea that his wife does not love him. If she
admits the plea, the state must grant the divorce ;

for love only is the ground of a legal marriage, and where there is no love the relation is merely a concubinage. What reasons could a woman have, indeed, to continue to live with a man whom she confessedly did not love? These reasons could only be of an external character, and the man can not allow himself to be made their tool. If she does not admit the plea, the state can not proceed directly, but must either wait to collect sufficient grounds for a divorce, or until both parties come to an agreement.

The refusal on the part of the wife of what has been very ignobly called "connubial duty," is a proof of want of love, and in so far constitutes legal ground for a divorce. For love proceeds from this submission of the woman, and this submission remains the constant expression of love. I have said *in so far* as it proves this want of love; for if sickness or some other physical obstacle can be proved, it does not prove want of love; and in such a case the suit of a man for a divorce would be mean beyond all expression. But supposing he is so mean? In that case the state can not consent to be the servant of his meanness; but neither is it to be hoped that the wife of such a man will oppose any obstacle to a divorce.

If the wife becomes subject to a criminal prosecution, the very facts of the case separate her from her husband; for the state takes her away from him. In all civil cases the husband is the legal representative of the wife; but in a criminal, that is, an exclusively personal case, he can not be so. She is reinstated in her full personality, and thereby divorced from her husband. If she is found to be innocent, she returns under the jurisdiction of the husband. If the husband wishes to take her back again, after she has been found guilty and suffered punishment, he may do so; but he can not be compelled to do it, for she has dishonored him.

XX.

Let us now assume that the wife sues for a divorce on the plea of her husband's adultery. We have shown that it is certainly possible, nay, even honorable, to the wife to pardon her husband in such a case. Hence, it is advisable to dissuade her, or to let her wait awhile. But if she insists, the divorce must be granted; for she alone knows her own heart, and alone can decide whether the infidelity of her husband has rooted out all her love for him or not; and it would be utterly unjust to force the wife to submit herself to her husband after her love has expired.

The state, indeed, is generally obliged to grant a divorce to the wife, if she insists upon it. The female sex must be favored by the law to this extent, for the reason that, although the suit of the wife may prove nothing against the husband, it proves, at least, the absence of love in her, and no woman should be forced to give herself up without love. But as women often do not know their own heart, and love more than they are aware of, it is advisable, as we have said, to first use dissuasion or temporary separation, (from bed and board.)

That a woman should plead impotency, etc., on the part of her husband is a dishonor to her sex, a sin against nature, and it may safely be called barbarism, if the state—or the church—accepts such a plea. Experience confirms, moreover, that women are themselves ashamed of this plea, and usually put it forth merely as a pretense.

A criminal investigation, to which the husband becomes subject, does not necessarily cause a divorce. The relation here is a very different one. Nevertheless, such an investigation is a very valid reason for the wife to insist on a divorce, since she can not esteem a criminal. Should she choose, however, to remain with him, to bear his fate and relieve it as much as the law allows, she is free to do so.

Willful desertion, where the deserted party has not been made aware of it or of its grounds, is of itself a divorce, if used as a plea ; for the missing party must be regarded as having pronounced a divorce, and hence as consenting to it.

XXI.

The final question is : How shall the property be divided in cases of divorce ?

As my principles on this subject differ from those usually entertained, I would ask my readers well to consider the grounds of my decision.

The wife, together with her personality, submits all her possessions to the husband; and he can repay her love only by also submitting his person and freedom, as well as all his possessions, to her, with this difference, however, that he retains external control over the whole. The union of hearts necessarily involves union of possessions under the chief control of the husband.

A divorce separates this union; but when the ground ceases, so also does the grounded. It seems, therefore, at first sight, as if each party ought to be placed back again in its original position, and ought to receive back what it contributed to the common property.

But there is this to be considered: both parties have for a certain time administered, enjoyed, increased, or diminished their property, presumptively under one will and as one subject. The effect of this common administration can not be canceled; is necessarily common to both, and remains common to both. It is impossible to make a close calculation as to what amount of attention and care the one and the other party has stood in need of, etc.; for, if it has been a true marriage, the needs of the one party were those of the other, and the gains of the one party those of the other. Both were but one legal person. It is as impossible for husband and wife to make such a settlement with each other or to sue each other as it is for one individual to settle with or sue himself. True, this relation is now canceled, but it was not canceled before, and the effect of that relation can not be annulled.

Now, the external condition of this effect is the amount of property each party had before the marriage. According to the ratio of the property thus contributed, the whole amount of property at the time of the divorce is to be redivided, as effect. If the wife, for instance, contributed one third of the common property at the time of marriage, and the husband two thirds, then at the time of divorce the whole common property must be estimated, and one third given to the wife and two thirds to the husband. The wife does not get back the amount of her original third, but *plus* its gains or *minus* its losses during the time of marriage. Other law provisions may have excellent political reasons, but they are not just.

To whom the children are to be assigned we shall see hereafter, when we come to speak of the relation between parents and children.

§ 3.

CONCERNING THE LEGAL RELATION OF BOTH SEXES IN GENERAL TO EACH OTHER IN THE STATE.

I.

Has woman the same rights in the state which man has ? This question may appear ridiculous to many. For if the only ground of all legal rights is reason and freedom, how can a distinction exist between two sexes which possess both the same reason and the same freedom ?

Nevertheless, it seems that, so long as men have lived, this has been differently held, and the female sex seems not to have been placed on a par with the male sex in the exercise of its rights. Such a universal sentiment must have a ground, to discover which was never a more urgent problem than in our days.

If we grant that the female sex, so far as its rights are concerned, has really been thus treated, it by no means suffices to assign as ground a less degree of mental and physical power. For women would reply : "Firstly, you men do not give us the same degree of culture which you extend to your

own sex ; and secondly, that statement is not even
true ; for if you will make a list of the men who
are the pride of their sex, we can make one of
women, who will, justly estimated, be their peers
in every thing ; but finally, even if this inequality
were as you state it to be, it would on no account
involve such a decided inequality of rights, since
there is also among men a great distinction of mental and bodily powers, which does not involve such
an oppressive inequality of rights."

Hence, it will be necessary, above all things, to
investigate whether women are really treated so
badly and unjustly as some of them, and, still more,
some uncalled-for advocates of their cause, assert.

II.

The question, whether the female sex has really
a claim to all the rights of men and of citizens
which belong to the male sex, could be raised
only by persons who doubt whether women are
complete human beings. We do not doubt it, as
appears sufficiently from the above. But the question may certainly be asked, whether and in how far
the female sex *can desire* to exercise all its rights ?
To facilitate the answering of this question, we shall
consider the several conditions of women.

III.

As a rule, woman is either a maid or married.
If a maid, she is still under the care of her father,

precisely as the unmarried young man. Herein both sexes are perfectly equal. Both become free by marriage, and in regard to their marriage both are equally free ; or if there is to be a favor shown, it should be shown to the daughter. For she ought not even to be persuaded to marry, which may be permitted in the case of the son, as we have shown heretofore.

If she is *married,* her whole dignity depends upon her being completely subjected, and seeming to be so subjected, to her husband. Let it be well observed, what my whole theory expresses, but what it is perhaps necessary to repeat once more emphatically—woman is not subjected to her husband in such a manner as to give him a *right of compulsion* over her ; she is subjected through her own continuous necessary wish—a wish which is the condition of her morality—to be so subjected. She has the *power* to withdraw her freedom, if she could have the *will* to do so ; but that is the very point : she can not rationally will to be free. Her relation to her husband being publicly known, she must, moreover, will to appear to all whom she knows as utterly subjected to, and utterly lost in, the man of her choice.

Her husband is, therefore, the administrator of all her rights in consequence of her own necessary will ; and she wishes those rights asserted and exercised only in so far as *he* wishes it. He is her natural representative in the state and in the whole society. This is her *public* relation to society.

She can not even allow herself to think for a moment that she should exercise herself her rights in the state.

So far as her *private* and *internal* relation in the house is concerned, *the tenderness of the husband necessarily restores to her all and more than she has lost.* The husband will not relinquish her rights, because they are his own ; and because, if he did so, he would dishonor himself and his wife before society. The wife has also rights in public affairs, for she is a citizen. I consider it the duty of the husband—in states which give to the citizen a vote on public matters—not to vote without having discussed the subject with his wife, and allowed her to modify his opinion through her own. His vote will then be the result of their common will. The father of a family, who represents not only his own but also the interests of his wife and children, ought indeed to have a greater influence and a more decisive vote in a commonwealth, than the citizen who represents only his own interests. The manner of arranging this is a problem for the science of politics.

Women, therefore, do really exercise the right of suffrage—not immediately, however, in their own person, because they can not wish to do so without lowering their dignity, but—through the influence which results from the nature of the marriage relation. This is, indeed, proved by the history of all great revolutions. They either emanated from, or at least were led and considerably modified by, women.

REMARK.

If this must be admitted to be the case, what, then, do women and their advocates really demand? What is it whereof women are deprived, and which must be restored to them? The rights themselves? They are completely possessed of them, as we have shown. It can only be the external show of those rights. They not only want to accomplish, but also to have it known that *they* accomplished it. They not only want their ideas to be carried out, but also to have it publicly known, that *they*, even they, carried them out. They long for celebrity during life, and after death in history.

If this alone is and can be their object in preferring those complaints, then their complaints ought to be unhesitatingly rejected; for they can not prefer them without renouncing their whole female worth. The fewest, however, who prefer them, do so seriously. Most of them have been persuaded to utter such wonderful words, which they can not *think* without dishonoring themselves, by a few crack-brained men, most of whom have never thought sufficiently high of a woman to make her their companion through life, and who are therefore anxious to remedy the matter by having the whole sex, without exception, immortalized in history.

Even the man who makes glory the chief or but one of the ends of his life, loses the merit of his acts, and sooner or later, also, that very glory. Women ought to be grateful that their position precludes the very suspicion of such a motive. But what is far more : by such thirst for glory women sacrifice the amiable modesty of their sex, which nothing can more disgust than to be put up for a show. Ambition and vanity are contemptible in a man ; but in woman they are corrupting ; for they root out that modesty and self-sacrificing love for her husband, upon which her whole dignity rests. A rational and virtuous woman can be proud only of her husband and children ; not of herself, for she forgets herself in them. Add to this, that those women who seriously envy men their celebrity, are deceived concerning the true object of their wish. Woman necessarily desires the love of some man, and, in order to attract it, she is anxious to attract the attention of the male sex. This is natural and very proper in an unmarried woman. But those women calculate to increase the charms of their own sex—perhaps not having much confidence in them—by that which attracts the attention of men to men, and seek in celebrity merely a new means of captivating men's hearts. If those women are married, their object is as contemptible as the means are unsuited to accomplish it.

IV.

If the husband can not or refuses to vote, there is no reason why the wife should not appear in his place and cast their common vote, but always *as the vote of the husband.* (She could not cast it as her own without separating herself from her husband.) For the grounded extends no further than the ground; and the ground why the wife could not vote was, because the husband voted for both. If he does not, she can, therefore, vote.

This furnishes us the principle applicable to widows and divorced women, and to maids who are no longer under paternal authority and yet have never been married. All these classes of women are not subjected to a man; hence there is no reason why they should not themselves exercise all civil rights precisely as men do. In a republic they have the right to vote, to appear in court, and to defend their own cause. If from natural bashfulness and modesty they prefer to choose a guardian, they must be permitted to do so, but there is no legal ground why they should be forced to choose one.

V

Every citizen in the state is to possess property and to administer it according to his will; hence, also, the woman who has no husband. This property need not be absolute property, money or valuables, but may also consist of civil rights or privileges. There is no reason why women should not have these. Woman can own land and carry on agriculture. Or she can carry on an art, or a profession, or some commercial business.

√I.

Women are ineligible to public offices for the following simple reasons : public officers are responsible to the state ; and hence must be perfectly free, and dependent always only upon their own will ; otherwise such a responsibility would be unjust and contradictory. Woman, however, is free and independent only so long as she has no husband. Hence the exclusive condition under which a woman might become eligible to office, would be the promise not to marry. But no rational woman can give such a promise, nor can the state rationally accept it. For woman is destined to love, and love comes to women of itself—does not depend upon her free will. But when she loves, it is her duty to marry, and the state must not form an obstacle to this duty. Now, if a woman, holding a public office, were to marry, two cases are possible. Firstly, she might not subject herself to her husband so far as her official duties were concerned. But this is utterly against female dignity ; for she can not say then, that she has given herself up wholly to the husband. Moreover, where are the strict limits which separate official from private life ? Or, secondly, she might subject herself utterly, as nature and morality require, to her husband, even so far as her official duties are concerned. But, in that case, she would cease to be the official, and he would become it. The office would become his by marriage, like the rest of his wife's property and rights. But this the state can not permit; for it must know the ability and the character of the person upon whom an office is conferred, and can not accept one chosen merely by love.

VI.

This fact, that women are not intended for public offices, has another consequence, which the advocates of woman's rights put forth as a new complaint against our political institutions. For, very naturally, they are not educated for duties they will never have to perform ; are sent neither to colleges, nor to universities. Now they cry out, that men neglect their minds, and enviously and cunningly keep them in ignorance, and hold them removed from the sources of enlightening culture. We shall examine this charge carefully.

The learned man by profession studies not merely for himself; *as* student he studies, on the contrary, not at all for himself, but for others. If he wishes to become a preacher, or statesman, or doctor, he studies for the purpose of immediately applying what he has learned ; hence he learns at the same time the form, or the manner of applying his science. Or if it is his intention to become a teacher of future students in schools or universities, it is also his intention to communicate again what he now learns, and to increase the stock of his knowledge by discoveries of his own, so

that culture may not come to a stand-still. Hence
he must know *how* to make these discoveries, and
how to develop them out of the human soul. But
this acquiring a knowledge of the *form* of science
is precisely what they, women, can not make use of,
since they are to become neither teachers, preach-
ers, doctors, or lawyers.

For their own intellectual culture, men only require the *results* of culture ; and these results women
learn also in society : in each condition of society
the results of the whole culture of that condition.
That which they envy us is, therefore, the unessen-
tial, the formal, the mere hull. By their position
and by our conversation they are saved the trouble
of working through this hull, and can receive its
contents directly. They could not, indeed, make
use of the form at all. Women are not habituated,
and can not be habituated, to look upon the form as
means, because they could be accustomed to do
so only by making use of the form. Hence they
look upon it as an end in itself, as something noble
and excellent in itself. This is the reason why
really learned women—I do not speak of those who
reason purely through their common sense, for
these are very estimable—are usually pedantic.

To prevent my being misunderstood, let me explain this further. It can not be maintained that
woman is inferior to man in regard to talents
of mind ; but it can certainly be maintained that
the minds of man and woman have, by nature, a
very different character. Man reduces all that is

in and for him to clear conceptions, and discovers it only through reasoning—provided, of course, his knowledge is a true conviction, and not a mere historical knowledge. Woman, on the other hand, has a natural sentiment of what is good, true, and proper. Not as if this were given her through mere feeling, for that is impossible ; but when it is externally given to her, she has the faculty of judging quickly through her feelings, and without clear insight into the grounds of such judgment, whether it be true and good, or not. It may be said, that man must first make himself rational ; whereas, woman is already rational by nature. This is, indeed, clearly to be deduced from the fundamental distinction between woman and man. Her fundamental impulse originally unites with reason, because it would cancel reason unless it did so unite ; it becomes a rational impulse. And this is the reason why woman's whole system of feeling is rational, and made to correspond to reason, as it were. Man, on the contrary, must first subordinate all his impulses to reason, through exertion and activity.

Woman, therefore, is especially practical, and not at all speculative in her womanly nature. She can not and shall not go beyond the limit of her feeling. (This explains the well-known phenomenon, why some women have been known to become distinguished in matters of memory, as languages, and even in mathematics, so far as they can be learned through memory ; and some also in matters of invention, in the gentler forms of poetry, in novel-

writing, and even in the writing of history. But
no women are known to have been philosophers, or
inventors of new theories in the mathematical
science.)

A few words more concerning the passion of women to become authors—a passion which is constantly on the increase among them in these our
days.

Literary labor can have only two ends in view:
to make known new discoveries in sciences for the
examination of the learned, or to communicate
that which has already been discovered to the people at large by means of popular representations.
We have seen that women can not make discoveries. Popular writings for women, writings on female education, moral books for the female sex, as
such, etc., can certainly be most properly written
by women ; partly because they know their own
sex better than man ever can know it, (that is, if
they have the gift, also, of rising in part above their
sex,) and partly because such books are generally
more read by women. Even the learned man can
extend his knowledge of female character from
such writings. Of course, the woman must write
as a woman, and must not appear in her writings
as a badly disguised man.

I have presupposed, as it will be seen, that a woman will write only for her sex, and only for the
purpose of being useful and to alleviate a discovered
need of her sex ; but on no account for our sex,
or from motives of vanity or ambition. Not only

would her works have little literary value in the latter case, but the moral character of the authoress would also be greatly injured. Her authorship would be nothing but another means of coquetting. If she is married, she receives, through her literary celebrity, an independence which necessarily weakens and threatens to dissolve her relation to her husband; or, if criticism is unfavorable, she will feel the reproof as an insult to her sex, and will embitter the days of herself and of her husband.

§ 4.

CONCERNING THE LEGAL RELATION BETWEEN PARENTS AND CHILDREN IN A STATE.

I.

The original relation between parents and children is not merely determined through the conception of rights, but chiefly through nature and morality, precisely as the relation between husband and wife. Hence, our present investigation requires, as our previous investigation required, that we proceed from principles which are higher than those of law, in order to obtain, first of all, an object for the application of law. For this natural and moral relation may very possibly involve further determinations, which the conception of law has to regulate.

The attempts to constitute the whole relation a simply legal one have failed by reason of their absurd presuppositions ; as, for instance, that children are *property* of the father, by reason of the act of generation being a species of manufacture, etc.

II.

The fruit generates itself in the womb of the mother as a part belonging to her. Her own health and life are conditioned by those of the fruit ; and, what is important above all things here, in the case of the mother, this condition *is* not merely so, as in the irrational animal, but is, moreover, *known* to be so.   It is not merely mechanically necessary that she should generate the fruit out of herself, and form it in her womb, but her own consciousness forces upon her considerate care of its preservation.

In virtue of a law of nature, which is most assuredly universal, the child is not born without pain. The moment of the child's birth is for the mother a moment of relief from pain, and hence, necessarily, a joyful moment. Joy connects the mother with the existence of the child.

Even after the child is born, the organic tie which connects mother and child is not yet dissolved. The mother continues to furnish the food from her body, which she finds the same need to give to the child as the child to take it.

(An organic body comprises all those parts, in

one of which is an impulse to satisfy a need in the other, which that other part can not satisfy of itself; and the other of which is an impulse to satisfy a need of the first, which the first can not satisfy of itself. And this relation I call the organic tie of the parts. Since it is only in the body of the mother that nature prepares the food which is most advantageous for the child, and since nature has provided no other way of relieving the mother of her milk than through the mouth of the child, an organic tie connects them even after they have become two separate bodies. It appears to me worth while to observe, how far this law of nature prevails also in the vegetable kingdom, since the young plant does not separate at once from the mother-body.)

III.

This law of nature, operating in the animal and vegetable kingdom, impels animals and plants to assist in the growth of external bodies. This impulse impels them necessarily; the impulse and the activity required by it arise at the same moment. But in intelligent beings there arises between the impulse and the act required by it a third link—consciousness. The intelligence becomes conscious of this natural impulse, as of a sentiment. This sentiment is the necessary product of the natural impulse, and succeeds it immediately; or, to speak still more strictly, this sentiment is the natural impulse in the intelligence.

The act required by the impulse or sentiment, however, does not succeed in this necessary and immediate manner, but is conditioned by an application of freedom.

The natural impulse in animals and plants impelled them to take care of a strange body as of their own. How is this impulse likely to manifest itself in human intelligence? Doubtless as *a feeling of the needs of another body; precisely as the mother feels her own needs.* Such a feeling is called sympathy. Sympathy, therefore, is the form in which the natural instinct of the mother for her child manifests itself; and this sympathy has the same end which the instinct of nature has—the physical preservation of the child.

A mother is impelled by the sympathy which is an instinct of her nature to take care of the preservation of her child. Nature and reason combined have established this mechanism for the preservation of the child. Of course, a mother may resist it, since reason or freedom assists also in this mechanism, but only by becoming unnatural. Naturally, no mother resists it.

The question of rights does not occur yet at all. It is as absurd to say that the child has a right to demand this physical preservation from its mother, as it is to say that a branch has the right to grow on the tree; and as absurd to say a mother must be compelled to preserve her child, as it is to say the tree must be compelled to bear the branch. It is a law of nature, although connected with reason.

IV.

There is an impulse in human nature generally, and hence, also, in man, to take care of the weak and helpless. This universal impulse will doubtless speak in the *father* for his child; but since it is a universal impulse, based upon the mere sight of helplessness, it will speak for every child, and there is no reason why a father should feel a particular preference for *his* own child. Such a preference, however, we must discover; and since the whole relation is a physical one, this love can only have a physical ground. But there is no physical tie to connect father and child; and hence it is to be assumed that the father has no immediate love for his child. For the natural relation in the act of generation does not involve it, since as such act, as generation of a particular individual, it does not occur in consciousness at all.

The special love of a father for his child results *originally*—what its sources may be in our *opinion* as influenced by our social institutions, we do not investigate here—from his tenderness toward the mother. This tenderness makes all the wishes and desires of the mother his own, and hence, also, her wish to take care of the preservation of the child. Precisely as this is naturally the necessary duty of the mother, so does it now, by transfer, become that of the father also; for both are only one subject, and their will is one.

It is absurd to speak of the right of the mother

to compel the father to maintain the child. The ground upon which it has been believed that such a right could be based is not sufficient. It was believed that the mother might say to the father: " Thou art the cause of my having a child ; assume, therefore, the burden of taking care of it." But the father can justly reply : " Neither I nor thou intended it ; nature gave the child to thee, not to me ; bear the results which have fallen upon thee just as I should have had to bear the results which might have fallen upon me."

It would be different if both parties had arranged a contract about the maintenance of the child. But even in such a case the state must have guaranteed the contract to make it legally binding.

V.

The parents live together, and the child, recommended to the care of both by nature, must also live together with them.

A natural impulse leads man to apprehend reason in all external nature so far as it is any way possible, and to treat objects (for instance, animals) as if they had reason. The parents will doubtless treat their child thus, and induce it to manifest free activity ; and the child will assuredly, under such treatment, soon manifest reason and freedom. According to the necessary conceptions of men, freedom appertains to welfare, and hence the parents, who desire the welfare of their child, will doubtless give him freedom. But many a use of freedom might be detrimental to the preservation of the child's life and health, which are also objects of the parents. Hence, the parents will restrict that freedom to such an extent that its exercise may not endanger the preservation of the child. This is the first conception of education. The parents will educate their child, because they both love it and wish to preserve it from danger.

It can not be said that the child has a right to compel education, or that the parents are compelled to educate. Whether the state has any thing to do with the matter will appear hereafter.

VI.

It is the universal moral duty of every moral and good man, to diffuse and promote morality everywhere about him. Each free being, and hence, also, the child, is susceptible to morality. Living together with its parents, the parents, if they are moral themselves, will make use of all possible means to develop morality in the child ; and this is the conception of *higher education.*

(We do not teach morality here, and hence we can not say, they *shall* do it ; but only, they *will* do it. We merely state natural and moral facts in order to get objects for the application of the conception of rights.)

This education involves the following two conditions : 1st, the powers of the child must be developed and cultivated for various uses ; and 2d, the morality of the child must be awakened.

To attain the first object, the freedom of the child must be limited ; every use of this freedom which conflicts with the end of preserving the health and life of the child, and with the end of developing the powers of the child must be prohibited, and every use thereof which tends to promote these ends must be insisted upon. It is only for the purpose of awaking the morality of the child, that its freedom must not be restricted ; for morality develops itself in man of itself, and can not be produced by force or artificial measures.

VII.

Only the parents have a full knowledge of the end of the children's education ; not the children themselves, who are to be educated. Hence, only the parents, and not the children, can judge what measures are necessary for that end. They are their own judges in their own case so far as the child is concerned ; they are sovereign and the child is unconditionally subject to them, in so far as they educate it. It is for their own conscience to tell them that they must use this sovereign power only for the purpose of educating the child as they deem best.

VIII.

The possibility of a state depends upon the fact that its population remains pretty nearly the same numerically; for all its measures of protection, taxation, etc., are calculated with a view to that specific number. If mortality should constantly decrease that number, the calculation would turn out wrong, disorders would ensue, and finally the state would utterly perish. The numerical equality of population, however, is conditioned by the fact that the dying-out generation is replaced by new citizens.

Each citizen of a state promises, in the original compact, that he will promote, as far as lies in his power, all the conditions of the possibility of the state; hence, also, the condition just mentioned. This he can best do by educating children who may grow up to realize various ends of reason. The state has the right to make this education of children a condition of the state-compact, and thus education becomes an *external*, legal obligation, which the parents owe to the state.

I have spoken of the education of *children generally;* for the end of the state is realized by it. Now, it can not be left to the arbitrariness of the citizen what particular child he chooses to educate, since this would involve endless and unsolvable law disputes. A general law must be made to settle this matter, and the most rational provision is, that the parents should be obliged to educate *their own* children.

IX.

If the children are the offspring of a lawful and rational marriage, there is no difficulty about this. If, however, they come from a marriage which has not been legally solemnized at first, and which, after having been solemnized, was followed by an immediate divorce, or if they are the offspring of a concubinage, the care and education of the child devolves upon the mother as the one whom nature herself has intrusted with it ; for both parents—if separated—can not educate it. The father, however, contributes his share to the child's maintenance and education in money.

X.

Infanticide committed by the mother is doubtless a monstrous, unnatural crime ; for to commit it the mother must have silenced all the feelings of nature ; it is, however, no offense against the external rights of the child. The child has no *legal* rights upon its mother. It is an offense against the laws of the state, which provide that all children must be educated, and in so far it is to be punished. This crime belongs to the class of crimes which exhibit an unnatural brutality and savage disposition, and hence to that class for which the state must provide institutions of correction. Infanticide is, therefore, to be punished with imprisonment in such institutions until reform has taken place.

(Some ancient republics, fearing too large an increase of population, especially of their privileged classes, their real citizens, permitted the exposition of infants, particularly if they were weak ; and hence, indirect infanticide was allowed by law. To *command* it, no state has a right; for it has no right to command any thing that is immoral or is a sin against nature. Nor has the state even a right *expressly* to permit it ; for such a permission is immoral, and dishonors the state and its citizens. But if a state *tacitly* permits it, no legal objection can be raised ; for it is not the state's business to take positive care of the *morality* of its citizens ; and new-born children have no external rights except in so far as the state guarantees them their life, which the state is bound to do only so far as the possibility of its own preservation depends upon it.)

XI.

The state has, therefore, the right to provide that children are kept alive, fed, clothed, and raised among men; for these are exclusive conditions of their becoming eventually men and citizens.

XII.

The state makes it the duty of parents to educate their children. Hence, the state necessarily guarantees to them the conditions of the possibility of such education. One of these conditions is, that no other citizen shall be allowed to take their children from them in order to educate them. Hence, *the state necessarily guarantees to all parents the exclusive right to keep their own children.* If a law dispute arises, the law must decide in favor of the true parents.

Education requires also a fixed plan and uniformity of principle, according to which the children are to be educated. This plan would be disturbed if strangers had a right to interfere, and to influence the children. Complaint can be preferred against such interference, and the law must decide in favor of the true parents.

XIII.

If the parents are moral, the education of their children is to them a matter of conscience. They wish to educate them as morally good as possible ; but each one necessarily considers his own principles the best and most correct; for if he did not, and retained them, he would act immorally. Now, the state can not interfere in matters of conscience. The state itself can not, therefore, interfere in education. The state has the right to establish public schools ; but it is for the parents to decide whether they will take advantage of them or not. The state has no right to compel them to do so.

XIV.

Neither the state, nor any citizen, nor the child itself—since it is the object of education—has a right to decide upon the principles which are to govern the education of the children ; hence, the parents are the sole judges. No law dispute can arise between children who are being educated and their parents. The parents are, in this matter, the final appeal, and sovereign. The state has no more right to regulate this relation than that between husband and wife by law.

XV.

Hence, the control of parents over children is based solely upon the parents' duty to educate them. This duty of education is established by nature and is guaranteed by the state. To consider the children as property of the parents is absurd.

XVI.

The state has the right to watch that the child is educated ; hence, also, the right to prevent any use of the child which would evidently annul all education. The state can not, therefore, allow children to be used as property ; for example, a son to be sold into slavery.

XVII.

Only free persons are responsible before the law. Children are not free, for they are under the guardianship of their parents. Their father—as equally the representative of their mother—is thus their legal guardian. They have no rights for him to defend, since they are not yet themselves citizens; but when they have committed any trespasses, the father is justly held responsible; for the children are under his supervision, and he ought to have prevented them from committing such trespasses.

Children can be subjected to no public punishment; for they are not subject to the penal laws of the state. They are subject only to the penal laws of their parents, who punish them as they see fit.

XVIII.

The only ground for the control of parents over their children is the need of education. When the ground ceases, so does the grounded. When the education is completed, the child becomes free. But only the parents can decide when it is completed, since only they have preëstablished its final end. If they hold that the child is sufficiently educated, they voluntarily give it freedom. They should, indeed, increase the freedom of the child constantly during the progress of education, as one of the rules of such education, and not as a right which the child has ; and when they cut the last tie, the child is wholly free.

Or this tie may be cut when it appears, from the nature of the case, that the end of education is accomplished. The general end thereof is the utilizing of our powers for rational purposes, and the external judge of the matter is the state. True, the state can not directly liberate the children ; for that would be interfering with their education ; but it can do so indirectly, by giving to the son a civil office or some other civil right or privilege. Such an office liberates the child from parental authority.

Or, finally, the education, and hence, the subjection of children may be annulled, by making it, from the nature of the case, no longer possible. This occurs in marriage. The daughter is now unlimitedly subjected to the will of her husband, and can therefore no longer be subjected to the will of her parents. The son has now to care for the happiness of his wife with unlimited tenderness, and can not, therefore, allow himself to be disturbed in this care by the will of his parents.

But precisely because marriage puts an end to education, and because parents alone have a right to decide when the education is finished, the parents must also have the right to refuse their consent to the marriage of their children for a time, or to postpone their marriage.

They have not, however, the right to prohibit marriage generally to their children, nor to choose

for them in marrying, from the reasons stated heretofore.

XIX.

Husband and wife have their property in common. Children have no property. Where should
they get it? Their parents owe them food and
clothing, as means of education; and it is a duty
they owe to the state, and which the state may enforce, to thus provide for their children.

But children work, it is said, and thus acquire
property. This would be correct under the presupposition, which we have shown to be wrong, that
formation gives title to property. But the object
of this labor is merely to exercise their powers for
educational purposes, and hence, the parents very
properly take hold of its results as their property.
The child can do nothing without the will of the
parents; it can not, therefore, acquire property
without their consent. Or does any one pretend
that the right of property is founded upon a contract with the parents? Only free persons can
make a contract; but children are not free in their
relation to parents.

XX.

Each independent citizen must have property of
his own, and must be able to tell the state what he
lives from. Hence, the state can justly demand of
the parents, who allow a child its full freedom, that

they shall give a certain amount of property to it, or, to use a very characteristic word, that they shall endow it. How much they ought to give it depends upon their own discretion.

When two persons marry, the parents of both parties must agree as to whether both shall receive something, or only one of them, and what the amount shall be. It is no business of the state who furnishes the property, provided the new family can subsist.

XXI.

It is altogether arbitrary with the parents whether one of the children receives more than the other or not. It may be unfair, but it is not illegal. What legal ground could the child have to complain? All that it gets, it gets through the voluntary kindness of its parents.

XXII.

When the parents die, their rights in the sensuous world, and hence, also, their rights to property, utterly cease. It depends altogether upon the positive legislation of a state whether laws of inheritance shall be established or whether parents shall have the right to make wills ; and if so, to what extent they may will away their property to strangers, etc. These are questions purely of expediency, and not of *a priori* law.

XXIII.

We have deferred to reply to the question, To whom children are to be assigned when their parents are divorced ? because the reply was not well possible before we had a thorough insight into the relation between parents and children.

Since parents have unlimited control over their children, parties who are being divorced must have the right to come to an agreement about it among themselves. The state has nothing to say in the matter, provided the education of the children is secured. It is only when the parents can not agree that the state decides. Only two grounds of such a dispute among parents are thinkable. Either neither of them wishes to undertake the care of the children, or both wish to retain the children.

In the former case the decision is this : The duty to take care of the children is immediate duty only for the mother, and for the father it is only a mediate duty derived from his love for the mother. The latter, and hence the natural, ground of his paternal tenderness having ceased, the children are to be returned to the personal care and attention of the mother ; but the father must contribute to their maintenance ; and the state has to see that he does so according to his means.

In the second case, the decision is this : The legally grounded object of the state is, that the children shall be educated in the best possible manner. As a rule, the mother is the most proper person to educate daughters, and the father the most proper person to educate sons. General laws can take cognizance only of such rules ; and hence the mother receives the daughters and the father the sons.

As a matter of course, the child generated in adultery is not to be maintained by the husband, but by its true father.

SECOND APPENDIX

TO THE

SCIENCE OF RIGHTS.

———◆———

INTERNATIONAL

AND

COSMOPOLITAN LAW.

§ I.

CONCERNING INTERNATIONAL LAW.

I.

EACH individual, as we have shown, has the right to compel each other single individual to enter into a legal relation (state) with him or to remove from his sphere of activity. If one of the two is already a resident of a state and the other one not, then the former compels the latter to become a citizen of his state. If neither is as yet a resident of a state, both unite to form at least the beginning of a state. From this it follows, that whosoever is not yet a citizen of a state can be legally compelled, by the first state which chooses to do so, either to submit to its laws or to remove from its limits.

The natural result of this proposition would be gradually to unite all men who inhabit the earth under one single commonwealth.

II.

But it is equally possible that separate masses of men, unknown to each other, may gather together at various places of the earth and unite themselves.

This place has such requirements, and another place has other requirements, and these requirements are alleviated in each case without either party becoming aware of the requirements of the other. In this manner various states would arise on the earth.

It is a proof that the state is not an arbitrary invention, but is established by nature and reason, when we actually find that, in places where men have lived together for a time and have become educated, states are erected, although the people in the one such place know not that the same thing has been done in other places.

The surface of the earth being, moreover, separated by seas, rivers, and mountains, this formation of separate states became necessary likewise from geographical reasons.

III.

The people in these several states know not of each other ; and hence are in no true legal relation to each other, since the possibility of a legal relation is conditioned, as we have seen, by actual and conscious reciprocal influence.

IV.

Two citizens from these different independent states meet each other. Each one will require of the other a guarantee for his security, and has a perfect right to do so ; which security consists in their both subjecting themselves to the chief government. But each one has a chief government; hence, each one has the same right to make the same request, and their rights thus canceling each other, neither party has a right to make it.

Nevertheless, they must give each other mutual guarantee. Since this can not be done in the manner suggested, how can it be done? Both are to submit to a common judge; but each one has his particular judge. Hence, their judges must agree among themselves, and must become the One common judge of both in matters which concern both; that is, both their states must mutually agree to punish the injury done by one of its citizens to a citizen of the other country, as if it had been inflicted upon one of its own citizens.

COROLLARIA.

1. The whole relation of states is based upon the legal relation of their citizens. The state in itself is nothing but an abstract conception; only the citizens, as such, are actual persons. Again: this relation is based expressly upon the law, necessity, that citizens who meet each other in the sensuous world must guarantee security to each other. Hence, only those states are related to each other which are adjoining. How states, separated by space, may nevertheless be related to each other, we shall soon see.

2. This relation of the states consists in their

H H

mutually securing to each other the security of their citizens. And the formula of the contract is as follows : I agree to hold myself responsible for all the damage which my citizens may do to your citizens, provided you will make yourself responsible for all the damage which your citizens may do to mine.

3. Such a compact is not involved in the original state organization, but must be specially concluded, and must be made publicly known to all citizens. The citizen satisfies all the conditions of the state compact by simply refraining from violating the rights of his fellow-citizen ; and it is only in virtue of this special compact that he is obliged by law also to respect the rights of citizens of adjoining states, and that he makes himself liable to punishment if he does not do so.*

V.

Such a compact of states necessarily involves their *mutual recognition,* since this is the presupposition of the possibility of such a compact. Both states accept each the guarantee of the other for its citizens, and hence assume each that the other has a legal constitution and can be held responsible for its citizens.

---

* (It is sufficiently clear from what we have before said regarding the confederate form of government as applicable to the whole earth, how this doctrine of international law must be modified to become absolutely rational.—TRANSLATOR'S REMARK.)

Each state has, therefore, the right to judge about the legality of another state, with the citizens whereof its own citizens are likely to come into contact. But this right of judgment extends only to the external, not to the internal, administration of such state.

This is what is signified by the *independence* of states.

VI.

Each people, which does not live in a condition of nature, but has a government, no matter how constituted, has a right to compel its recognition from all adjoining states. The proof of this is indeed contained already in the preceding paragraph. Not to recognize a state signifies, to proclaim its citizens as not possessing any legal form of government; and this involves the right to subjugate them. A refusal to recognize is, therefore, sufficient ground for war.

States are necessarily independent of each other.

VII.

When a people has no government, and hence does not constitute a state, the adjoining state has a right either to subjugate it under its own jurisdiction, or to compel it to establish some form of government, or to expel it from its neighborhood. The reason is, that he who can not offer to the other any guarantee for the security of his rights, has himself no rights. Such a people, therefore, has no rights at all.

(Let no one fear that this proposition is favorable to ambitious nations. A people such as we have described most likely does not exist anywhere, and we have established this theory more to complete our argumentation than for the sake of its application. If a people has only a leader in war, it has doubtless a government. The French Republicans whipped the armies of the Coalition again and again, while the latter doubted whether the Republicans had any government, and were asking, "With whom shall we conclude peace?" Why did they not ask those who had beaten them the name of their commander in battle? Perhaps the men who had issued the command to beat the Coalition could also have given the command to cease beating them. At present, when they have been sufficiently beaten, the Coalition has finally hit upon this idea, and has thus discovered that the French have, after all, some kind of government.)

VIII.

Adjoining states guarantee to each other the rights of property of their citizens. Hence, they must have come to some agreement as to the limits of these rights. These limits have already been fixed in each state by the property compact of all citizens; and the treaty between the states only adopts those limits. Thus, what before concerned only the citizens of the one state has become obligatory, likewise, upon those of the adjoining states. Possible disputes must be settled by compromise, since there are no *a priori* legal grounds why one piece of property should belong to this citizen and not to the other. Hence, the first condition of a legal relation between two states is the fixing of their boundaries ; and not only of the boundaries of the land itself, but also of certain rights, as, for instance, of fishing, hunting, navigation, etc. The boundaries of the property of their citizens becomes for the states the boundaries of those states.

IX.

In this treaty both states are perfectly equal. What the one state does to protect the citizens of the other state from damage, the other must also do in regard to the former ; but neither is obliged to apply greater care than the other. Hence, it is very possible that in some states the rights of their own citizens are more protected than those of strangers—perhaps because the other states refused to afford sufficient protection on their side ; nay, it is even possible that the property of strangers from *one* adjoining state may be better protected than that of strangers from another state, because the other state, on its side, affords more protection. The whole relation is one which is based purely upon an agreement.

X.

Through this compact the states which are a party to it attain the right of mutually watching each other, to see whether its provisions are conformed with and carried out or not. The ground of this right is clear enough. The agreement is valid only if both parties conform to it; hence each party must have a right to know whether the other has complied with it or not.

This watch can be realized only in the state which is watched. Hence the states send ministers to each other to conduct this surveillance. It is true, states also send agents to conclude treaties; but the office of such agents is partly temporary and partly accidental. To distinguish both, the latter are usually called ambassadors. The original character, however, of a permanent, resident minister *(chargé d'affaires)* consists in keeping watch as to whether the state to which he has been sent conforms to its obligations or not, and perhaps in reminding it of its duties. Of course, he has no right to interfere in the internal arrangements of such a state, since his own state has not even the right to interfere in them.

XI.

Holding this office of watching the conduct of the state to which he has been sent, of course the minister can not be dependent upon it, since, otherwise, he would have to render it obedience, and since thus the object of his mission would not be accomplished. Hence, so long as he preserves the character of mere minister, he is subject only to the authority of his own government. He is, for the state to which he has been sent, a holy and inviolable person; he represents his own independent state. Taxes, of course, he has none to pay; for taxes are a contribution to the support of a government; but he is not a citizen of this government. If the minister steps beyond the limits of his official duties, either by seeking to acquire an influence in the internal affairs of such a state or by creating disturbances through bad behavior otherwise, the state which has received him does not become his judge, but may send him back and demand satisfaction.

XII.

If the treaty between both states is clearly and plainly written—and since it only comprises few matters, it is easy to make it clear, and any indefiniteness would at once indicate some evil intention not to observe its provisions—error and injustice are almost impossible. Nevertheless, violation of the treaty certainly gives a right to declare war, precisely as a refusal to recognize a state gives such right. For in either case, the state which is thus made war upon, shows that a legal relation with it is impossible, and hence that it has no rights at all.

XIII.

The right of war, like all rights of compulsion, is infinite. The opponent has no rights because he refuses to recognize the rights of the war-making power. True, he may afterward sue for peace, and promise to recognize those rights. But how shall the other party be convinced that he is in earnest and is not merely looking out for a better opportunity to subjugate him? Hence, the natural end of war is always the *annihilation of the opponent ;* that is to say, the subjugation of his citizens. True, a peace (or rather merely an armistice) may be concluded, because one party or both parties are too much weakened ; but mutual distrust remains, and the object of subjugation remains also.

XIV.

Only the armed powers of both states carry on the war, not the unarmed citizens ; hence, the war is not made upon them. That part of a state's territory which its troops no longer protect is an acquisition of the conqueror, the object of the war being the subjugation of the hostile state ; and the conqueror can not plunder his own citizens or devastate his own possessions without acting irrationally, and hence, also, against the laws of war. As soon as the conqueror has driven away the enemy's armed troops, the unarmed citizens of the enemy are his subjects. That part of the state's territory,

however, which its troops still protect, is not subject to the enemy. The former part the enemy
can not devastate, because it is its own ; the latter
part he can not devastate, because it is physically
impossible, being held by its troops.

The usual manner of carrying on war is certainly
irrational and barbarous. The conqueror devastates
the subjugated provinces in order to plunder them
in all haste, as much as possible, and to leave as
little as possible to the enemy. He does not,
therefore, calculate upon keeping possession of
them. But why, then, does he carry on war ?

The disarmed soldier is also no longer enemy,
but subject. Our mode of considering him as a
prisoner of war and keeping him for exchange, is
an arbitrary arrangement of modern policy, which
has no thorough, independent object in prosecuting
war, and hence at all times considers the possibility
of treating with the enemy.

The object of war is not to kill, but merely to
drive away and disarm the armed force which protects the country and its citizens. In a hand-to-
hand fight, one man kills another to escape being
killed himself, and hence, in virtue of *the right of
self-defense,* but not of *any right conferred by the
state to kill the enemy;* which right, indeed, no state
has, and hence can not, either, confer. In the same
manner we may regard the modern manner of con-
ducting war by means of cannons, guns, etc. It is
not the object to kill with the bullets, but merely
to drive the enemy away from the place covered by

the cannons or guns. If, nevertheless, the enemy remains, it is his own fault if the balls kill him. (Reason would seem to require that we should always advise the enemy when we intend to open a fire upon his posts; precisely as we first send a demand to fortresses to surrender before opening fire upon them.)

The only thing in our modern mode of warfare which is downright illegal, is the *sharp-shooters*, who from hidden places, where they are safe themselves, cold-bloodedly take aim upon a man as upon a target. With them murder is end. (The first use of sharp-shooters, by Austria against Prussia, did, indeed, create universal indignation throughout Europe. We have now become accustomed to it, and imitate it; but it is not to our honor.)

XV.

The aggrieved state has a perfect right, as we have seen, to make war upon the unjust state, until it has subjugated it and united its citizens with its own. War would, therefore, seem a sure and legal means of securing the legal relation between the several states, if it were only possible to invent a contrivance by means whereof the party which has the just cause at hand would always be victorious. But since every state has not the same amount of strength as of right, war may promote as often, if not oftener, the cause of injustice as the cause of justice.

But war is the only means to compel a state ; and hence the problem must be to arrange matters in such a way that the just cause will always be victorious in war. Strength arises from the masses ; hence a number of states must *confederate* among themselves for the maintenance of law and for the punishment of all unjust states. It is clear that such a combination will result in a power always victorious ; but the far higher question is, how can it be arranged that this combination of states always will decree justly ?

XVI.

Many states unite and guarantee each to the other their independence and the inviolability of the compact just described. The formula of such a confederation would be as follows : We all promise to exterminate with united force any state, whether it belong to this confederation or not, which shall refuse to recognize the independence of any one of us, or which shall violate a treaty concluded between it and one of us.

I say the formula of this *confederation*, for it would be a *confederacy*, not a *state*. The distinction is this : Each individual can be compelled to become member of a state, since otherwise it is impossible to establish a legal relation with him. But no state can be compelled to enter this confederation, because it can establish a legal relation with for-

eign states without entering it.* To establish such
a relation it suffices, indeed, to recognize them and
conclude a treaty with them. No state, however,
has the right to compel other states to furnish to it
positive protection. Hence the confederation is an
arbitrary, and not a compulsory union, and such a
union is called a Confederation.

XVII.

Whether one state has recognized the independence of another state, appears from the fact whether it has concluded a treaty with it or not. Hence,
the confederation has a sure means of deciding this
question ; and it is not to be presumed that this
confederation will knowingly and intentionally pronounce a wrong judgment, since all the world
would see immediately the injustice of such judgment. The question whether a state has fulfilled
the conditions of its treaties or not, the confederation must decide partly from the facts brought to
its notice and partly from the terms of the treaty.
So far as the facts are concerned, each state being
obliged to conduct its matters publicly, it will not
be difficult to obtain reliable knowledge concerning

---

* Here we meet again the oversight which limits Fichte's whole
application of his Science of Rights. No state can establish a
legal relation with foreign states, as we have shown, unless it establishes also a common government and a supreme judiciary, that is,
a confederate republic. Hence, every state can be *compelled* to
become a member of a confederate republic.—TRANSLATOR'S RE-
MARK.

them. A state charged with non-compliance with an obligation of its treaties must furnish positive proof that it has complied with it. If a state does not appear before the confederation to justify itself, it thereby virtually admits its guilt. True, a state not belonging to the confederation might say : What have I to do with this confederation ? It is not my judge. But the answer is : You are at least responsible to the state with whom you have made the treaty, and that state has, doubtless, a right to appeal to us.

The confederation being the judge of violations of treaties, must also supervise their original construction so as to have them made clear and definite. This appears, already, from the fact that all treaties are concluded under its guarantee. Indefiniteness in the treaties can not be tolerated, because there must be left no room for error of judgment. Any injustice will thus be flagrant to all the world. Such a confederation, however, composed of states which all have private interests of their own, can not well have a common interest to act unjustly. An unjust sentence turns against the states themselves. For the principles which they apply to others will be applied to them.

XVIII.

The confederation must have the power to execute its decisions. This is done, as appears from the above, by a war of extermination against the state condemned. Hence, the confederation must be armed. The question may arise, whether a special standing army shall be established, or whether such an army shall be called out only in times of war by contributions from the separate states? Since it is to be hoped that war will rarely occur, and in future never, I should vote for the latter; for why have a standing army, when it will probably be idle most of the time?

XIX.

The absolute impossibility of an unjust decision by the confederation has not yet been established. Nor can it be established, as we also could not show the absolute impossibility of an unjust decision by the people assembled in convention. Until reason herself appears in person upon earth and assumes judicial power, we shall always have a supreme court, which, being finite, is liable to error or to evil motives. The problem is simply to discover a tribunal from which there is the least likelihood to expect this; and such a tribunal is for civil relations the nation, and for the relations of states, the just-described confederation.

XX.

As this confederation extends and gradually embraces the whole earth, *eternal peace* will be established— peace, the only lawful relation of states, since war is as likely to give victory to the unjust as to the just, or, at the very best, under the direction of a confederation of states, is only a means for the ultimate end—the maintenance of peace.

§ 2

CONCERNING COSMOPOLITAN LAW.

I.

Each citizen has the right to practice his occupation throughout the whole territory of his state. This right is a part of the rights guaranteed to him by the state. The minister of a foreign state has a right, by virtue of the treaty between both states, to travel also throughout that foreign state, this being the means for his end—to watch over the performance of the treaty stipulations. He shows his pass at the boundaries, and it is the duty of the state to which he is accredited to admit him. His unconditional rejection would be ground for a war. Private persons of one state visit another state either on business or pleasure. Their residence in foreign states is regulated by the treaties with such states. If both states have guaranteed to each other the safety of their citizens, the traveler-citizen is safe by virtue of the treaty. His position as citizen of his own state he proves by showing his pass.

But how, when a stranger, who is neither the ambassador from some state nor citizen of a state which has a treaty with it, enters a foreign state? The reply to this only remaining question of law furnishes the ground of the Cosmopolitan law.

II.

All positive rights, rights to *something*, are based upon an agreement. Now this stranger has made no agreement at all with the state visited by him, nor does he belong to a state which has made an agreement with it, for such is the presupposition. Has he, then, no rights at all? or, if he has any, upon what are they based? He has that original right of man, which precedes all law-agreements and first makes them possible, namely, *the right that all men must presuppose the possibility of entering into a legal relation with him?*

This alone is the true right of man, which belongs to man as man; the possibility to acquire rights. This, and only this, right must be granted to every one who has not expressly lost it through his actions. Let us illustrate it more clearly by opposition. The person whose citizenship in a state is cancelled by that state on account of a crime committed by him, thereby loses all his positive rights, and not only them, but also the right to acquire rights in that state, he having shown himself absolutely unfit for a legal relation. A new stranger has also no positive rights in that state ; *but he has the right to acquire rights* within that state, and to insist upon that right.

From this right is derived his right to enter the territory of a foreign state ; for to have a right to the end is also to have a right to the means ; and the attempt to enter a legal relation in that state can not be made without entering its territory. It is this right to wander freely over the whole earth, and to offer himself anywhere as candidate for a legal relation, which constitutes the right of the mere *cosmopolitan.*

III.

The ground of a stranger's right to enter the territory of a state is his right to attempt and offer to the citizens of such state a legal relation. That state has, therefore, the right to ask the stranger what he desires, and to force him to declare his object. If he does not do so, the ground of his right ceases, and he is expelled from its boundaries. Again : If he does declare himself, but if his proposal is rejected, the ground of his right also ceases, and he is justly expelled. But he must not be otherwise harmed. For the possibility remains that he may become citizen of another state. The right to this possibility can never be taken away from him.

IV.

If his proposal is accepted, he then occupies an *immediate* relation to such state and the rights of both parties are determined by this relation. By recognizing the state, he has already recognized the right of property of all its citizens. This he does not need expressly to reiterate, for it follows from the act of his entering into an agreement with the state. He is subject to the other laws of the state precisely in so far as he has subjected himself to the state.

Of course, the state thus becomes his judge, for no other state protects him. Disagreeable as this circumstance may be, he must submit to it, for it is unavoidable.

CONCERNING

THE

NATURE OF ANIMALS.

CONCERNING THE NATURE OF ANIMALS.*

I.

ACCORDING to the Science of Knowledge, I transfer to nature the conception of myself as far as I can do so without canceling nature herself in her own character, or in other words, without making nature an intelligence, that is, an Ego, or a Self-positing.

II.

To say the intelligence is a higher power or manifestation of nature may signify two things:

I. If I arbitrarily gather together all that is thinkable, as known to me already empirically; and if I rise higher in this gathering together of all the empirically known, I discover that man has in him altogether *all* that which nature contains; but that man has, moreover, in him *something else besides;* in other words, that man has in him a *natural*—the mere determinability of articulation,

---

* The following few pages of a fragment to the *Science of Rights* are appended as complementing the deduction of nature contained in the first part of this science.—TRANSLATOR'S REMARK.

which connects nature and freedom—and a *super-natural*. In so far it may be said in such a *System of the Thinkable* that the intelligence is a higher manifestation of nature ; for in such a system, which merely *narrates,* but does not *furnish grounds,* nature and intelligence connect with each other, and there is no absolute *hiatus*.

II. But when that proposition is made to signify that in a system of nature the intelligence is itself a higher power or manifestation of nature, then it is evidently incorrect, and is refuted thoroughly in transcendental philosophy. For the latter shows nature to be product of the intelligence ; how, then, can the intelligence again, through an evident circle, be product of nature? On the contrary, in man himself, so far as he is nature, the power of nature has not gone to its ultimate extent, for the very sake of man's freedom.

III. It is only in a system of the intelligible world that this proposition would have any significance. For the finite intelligence is certainly a lower power of the absolute intelligence. But this absolute intelligence involves, also, a merely *determinable,* whereof the actual intelligence, or the empirical Ego, is the higher power. This merely determinable is nature in her utterly unexplainable and incomprehensible fundamental elements. These latter elements, however, do not belong in a philosophy of nature, the business whereof it is to comprehend nature only in so far as nature has become *determined* in actuality, or received into the ground

form of the intelligence; in other words, in so far
as nature has again become product of the absolute
intelligence.

Hence, the above proposition is not really philosophical, but merely realistical and encyclopædical.
In a philosophy of nature, it is clearly false. It
attracts only through its very poetical side, which
poetry is always a presentiment of the intelligible;
as, for instance, in Jacob Boehme.

III.

This transferring of my own character into nature I always sensualize *singly* in contemplation.
Thus it becomes my experience.

IV.

The highest within me, independently of consciousness and the immediate object of consciousness, is the *impulse*. The impulse is the highest representation of the intelligence in nature. Hence,
the impulse is the immediate *feelable*, (substance or
element of feeling,) but on no account feeling itself,
since feeling is already a consciousness.

V.

The intelligence attributes to each atom in nature impulse; or, to speak more strictly, through
positing and realizing an impulse outside of itself,

there arises for the intelligence a world of nature. Impulse is, therefore, a tendency to have externally causality, and to be the object of an external causality ; which latter two links are, indeed, exchangeable, and differ only in accordance with the degree of the product of nature. We shall find instances very soon—as, attraction and repulsion ; polarity in general ; chemical affinities and hostilities.

VI.

Through this internal and immanent impulse, the nature of every atom is absolutely determined. This nature of the atom I shall for the present call its *chemical* nature, according to my own interpretation of the word.

VII.

It is clear that these chemical forces in nature will remain without manifestation—precisely like the impulse in man—and that, hence, they are *posited* merely abstractly, unless the condition of their realization is posited at the same time. Posited thus abstractly, they result in the conception of *raw matter*, which is nothing but an empty abstraction from the causality of the impulse—as again, the impulse in general, as not throughout determined, is also nothing but an abstraction. (Every thing posited in the intelligence must appear *in concreto.*)

VIII.

This conception of raw matter is an abstraction of lower degree, because the impulse is put into operation by a union of atom-affinities.

It may thus be put into operation in a twofold manner:

I. *One-sidedly :* in which case the impulse is posited as mere *causality,* resulting in a product which does not retroact upon the impulse, and in which product the impulse, therefore, posits only a quiet residuum of exhausted power. The product arising from such one-sided causality of the impulse we call *minerals*—crystallization of earths and metals—which, for that very reason, join in *straight lines.* For here there is mere result and no organization whatever ; hence, also, no continuous and thus itself-renewing reciprocity with the rest of the universe. The chemical force—speaking abstractly—is as yet held in confinement by the impenetrated and throughout similar mass.

II. *Reciprocally :* in which case both or all chemical forces intimately penetrate each other, dissolve into each other, and melt together into a new whole. The product of such a reciprocal causality of the impulse is *organization,* as exemplified in its simplest abstraction in the *plant.* Such a new whole, which is neither *a,* nor *b,* nor *c,* but rather the result of all of them in their closest union—such a separate organization (or plant) forms a higher power within nature—a nature of its own, finished and completed in itself.

IX.

But *nihil per saltum.* The *union* is absolute; the *interpenetration*, however, proceeds gradually. In this work of *interpenetration* each force draws unto itself from surrounding nature that which is homogeneons to itself, and repels that which is averse to the tendency of the interpenetration. Thus it influences as a totality the surrounding chemical nature as far as its sphere of causality extends; and the result of this infinite reciprocity within itself, and with the external world, we call *life:* here the life of the plant, or *growth,* and the absolute interpenetration manifesting itself, we call here *blossom.*

X.

From the moment of this highest penetration the organic forces, as separates, are canceled, since they are concentrated in that product, the blossom. Hence, with it expires the impelling power of development, and the plant ceases to grow, as, indeed, it grows less toward the time of bloom. By this stoppage of life and the expurgation of that which can not be used in the absolute interpenetration, the plant retires from its reciprocity with the rest of the world; and while the result of the interpenetration remains as dry seed, the plant itself dies as such separate plant.

(Objections from actual life do not invalidate this conception. Even those seeming exceptions will be found to express the same conception, only in a somewhat weaker degree.)

XI.

The seed is again awakened into life through the universal movements of development in nature, warmth and wet; and the same circle begins anew. The chemical components lie in the seed; and that influence of nature, which may be akin to fermentation, places them again in conflict with surrounding nature. The way of nature is an everlasting circular movement of analysis and synthesis. Fermentation is analysis; development of the individual, and self-assertion thereof, is synthesis. Hence the fruitfulness of plants; many of them working together with united power against the influence of surrounding nature. Here also can be established the distinction between dead (artificial) and living chemistry. The former has only results, and not any separate forces; it analyzes, but does not synthesize; and hence it can not produce the conditions of nature.

XII.

The plant is, therefore, a central point of a chemical-organic circle of attraction and repulsion, which we may conceive as internal motion. This motion must be realized as posited in the impulse ; in other words, this motion must appear in nature as an independent principle.

XIII.

An in-itself-returning, and hence itself-determining *impulse of motion*—which arises through a synthesis of parts working together into a totality, and which is a system of a more complex organism, to be conceived as *articulation*—we call an *animal.*

XIV.

What, then, is the animal ? First of all, a system of plant-souls. The unity of those plant-souls, which unity nature itself produces, is the soul of the animal. Its world is therefore partly that of the plants—its nourishment, for instance, it receives partly through synthesis from vegetable, and through analysis from animal nature—and partly that of the animals, whereof we shall speak directly.

XV.

To describe the relation of the animal to the world, we must first recapitulate previous points :

The sphere of causality of a growing plant is an everlasting vortex* of a chemical attraction and re-

* Compare Swedenborg's *Principia* and the theories of Des Cartes and Leibnitz.—TRANSLATOR'S REMARK.

pulsion, the central point whereof (or, ideally expressed, the soul whereof) is the one force of the plant itself. This everlasting appropriation of foreign elements, and expurgation of what does not harmonize with the organism, we can not think otherwise than as an invisible movement in space. Hence, the soul of the plant is not only the principle of a determined organization, (is not only the interpenetration and union of different chemical forces,) but is, moreover, the first principle of a *motion* in nature ; it is the moving principle.

XVI.

But, in the case of the plant, motion is altogether a passivity, a being driven or dragged onward, and hence it is not the predicate of an absolutely independent organization. This motion in nature must also be organized, and must occur in a complete system of nature as impulse and as a peculiar force. How is this achieved ?

XVII.

Each product of nature is an organically in-itself completed totality in space, like the plant. Hence, the unknown *x* which we are looking for must also be such a whole or totality, and in so far it must also have a principle of organization, a sphere and central point of this organization ; in short, the same which we have called the soul of the plant, which thus remains common to both.

But it is, moreover, realization of a movement in nature ; first of all within itself. This can signify only that the principle of the original motion, already discovered in the plant, is posited in every part of its organic body, and that, hence, so far as determinability is concerned, this motion is thus in every part of its body ; and that this mobility is thus in every part of its body by virtue of its own nature, as involving an *impulse ;* and hence, that part of its body can draw along another part, or the whole of the body.

This is clearly the conception of articulation, as explained in the Science of Rights in relation to man. But in the present case the principle of an actual movement is to be—not, as in man, the free-will, for in that case the body under consideration would not be *merely* nature ; it is to be nature itself determining itself with necessity ; and thus the body is not man, but an *animal.*

XVIII.

Abstracting from the fact that the animal is a plant—which word may here receive another signification—let us now compare this conception with the above-established conception of a plant. In the plant and its sphere of causality, all motion proceeded from one central point and returned into it. But in the animal every possible point, involving, as it does, a peculiar principle of motion, is the central point of a plant-atmosphere as its lower world.

Hence, the animal is a system of plant-souls, and the plant is a separated, isolated part of an animal. Both reciprocally affect each other.